HEAVEN IN CONFLICT

Heaven *in* Conflict

FRANCISCANS AND THE
BOXER UPRISING IN SHANXI

Anthony E. Clark

UNIVERSITY OF WASHINGTON PRESS
Seattle and London

Publication of this book was made possible in part by

THE DONALD R. ELLEGOOD INTERNATIONAL PUBLICATIONS ENDOWMENT

and a grant from the

CHIANG CHING-KUO FOUNDATION FOR INTERNATIONAL SCHOLARLY EXCHANGE

UNIVERSITY OF WASHINGTON PRESS
www.washington.edu/uwpress

LIBRARY OF CONGRESS CATALOGING-IN-PUBLICATION DATA
Clark, Anthony E.
    Heaven in conflict : Franciscans and the Boxer uprising in Shanxi / Anthony E. Clark. — 1st edition.
        pages   cm
    Includes bibliographical references and index.
    ISBN 978-0-295-99400-0 (hardover : alk. paper)
1. Franciscans—China—History—19th century.   2. Franciscans—China—History—20th century.   3. China—History—Boxer Rebellion, 1899–1901.   I. Title.
    BX3646.C5C53 2014
    951'.035—dc23

                                                                    2014007525

The paper used in this publication is acid-free and meets the minimum requirements of American National Standard for Information Sciences—Permanence of Paper for Printed Library Materials, ANSI Z39.48-1984.∞

For Amanda
and for il Poverello,
who was an instrument of peace

Contents

Acknowledgments

THIS book began to form in my mind while I worked in my Beijing apartment during the Olympics in 2008; I read through materials related to the Shanxi Sino-missionary conflicts of 1900 while China spun around me, and while the city skies were lit with fireworks during the closing ceremonies. Looking back, this was an appropriately dramatic backdrop to the narratives I was reading for the first time, of warm friendships, growing tensions, tragic violence, and hopeful reconstruction. As I continued to conduct research in Beijing, Taiyuan, Rome, and Paris, and in university archives in my native United States, the principal themes of religious and cultural resistance, defiance, and accommodation persisted as I confronted the history of Franciscan encounters with Boxers during the Boxer Uprising. In his famous classic work on military strategy, Sunzi (ca. 554–496 BCE) wrote that "supreme excellence consists in breaking the enemy's resistance without fighting." As I sought to bring light to these haunting reflections, I received the unselfish and generous assistance of several people, institutions, and granting agencies. While I researched and wrote about tension and conflict between peoples, I encountered only warmth and hospitality, and to the following friends I render my warmest gratitude.

Generous grants from the National Endowment for the Humanities/American Council for Learned Societies and the Chiang Ching-Kuo Foundation allowed me to remain in China during the 2012–2013 academic year while on a leave of absence from my busy teaching schedule at Whitworth University; without the kind support of these agencies this project would likely still be "on the back burner." Previous manifestations of this research were facilitated by the substantial support of the William J. Fulbright Foundation as I completed a year of work as a Fulbright scholar, and by the National

Security Education Program, the Congregation of the Mission Vincentian Studies Institute (DePaul University), and the Weyerhaeuser Foundation Research Grant provided by my home institution. I thank my colleagues at Whitworth University, especially my friends in the Department of History, whose support and encouragement remind me often how fortunate I am to work and walk beneath the tall pines that shelter our campus.

The American poet and essayist Ralph Waldo Emerson (1803–1882) once wrote, "The mass of men worry themselves into nameless graves while here and there a great unselfish soul forgets himself into immortality." There are more "unselfish souls" who made this work possible than I can acknowledge here. Leland and Carol Roth are among them, Lee for scanning rare documents and Carol for helping make sense of them; especially Carol's fierce editorial pen has solicited from me many a grateful sigh. My understanding and navigation of the complex ecclesial and scholarly landscape of Taiyuan and surrounding locations related to this study were facilitated by Liu Anrong and my dear friends Anthony and Veronica Fok, who accompanied me on many trips here and there in Shanxi and Hebei. Michael Kelly's expertise was most welcome in helping me understand the labyrinthine Latin documents from the Vatican Archives. Dale Soden was a much-needed sounding board for ideas as I worked through some perplexing assessments, and his assistance with a scholarly grant allowed me to make important visits to archives in both Taipei and Rome. James Fox, Cassie Schmitt, Tanya Parlet, and Bruce Tabb at the University of Oregon Special Collections tolerantly helped me locate and consult the exceptional China missions collection in their archive. Martha Smalley at the Yale Divinity School Library generously provided me with access to critical materials held at Yale. Wang Renfang and his assistants at the Xujiahui (Zikawei) library, the former Jesuit library in Shanghai, especially Shen Shuyin and Ming Yuqing, were most accommodating as I perused and photographed the vast collection of materials there related to Roman Catholic "missionary cases" in late-imperial China. Wu Yinghui and Sun Miqi at Minzu University of China very generously helped manage the complicated process of securing a visa and lodging in China for me to use while writing this book as a visiting scholar. In significant ways, friendship and intellectual repartee with Stephen Durrant, Lionel Jensen, Eric Cunningham, Matthew Wells, and Wu Xiaoxin have influenced the narrative of this work. Shan Yanrong and Jean-Paul Wiest at the Anton Chinese Studies Library at the Beijing Center selflessly provided helpful advice on where to locate important documents. The works of and my correspondence with Henrietta Harrison have helped direct this work in unexpected directions. The assistance of Tulia Barbanti was gratefully received, for without her decryption of the attractive but impenetrable French cursive of the Franciscan Missionaries of Mary (FMM) correspondence in Shanxi, my understanding of the letters would have been nearly impossible. Georges Hauptmann has provided me with enlightening materials related to the architectural work of the Franciscan friar Barnabas Meistermann, OFM, who designed the convent of Dongergou in Shanxi. Thomas Reilly, Christopher Johnson, and Susan Gorin-Johnson all saved me from embarrassing errors and recommended valuable new directions of inquiry as they read through drafts of this book. Riccardo Pedrini, at the Archivio Storico della Provincia di Cristo Re dei Frati Minori dell'Emilia Romagna, very generously searched for and sent to my office rare photographs of the Franciscans discussed in this book.

I thank my editor, Lorri Hagman, the anonymous reviewers, Bonita Hurd, and the patient and gifted staff at University of Washington Press, including Jacqueline Volin, Rachael Levay, Beth Fuget, Kathleen Jones, and Tim Zimmermann, who deserve much more thanks than I can render here. The process of bringing this work from desk to bookshelf was made more pleasant, and was much improved, by their invaluable contributions.

After writing a Catholic archive seeking permission to access their voluminous collection of letters, records, and images, I received an unexpected reply: "You are welcome, Professor," the letter began, "but please, please remember our goal was always to honor God and serve people in need." As I later worked through their materials I understood the impulse behind the archivist's reply; several researchers before me had written what the archivist believed were unfairly biased, scathing accounts that perhaps misrepresented what the missionaries had written and done in China during the late-imperial era. I hope that my representation of the sources I consulted for this project fairly and accurately depict the foreign missionaries I studied, and that what I have written represents an objective engagement with the many heartrending personal accounts, both Western and Chinese.

The generosity and open-armed welcome I received from the Roman Catholic archives I consulted were inspiring, and by and large, photocopies and permissions were freely granted with no or minimal fees. Pedro Gil, OFM, with whom I grew to share a common respect for the Franciscan friars who served and died in Shanxi, allowed me unlimited access to the copious materials at the General Curia of the Order of Friars Minor Archives in

Rome. Li Jianhua, SVD, kindly granted me access to his private collection of materials related to the Franciscan mission in Shanxi. Augustine DeNoble, OSB, spent countless hours locating, photocopying, and annotating materials held in the vast collection at Mount Angel's Benedictine Library. The kind and hospitable Dominican Fathers of Blessed Sacrament Priory in Seattle, Washington, provided me with needed accommodations and meals while I worked in the collections of the University of Washington. Roberto Ribeiro, SJ, Thierry Meynard, SJ, and Jeremy Clarke, SJ, all offered support and friendship as I lived and wrote in Beijing, and Fr. Meynard unselfishly provided me with access to, and a working space in, the impressive Sino-missionary collection at the Beijing Center. I thank Paul Mariani, SJ, for accompanying me on remote treks through China to gather materials and for his constant friendship. Daniel Peterson, SJ, provided some helpful correspondence regarding the Jesuit enterprise in China. Robert Danieluk, SJ, and Mac Cuarta, SJ, at the ARSI Jesuit Archive in Rome were helpful as I worked in the Eternal City during a research sabbatical in 2012. Elias Cerezo, SJ, at the China Province Jesuit Archive offered me a working space at the China Province Archive in Taipei and helped locate important materials held in the Jesuit library at Fu Jen University, also in Taipei. Jack Clark Robinson, OFM, and Pat McCloskey, OFM, provided an important and corrective reading of this book from the Franciscan perspective. And finally, Merlyn D'Sa, FMM, the secretary general at the Archive of the Franciscan Missionaries of Mary, sent to my U.S. office several parcels and kindly provided important materials that have enriched this study.

While the situation for scholars of China's missionary history has improved considerably in the last several years, obstacles remain when working on the mainland; archival materials—some as mundane as the musical scores produced by early Qing missionaries—are still, unfortunately, held behind inaccessible archive doors, listed as politically sensitive. This can be constantly unnerving for the Western scholar who finds other archival collections completely open, well documented, and well preserved. I have benefited from many letters and inquiries rendered by ecclesial hierarchy with better connections to these sources. Letters of introduction and support have been provided by Bishops Blase Cupich, Robert Baker, and William Skylstad, and especially by Raymond Cardinal Burke, who provided important words of support in two brief encounters, one in the United States, and another in Rome after a long day that I spent reviewing documents at the Jesuit archive near Saint Peter's.

Johann Wolfgang von Goethe (1749–1832) once wrote, "The moment one commits oneself, then providence moves too. All sorts of things occur to help. A whole stream of events issue from the decision, raising in one's favor all manner of incidents and meetings and material assistance which no one could have dreamed would come his way." It is rare indeed when providence launches two academics in the same direction, especially when their respective disciplines are as far apart as the Sino-missionary history of late-Qing China and the development and history of book arts in U.S. libraries and museums. Just as I received the welcome news that I had received two generous research grants to live and work in China, my wife, Amanda, providentially completed the research portion of her doctoral work and happily embraced a year free of teaching obligations to write her dissertation. We both benefited from an unencumbered year in which to work side by side, punctuating our long, solitary spells of writing with animated discussions about our discoveries and mutual readings, during which we gratefully exchanged invaluable "slash-and-burn" editorial ideas. To Amanda, and to her work, this work is dedicated.

Abbreviations

Dramatis Personae

Adolphine, Marie, FMM . . . . Shanxi missionary

Amandina, Maria, FMM . . . . Shanxi missionary

Balat, Théodoric, OFM . . . . Shanxi missionary

Bauer, André, OFM . . . . Shanxi missionary

Capozi, Bishop Domenico Luca, OFM . . . . Shanxi missionary

Chiara (Nanetti), Maria, FMM . . . . Shanxi missionary

Cixi . . . . Empress dowager, aunt of Emperor Guangxu

de Doullens, Hugolin, OFM. . . . . Shanxi missionary

de Jesus, Marie-Hermine, FMM . . . . Shanxi missionary

della Pace, Maria, FMM . . . . Shanxi missionary

de Sainte Nathalie, Marie, FMM . . . . Shanxi missionary

de Saint Just, Marie, FMM . . . . Shanxi missionary

Facchini, Elia, OFM . . . . Shanxi missionary

Fiorentini, Bishop Agapito, OFM . . . . Shanxi missionary

Fogolla, Bishop Francesco, OFM . . . . Shanxi missionary

"Goddess Yang". . . . . Shanxi Red Lantern

Grassi, Bishop Gregorio, OFM . . . . Shanxi missionary

Grioglio, Bishop Gabriel, OFM . . . . Shanxi missionary

Guangxu . . . . Emperor who reigned during the Boxer Uprising

Guo Qizi ("Old Man Immortality") . . . . Shanxi Boxer

Hao Nai, Joseph, OFM . . . . Vicar general of Taiyuan Diocese

Hu Xingyuan ("Old Man Immortality") . . . . Shanxi Boxer

Liu Dapeng . . . . Shanxi literatus

Massi, Bishop Eugenio, OFM . . . . Ordinary bishop of Taiyuan

Moccogatta, Bishop Aloysius (Luigi), OFM . . . . Shanxi missionary

Mother Mary of the Passion, FMM . . . Founder of the FMM Missionaries

Nanetti da Cologna, Barnabas, OFM . . . . Shanxi missionary

"Old Master Guan" . . . . Shanxi Boxer

Pallotta, Maria Assunta, FMM . . Shanxi missionary; Dongergou convent

Ricci, Giovanni, OFM . . . . Shanxi missionary

Saccani, Francesco, OFM . . . . Shanxi missionary

Yuxian . . . . Provincial governor of Shanxi

Zhao Yuqian, Peter, OFM . . . . Shanxi priest

Chronology of Franciscans in China

1245–ca. 1370	First Franciscan friars arrived in China
1624	First Catholic chapel built in Shanxi, by Nicolas Trigault, SJ
1716	Shanxi mission assigned to the Franciscans
1886	First Franciscan Missionaries of Mary sisters arrived in China
1890	Taiyuan, Shanxi, made an independent apostolic vicariate
1898	Francesco Fogolla, OFM, appointed auxiliary bishop of Taiyuan, Shanxi
1899	Seven Franciscan sisters arrived in Taiyuan, Shanxi
1890–1900	Gregorio Grassi, OFM, served as bishop of Taiyuan, Shanxi
March 1900	Governor Yuxian appointed to Taiyuan, Shanxi
21 June 1900	Qing court declared war against all Western powers
9 July 1900	European and Chinese Christians massacred at Taiyuan
7 September 1901	Boxer Protocol signed in Beijing
1902–1909	Agapito Fiorentini, OFM, served as bishop of Taiyuan, Shanxi

1910–1916   Eugenio Massi, OFM,
                  served as bishop of Taiyuan, Shanxi

1916–1938   Agapito Fiorentini, OFM,
                  served as bishop of Taiyuan, Shanxi

1940–1952   Domenico Luca Capozi, OFM,
                  served as bishop of Taiyuan, Shanxi

1946   Taiyuan, Shanxi, made an autonomous diocese

1952   Domenico Luca Capozi, OFM, expelled from China

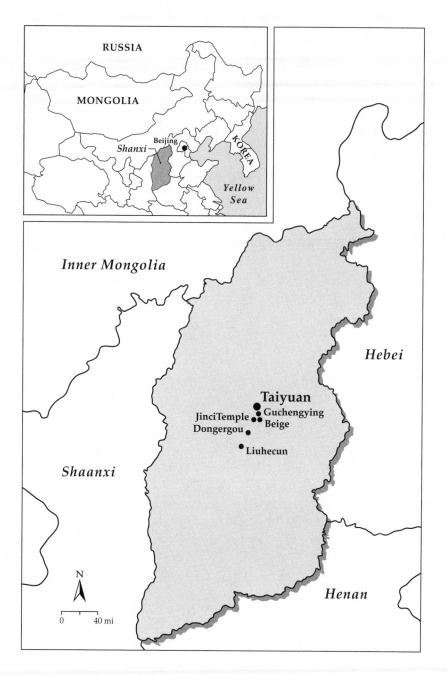

Labels within the map:

RUSSIA

MONGOLIA

Shanxi — Beijing

KOREA

Yellow Sea

Inner Mongolia

Hebei

Taiyuan
JinciTemple   Guchengying
Dongergou   Beige
        Liuhecun

Shaanxi

Henan

N

0   40 mi

SHANXI, showing key locations of Boxer and Catholic activities during the Boxer Uprising

HEAVEN IN CONFLICT

Prologue

WAR OF THE IMMORTALS

LORD GUAN

HEROIC role models were easy to find. China's historical legends are full of them. In Luo Guanzhong's (1330–1400) novel *Romance of the Three Kingdoms* (Sanguo yanyi), the epic general Lord Guan (d. 219) is memorialized as one of China's greatest champions:

> Wielding his green dragon halberd, Lord Guan mounted his horse, Red Hare, and rode out with his men. . . . Guan, on his saddle, briskly charged down the slope with his halberd pointed downward. His phoenix eyes rounded and his silkworm eyebrows bristled as he dashed through the enemy line. The northern army divided like waves as Lord Guan descended on Yan Liang. Yan was still beneath his standard when he saw Guan charging toward him. And by the time Yan knew who it was, Lord Guan and his swift horse, Red Hare, were already upon him. Yan Liang was too slow, and like a rising cloud Guan raised his halberd and pierced him. Quickly dismounting, Lord Guan decapitated Yan Liang. Tethering the severed head to Red Hare's neck, he vaulted to his saddle, raised his halberd, and fled through the enemy troops as if no one was there.[1]

Under the guidance of their leader, "Old Master Guan," a group of young men gathered at Lord Guan Temple in 1900 to practice martial arts, hoping that the spirit of Lord Guan would possess them and render them invincible to foreign bullets.[2] Old Master Guan's Society of Righteous Harmony had formed during the early summer months of 1900 in his native village, Beige, just south of Shanxi's capital city, Taiyuan. Nearly five hundred Boxers—local militias consisting largely of peasants displaced by drought and famine, and named thus by English missionaries who observed their martial arts practice—drilled with fists and swords in the courtyard of the temple, and their goal was to behead Europeans as Lord Guan had beheaded Yan Liang.[3]

SAINT MICHAEL

When Roman Catholic missionaries left their native countries for China, the "land of the dragon," they had countless times read passages in scripture and their breviaries (prayer books) about God's heavenly warrior, Saint Michael the Archangel. "And there was a great battle in heaven," wrote Saint John the Evangelist, and "Michael and his angels fought with the dragon."[4] Catholic convention ascribes four offices, or prescribed hours of prayer intoned using the breviary, dedicated to Michael: to do combat with Satan, to rescue souls from the power of the Enemy, to champion the people of God, and to summon souls to final judgment. In his role in spiritual confrontation, Saint Michael delivers the coup de grâce against enemy spirits: "O glorious prince, St. Michael, chief and commander of the heavenly hosts, guardian of souls, vanquisher of rebel spirits, servant in the house of the Divine King and our admirable conductor, you who shine with excellence and superhuman virtue, deliver us from all evil."[5] In 1844 the Catholic mission of Taiyuan was assigned to the Franciscan friars of the Roman Province, named after Saint Michael the Archangel, and the friars who went to Shanxi therefore traveled under the patronage and banner of heaven's most powerful warrior. As the friars passed over water and land to their missions in north China, they were accompanied by their divine protector, and as they arrived, non-Catholic Chinese offered incense and prayers to Lord Guan, their own divine protector. During the summer months of 1900 Guan and Michael, swords in hand, met in Shanxi.

THE FRANCISCAN EXPERIENCE IN SHANXI

The Franciscan enterprise in Shanxi played a key role in the conflict that spread across northern China at the end of the nineteenth century. Little attention has been given to these "sons and daughters of Saints Francis and

Clare" in previous studies on late-imperial China, and as I pursued their story I found myself often lingering on passages more curious than I had encountered in previous research. The account of these Franciscans in Shanxi during the Boxer Uprising is too important to overlook. As one examines most library shelves devoted to Sino-Western historical exchange, both in China and the West, monographs considering the Jesuit enterprise, especially that led by Matteo Ricci (1552–1610), predominate. The Franciscans, however, had been the first Catholic order to settle in China, following closely on the heels of Marco Polo (1254–1324) in the thirteenth century. Four centuries later, Shanxi's Franciscans were mostly Italian, and they followed a long line of friars who left Italy for the Middle Kingdom. Rome's Propaganda Fide, the Vatican's official agency in charge of foreign missions, sent the first large group of Franciscans since the Yuan dynasty (1279–1368) to China in 1684, and this first group was Italian. The Franciscans during the nineteenth century would come to be the most prominent Catholic mission order both in number of missioners and mission holdings.[6] When sisters and friars served in China, Franciscans from a particular ecclesial province—a district overseen by a bishop—were normally assigned to a *mission sui iuris*, or "independent mission"; Taiyuan was assigned to the Roman Province of Saint Michael.

This study adds to a growing number of works on Western missionaries in late-imperial China but moves beyond the preoccupation with Sino-Jesuit history. One important advantage of working in the archives of mendicant orders is that both Franciscans and Dominicans have included female members (unlike Jesuits), and thus the study of women can be given equal treatment. To date, most studies of Western women in China have dealt with Protestant women missionaries, and most studies of the China mission in general have considered the exclusively male Jesuit order.[7] While more difficult to study owing to comparatively limited sources, Chinese women figure as well in the following story, and their contribution to this narrative allows us to see more clearly how widespread their influence was on the central plains of Shanxi in 1900.

SOURCES

As I began my research for this book, I hoped that Chinese sources on Shanxi's Sino-missionary incidents during the Boxer Uprising would equal available Western materials, though I had been repeatedly warned otherwise. While I was able to discover new sources in Chinese, largely unreported in previous studies, Western materials do outnumber Chinese materials. The Vatican's collection of records on late-Qing Shanxi alone outnumbers the collective Chinese materials located in Taiwan, mainland China, and Hong Kong; and the Franciscan and Franciscan Missionaries of Mary collections outweigh those sources held by the Vatican. I should note, however, that while Western-language materials predominate in Western archives, I was able to locate an unexpected number of Chinese-language books and other materials in those Western archives. I discovered, for example, a loose Chinese pamphlet randomly placed between folio pages of the voluminous Vatican *processus*, compiled for the Causes (i.e., formal cause for sainthood) of the Boxer-era martyrs. Also, in the General Curia of the Order of Friars Minor Archives in Rome, I found attached to the end of the Latin *acta* on the Shanxi martyrs a Chinese biography of the Franciscan and Chinese Christians in Shanxi during the late Qing. This Chinese-language work was published in Shanxi during the republican era and, as far as I know, constitutes the only surviving copy. These materials appear here in the text and bibliography.

My research carried me to numerous archives in several cities outside my native United States, including Beijing, Tianjin, Taiyuan, Shanghai, Taipei, Hong Kong, Paris, and Rome. I was able to acquire considerable information about the Chinese participants in the incidents of late-Qing Shanxi, though more information is available on the Westerners who appear in this book, who wrote copious letters, kept diaries, and, as members of the Franciscan order, benefited from the exacting personnel records on the Shanxi mission kept in the General Curia archive. The only Chinese figure from Shanxi to have left behind a substantial amount of personal and historical information related to the Boxer era in Shanxi, especially around Taiyuan, where this study centers, was the local diarist and literatus Liu Dapeng (1857–1943).[8] The reader will see that Liu's richly embellished remarks on the local Boxers and Red Lantern women figure largely throughout the narrative of this book. Regarding the life of Shanxi's notorious governor Yuxian (1842–1901), some imperial records and edicts exist to flesh out his character, but by far the most exhaustive source of information about his activities in China during the Boxer era is the collection of subjective materials about him preserved in missionary records.

As for the Fists of Righteous Harmony (the Boxers) and their female members, the Red Lantern women, most of these persons were barely literate and thus unable to write their own stories for posterity. In addition, the massive anti-Boxer sweep across China in 1901 resulted in the executions of most Boxer leaders, and the Boxers who survived the punitive expeditions of Qing and foreign armies would have been too timid to reveal their identities, especially in writing. Several works later appeared in China about the Boxers once anti-Boxerism had waned. Most sources on the historical events of 1900 Shanxi are located in U.S. and European archives, especially the enormous archival collections held at the Vatican's Archivio Segreto and the repository located at the General Curia of the Order of Friars Minor Archives, just a short walk up a nearby hill from Saint Peter's Basilica.

CONFRONTATION ON THE MARGINS

In most Chinese history survey classes only cursory remarks are made about the events of the 1900 Boxer Uprising, typically centered on the siege of the foreign legations in Beijing. Although the central Chinese court was located in Beijing's Forbidden City, and Western diplomats were located in Beijing's foreign legations, most of the battles—both ideological and physical—between Boxers and foreigners occurred far from the empire's capital. Of all the Sino-missionary conflicts in China at that time, the bulk of Boxer violence was committed in far-off Shanxi against Franciscans and the Chinese Christians attached to their missions. While Shanxi was considered somewhat out of the way by the Western diplomats, merchants, and missionaries who occupied the comparatively Westernized coastal concessions, Shanxi had been the banking and cultural center of much of late-imperial China, and it was far from being a backwater in the mind of the court.

The Protestants, Franciscans, native Christians, women and men Boxers, and local Qing officials who were involved in the terrible violence in 1900 Shanxi were in the center of Boxer conflicts, and much of this book explores the motivations behind these confrontations. Scholars who study the Boxer Uprising disagree in their conclusions. Some suggest that certain areas were culturally predisposed to conflict, observing that some provinces, such as Shanxi, already had "a long-lived culture of violence" before the tensions of the late nineteenth century inaugurated the Boxer attacks on Christians.[9] Others argue that conflict between Catholics and local Chinese was brought about by the church's "confrontational stance taken against most of the cultural and religious traditions of Asian countries."[10] Surely, however, factors on both sides contributed to these disagreements.

Another scholarly dispute regarding the cause of Sino-Western and Christian/non-Christian hostilities during the Boxer era centers on the role of religious misunderstanding in these conflicts.[11] In the increasing discomfort between the Manchu court and foreign diplomats, and between missionaries and native Chinese religious sects, such as the Fists of Righteous Harmony and White Lotus sects, lay the origins of conflict.[12] Although it is unlikely that one can confidently attribute the violence of the Boxer Uprising to any single cause, religious or political, Shanxi may be among the best places to look for examples of the myriad factors that sparked the violence of 1900. If we wish to better understand the history of the uprising, then we must perhaps rearrange our view of the "margins"; neither Shanxi nor the Franciscans nor women were marginal in this confrontation, and this study gives these actors center stage. Perceived players also include Lord Guan, Saint Michael the Archangel, and countless other "heavenly participants" who influenced earthly actors in the events of 1900.

My previous book, *China's Saints: Catholic Martyrdom during the Qing*, centered on the causes and circumstances of Christian martyrdom during China's last empire. Some have referred to that book as a "history of Christian massacres." I have deliberately veered away from the historical question of martyrdom in this book, choosing rather to reposition my analysis on the antecedents of violence. My desire here is to recount the history of how religious ideas informed and influenced the impulse toward conflict during the Boxer Uprising. In doing so, I explore a multitude of views, detouring into the lives and letters of those present during the conflicts in 1900 Shanxi.

PART 1

The Drought and the Heavenly Battle

CHAPTER 1

Taiyuan, from Mission to Diocese

The fact I am gray is due more to work and troubles than to old age.
—JOHN OF MONTECORVINO, OFM, ON HIS LIFE IN CHINA

O N 10 October 1927, the Italian friar Father Antonio Santarelli, OFM, inscribed his signature on a list of questions related to the tragic events of the Boxer incidents in Shanxi. In article 8 he asked whether the anti-Catholic persecutions of 1900 were due to the rash of calumnies against Chinese Christians and the Franciscans, such as rumors that Chinese Catholics "follow a new and pernicious doctrine, assist the European political leaders, condemn ancestral veneration, produce discord among the people, and poison water." Was it also true, he asked, that popular rumors accused the Franciscan missionaries of "carving out the hearts and eyes of Chinese children"?[1] In his opening remarks in this document for the Vatican's Sacred Congregation for Rites (now the Congregation for the Cause of Saints), he noted that some 2,417 Catholics had been killed in Shanxi during the summer of 1900. It is possible that he had known several of the Franciscans who had left for China and died there during the conflicts of the late nineteenth century, and in his list of thirty-seven matters "to be investigated" (*ut probant*), he asks some probing questions, all revolving around one central issue: Was this conflict one of politics or religion? As far as we know, Father Santarelli had never been to China, but his order, the Order of Friars Minor, had made Shanxi one of its principal mission stations, and to this day it is often discussed and written about in Franciscan communities.

JESUIT FOOTPRINTS

The first Catholic to leave missionary footprints on Shanxi's fertile loess soil was a Flemish Jesuit, Nicolas Trigault, SJ (1577–1628), who established a chapel in Jiangzhou in 1624. Nicolas's nephew, Michel Trigault, SJ (1602–1667), was later the first to arrive at Taiyuan.[2] Most of China's Christians at that time had been "missionized" by the Society of Jesus, and by the time Jesuits settled in Shanxi, the number of priests in China was far too few to adequately attend to the pastoral requirements of the country's growing number of converts. By 1665 fewer than two dozen priests were in China to serve the spiritual needs of several thousand Christians.[3] Michel Trigault entered Taiyuan in 1633 and managed the budding mission there until 1665, quite alone and overworked.[4] The Church of the East, from Persia (the so-called Nestorians), had taught its version of Christianity in Shanxi as early as the eighth century, but record of the "Luminous Religion," as it was called in China, had faded from historical memory. When Michel Trigault entered Shanxi, his Christian religion was unknown to the deeply conservative denizens of Taiyuan, and following Matteo Ricci's example he adapted his teachings to those of Confucius and ingratiated himself with the local literati. He baptized two hundred new faithful soon after establishing a modest Roman Catholic chapel in Taiyuan.

The difference, or perhaps the conflict, between Western and Chinese gods was quick to emerge in Shanxi, and Trigault was an eager participant in the contest for souls. Three years before moving to Taiyuan, Trigault and his Jesuit *confrere*, Albert d'Orville (1621–1662), lived in the Shanxi town of Jiangzhou, where the Catholic God was rumored to be more austere than the comparatively congenial gods of China. As the Lantern Festival approached, celebrated on the fifteenth day of the first lunar month, the two priests heard of local gossip that Catholics enjoy "no such feasts or revelries" as do the Chinese on such holidays.[5] In response, Trigault and d'Orville orchestrated a special celebration of their own on the Feast of the Purification of the Virgin, which corresponded with the festivities of the Lantern Festival. They installed a special platform inside the Jiangzhou church and lavishly adorned the chapel interior with paper lanterns, flowers, silk streamers, and censers that poured out clouds of fragrant incense.[6] The Catholic God would not be outdone by pagan revelries—the church doors were ordered to remain open so that passersby could observe how extravagant Christian merrymaking could be. Inquisitive Chinese were invited to enter and see the lanterns, which were "dedicated to the Lord of Heaven and his Holy Mother."[7] China's traditional Lantern Festival was transformed into an opportunity for conversion.

After 1665, Shanxi's mission evaporated because of imperial Chinese court politics and the shortage of clergy, but when Rome divided China into two archdioceses in 1696—one see in Nanjing and the other in Beijing—new Catholic orders were dispatched to supplement the Jesuit mission. Shanxi was at first assigned to the Jesuits, and Shaanxi was given to the Franciscans, though Shanxi's capital city, Taiyuan, remained a missionary backwoods.[8] The Jesuits had earlier prepared Shanxi's Catholics to sustain their religious fervor through membership in confraternities such as the Association of the Holy Mother (Shengmuhui); women catechists, vowed to perpetual virginity, taught other women the rudiments of Christianity, and men promoted pious practices such as intoning litanies and performing severe penances, including self-flagellation in organized assemblies. The Jesuit Alphonse Vagnone (1568–1640) had created a number of such pious associations in Shanxi by the 1630s; and in an Annual Letter he submitted in 1630, Vagnone reported that Shanxi's Christians gathered in private homes, many with richly adorned oratory chapels, "to practice devotions, read holy books, and encourage each other to observe the Commandments." Since Shanxi's Catholics saw a priest for an average of only a few days each year, Jesuits commonly assigned a local church elder (*huizhang*) to "rouse their fellow Christians to practice acts of piety and devotion."[9]

Yongzheng (1678–1735), successor to the emperor Kangxi (1654–1722), was far less impressed by Jesuit learning and artistic training than his father and accepted a memorial (i.e., a formal report or communication) from an official in Fujian who recommended the wholesale proscription of Christianity in China and the expulsion of all foreign missionaries. In an imperial edict issued in January 1724, Catholicism (Tianzhujiao) was expressly listed among "perverse sects" and "sinister doctrines."[10] After Yongzheng ascended the throne, the persecuted Catholic Church went underground, while others apostatized as European missionaries were driven out.[11] Christianity in Shanxi after Yongzheng saw the development of Taiyuan Catholicism reach a low point; after Yongzheng's edict the activities of Taiyuan's Catholics essentially vanished.[12] Not only did Shanxi suffer from Yongzheng's anti-Christian edict, but in addition, more than a third of China's Catholics stopped attending religious meetings or simply reverted to popular Chinese folk beliefs.

Despite the capricious state of the mission in Shanxi during the early Qing, the Society of Jesus laid an enduring foundation there, and when the Franciscan friars began to replace them, they did so on trails already blazed by distinguished Jesuits. Nicolas Trigault, for example, had produced one of the first systems of Romanization while working in Shaanxi and Shanxi in his *Aid to the Eyes and Ears of Western Literati* (Xiru ermu zi); Giulio Aleni, SJ (1582–1649), taught Christianity in Shanxi before relocating to his more famous mission at Fujian; and Shanxi was the first mission post of the renowned Jesuit court astronomer Ferdinand Verbiest, SJ (1623–1688). The Franciscan mission in northern China did not begin in earnest until the eighteenth century, when Rome was still considering how to divide its attentions, and its boundaries, in China.

FRANCISCAN FOOTPRINTS

The first Franciscan to build a church in China predated the first Jesuit missionaries by three centuries. Giovanni da Montecorvino, OFM (1247–1328), established his mission cathedral in the shadow of Kublai Khan's (1215–1294) imposing palace in Beijing, then called Khanbalik.[13] Friar Giovanni's legacy figures so heavily in Shanxi Catholic identity today that the present diocesan seminary, near the center of Taiyuan city, is named after him (Giovanni Montecorvino Seminary, Menggaoweinuo Zongxiuyuan), and Montecorvino's biography is outlined in a chapter dedicated to him in the Taiyuan Diocese's centenary commemorative book, published in 2006.[14] Shanxi's Catholics presently envision Shanxi as a Franciscan rather than a Jesuit province, and churches there most typically bear the names of Franciscan saints, such as Saint Anthony and Saint Francis.

It is perhaps Friar Giovanni's missionary success that has historically appealed most to the Franciscans who later settled in Shanxi, and friars in China are quick to point out that Montecorvino holds the distinction of being China's first Catholic bishop. In a letter entrusted to a papal legate on 8 January 1305, Bishop Giovanni succinctly recounted his triumphs, and his challenges, in converting the residents of Beijing: "I have built a church in the city of Khanbalik [Beijing], where the chief residence of the king is, and I finished it six years ago; where also I made a bell-tower and put three bells there. I have also baptized there, as I reckon, up to today about six thousand persons. And if there had not been the above-named slanders I should have baptized more than thirty thousand; and I am often engaged in baptizing."[15] The "slanders" he mentions came from Eastern Christian, or Nestorian, detractors, competitors with the early Catholic mission.[16] The Nestorian clergy in China were displeased that Roman Catholics had quite unexpectedly occupied the mission ground, which previously had been occupied only by they themselves.[17] But who could have blamed them for their bitterness? Had not the Catholic Church condemned Nestorius (ca. 386–ca. 451), the archbishop of Constantinople, as a heretic and ejected him from his see? According to Friar Giovanni the Nestorians were anathema, and according to China's Nestorian community the Franciscan bishop was an interloper. Interdenominational politics aside, neither the Catholics nor the Nestorians did much to ingratiate themselves to the native Chinese, and once their Mongolian sponsors retreated in 1368, their churches and monasteries slowly faded from China's vast landscape. It was nearly four centuries before the Friars Minor, more simply known as the Franciscans, sent new missionaries to China in large numbers, and it was not until 1890 that Rome officially recognized Taiyuan as its own apostolic vicariate under Franciscan care.[18]

Before Shanxi was a Franciscan mission it was administered by the Italian Jesuit Antonio Posateri, SJ (1640–1705), who served as the apostolic vicar of Shanxi from 1702 until his death at Taiyuan in 1705.[19] By the time of Posateri's death, Shanxi boasted a Catholic population of around three thousand, clustered mostly around the urban centers of Jiangzhou and Taiyuan.[20] Posateri's position remained vacant for eleven years after his passing. When Rome combined Shaanxi and Shanxi into a single vicariate in 1716, it assigned the Order of Friars Minor to manage mission affairs there. The sons of Saint Francis, affectionately known among the friars as "il Poverello" (the poor man), had at last staked their enduring claim to Shanxi's abundant plains, and there could not have been a more striking distinction between the styles of these two orders. Jesuits had decided upon a cautious and measured process of introducing the culturally startling aspects of Christian doctrine to Chinese society; the Franciscans were less calculated in their approach. A 1639 letter by the friar Antonio de Santa Maria Caballero, OFM (1602–1669), noted that Catholic literati "were so hindered by their Confucian rites and those to ancestral tablets that they persisted in their beliefs for more that five centuries . . . and encouraged considerable opposition to our Dominican and Franciscan Friars."[21] In addition to denigrating Confucian rites, the friars also aggressively preached in public areas wearing "their habits of blue and white sack" and "brandished their crosses while preaching."[22]

The two provinces of Shaanxi and Shanxi remained bundled together into a single apostolic vicariate from 1716 till 1844, and its first vicar, Bishop Antonio Laghi, OFM (1668–1727), lived in Xi'an, Shaanxi.[23] The post-Jesuit Catholic mission in Shanxi can be divided into seven principal periods: (1) the era after Yongzheng's edict, from 1724 to 1860, during which Catholic activities were forced mostly underground; (2) the three decades from 1860 to 1890, following the Sino-French Convention, which reopened the empire to missionary efforts, and during which the Franciscan friars labored to strengthen and protect the mission's legal status; (3) the period from 1890, after which Taiyuan was established as an independent apostolic vicariate, until 1896, when the Franciscan mission focused its attention on training and stationing more native clergy; (4) the period of the Great North China Famine, in 1896–1897 (distinguished from the Great Famine of 1877), through which the Shanxi friars were occupied with relief efforts for those afflicted by the severe drought; (5) the survival of the mission during the violence of the Boxer Uprising, 1898 to 1900; (6) the post-Boxer era of Catholic restoration in Shanxi, from 1901 to the 1940s, which centered on remembrance, reconstruction, and vigorous proselytization; and (7) the period of resistance and survival while Taiyuan was elevated to an archdiocese (1946) and as the province entered the post-1949 communist era. The events from the Great Famine of 1877 until the post-Boxer reconstruction era are at the center of this work.[24]

After a series of unequal treaties in China, such as the Sino-British Treaty of Nanjing of 1842, the Sino-American Treaty of Wangxia of 1844, the Sino-American and Sino-French Treaties of Tianjin in 1858, and the Sino-French Convention in Beijing of 1860, Western Catholic missions were accorded unprecedented access to China's inland areas. Catholic orders such as the Franciscans, Vincentians, and Dominicans were then allowed to lease or purchase land to construct ecclesial buildings—churches, orphanages, schools, and hospitals—and local officials were obliged to treat sympathetically the foreign missionaries who entered their jurisdiction. During this time, leading up to the official founding of the Taiyuan Diocese in 1890, the Franciscan mission in Shanxi sought to salvage what Catholic presence remained after Yongzheng's proscription; and after they had returned to Shanxi in 1860, the friars ambitiously sought to better secure the legal footing of the Catholic presence in the province. They therefore directed their attention toward the Zongli Yamen, the Qing (1644–1911) bureau in charge of foreign affairs in the capital, Beijing, and began to aggressively lobby for concessions favorable to Catholic religious practice and expansion. What Shanxi's Catholics complained about most during their time "underground," from 1724 to 1860, was their legal obligation to pay taxes to local temples devoted to other deities. That was the first and most hotly debated issue the Shanxi friars confronted after settling in the province.

It was in the context of recovering the Shanxi Catholic community that the friars of Fengtai county, who lived in the region of the Hanging Temple and Datong Buddhist caves, pressured the authorities to outline "the rights and freedoms of Chinese Christians."[25] The Franciscans submitted a letter, which later was sent to the Zongli Yamen, that included five articles recommending policies that would exempt Christians from certain financial obligations. Article one asked that Christians (*jiaoren*) be released from legal requirements to help fund operas, temple sacrifices, or temple repairs, so that they could allocate those funds to the support of Catholic churches (Tianzhutang) and Catholic rites (*libai*). In general, the letter appealed to the government to release Shanxi Catholics from supporting anything contrary or offensive to Catholic religious sensibilities, and although that request seemed sensible from the friars' point of view, it did not account for how their demands might be contrary or offensive to native Chinese religious sensibilities.[26]

Temples, which were the center of social activities in imperial China and fundamental to social cohesion and the Confucian sense of cultural harmony, were maintained by organized temple events. The Franciscan demand to be released from temple support was interpreted as antisocial and, more profoundly, as a rejection of Chinese cultural identity. Further, temple taxes were used to support public relief during famines, and if these requested policies were enacted, native Christians would not have to contribute to the relief provisions they might then seek in times of need; that caused no small amount of resentment from citizens who had paid their own taxes. Shanxi magistrates initially vacillated about how to respond to the Christian refusal to pay temple taxes; but after 1860, legal cases suggest these officials had begun to support the temples more openly. One official asked a Chinese Catholic, "As you are a subject of the Qing, please tell me why you follow the rebellious religion of these foreign devils?" Understanding well how socially divisive the Christian practice of refusing temple support was, this official insisted to the Christian, "You must pay the fees for the [temple] dramas."[27] It was precisely such conventions, which separated Chinese Christians and non-Christians into two factions in Shanxi, that nourished the conflicts of the Boxer era.

SHANXI'S EARLY FRANCISCAN BISHOPS, 1845–1899

The other Franciscan activity that marked the post-underground era of Catholic reconstruction in Shanxi was the widespread building of churches and other mission-related structures. Between 1860 and 1890, Shanxi's landscape was increasingly punctuated by large Catholic churches crowned with towering steeples and a Christian cross. The most prominent Franciscan church was the Church of the Immaculate Conception, commissioned by the Italian bishop Aloysius (Luigi) Moccogatta, OFM (1809–1891), and built in the provincial capital, Taiyuan, at Dabeimen Street East, near the city's major north gate. The church's main entrance faced south, as did all imperial structures, and its tall steeple, or clock tower (*zhonglou*), as it is called in China, would have noticeably competed with the two fifty-two—meter-tall pagodas at Taiyuan's famous Twin Pagoda Temple.[28] Never before had a foreign building seemed to vie with the city's hallowed monuments, and it appeared to the Buddhists of Taiyuan that a religious contest was afoot. The monumentality of this church complex remained unchallenged until the complex was demolished by Boxers and Qing troops in the summer of 1900.

Another Catholic church that appeared in 1870, or reappeared, since it was initially built in the eighteenth century, was the Church of the Holy Mother in the Shanxi village of Geliaogou, which is today a Catholic community of nearly three thousand faithful.[29] Unlike Taiyuan's Church of the Immaculate Conception, originally built to harmonize with Chinese architectural tastes, the Geliaogou church was built in an Italian Renaissance Revival style with three high "clock towers," the middle tower soaring twenty-four meters high and crowned with a cross; its bells were rung several times a day.[30] The Church of Saint Joseph, located in Fengshenghe village, was erected in 1869 where a popular religious structure, the Jinzhong Temple, previously had been located.[31] Several more churches were built immediately after the friars moved to Shanxi in 1860, all of which made the Catholic presence conspicuously evident after its long semiabsence during the years of ostensible proscription.

Not only did churches begin to appear throughout the northern plains of Shanxi, but also Italian friars—bishops and simple priests—began to pour into the cities and villages. The Franciscans' effort to remissionize Shanxi after 1860 was successful; they were able to effectively persuade some Qing officials to exempt Catholics from paying temple taxes, and they accomplished their goal of making the church more visible throughout the province. The number of catechists in 1862 equaled 767, and there were 12,281 active faithful. By 1886, only four years before Taiyuan was recognized as an independent vicariate, the number had grown significantly.[32] That year, Franciscan accounts recorded 2,500 catechists and total of nearly 15,000 Catholics.[33] Once Pope Leo XIII (r. 1878–1903) made Taiyuan an independent apostolic vicariate in 1890, a new and influential Franciscan hierarchy shared status with local Qing officials in Taiyuan.

Recent historiography in Shanxi on this era of Catholic reconstruction has inherited much of the pejorative casting of the Maoist era; when describing this period, for example, one record states, "Foreign Christian missionaries brought to China knowledge of astronomy, calendrics, cartography (geography), medical science, and other natural sciences, which were objectively useful. But they also were deeply involved in the semi-colonialism of China, and these foreign missionaries made religion into an instrument of invasion and coercion. Some foreign missionaries were unruly and persecuted the common people, and every church they built occupied vast areas of good farmland."[34] Even today, some local residents resent the reappearance of the Catholic mission in Shanxi after 1860.

After 1890 the new bishop leaders of the apostolic vicariate of Taiyuan, led mainly by Bishop Gregorio Grassi, OFM (1833–1900), divided their time between two Franciscan Catholic mission stations in Shanxi: Taiyuan city, where the mother church was located, and the small Catholic village of Dongergou, where the Franciscan seminary was located. The Franciscan Holy Land scholar and architect Barnabas Meistermann, OFM (1850–1923), designed the seminary at Dongergou, which still stands today.[35] These two Franciscan centers would play important roles in the Boxer Uprising.

From 1844 until 1890, Shanxi was designated a vicariate apostolic, a region administered by a vicar apostolic, or a bishop with a titular see. The first Franciscan vicar was Bishop Gabriel Grioglio, OFM (1813–1891), who is perhaps best known in the West for his distinction as one of the Council Fathers at the First Vatican Council that convened in 1868. Grioglio, an Italian, took the Franciscan habit in 1830 and was ordained a priest in 1836. By 1845 Grioglio had been sent to Wenshui county, fifteen years before the Franciscan mission there was fully opened, and had devoted himself to editing Chinese catechetical works for use by Shanxi's Catholics.[36] Despite the constraint of operating somewhat unofficially, the church recorded eight thousand Catholics in Shanxi at that time, all under the pastoral care of Bishop Grioglio.[37] As one of only four foreign Franciscans in Shanxi, he collaborated with sixteen native Chinese priests, who were better able to function anonymously as they carried out their pastoral duties.[38]

Grioglio was among the more colorful characters in the history of the Franciscan mission at Shanxi, and his manner toward the native Chinese remains unpopular to this day. With newly acquired funds obtained from China's weakened court after the first Opium War, Grioglio built a new residence and church in the small village of Dongergou; these and other Western-style buildings he commissioned advertised an emerging Western dominance.[39] This was only the first instance of many in which Grioglio antagonized local Chinese, especially his own clergy. Accounts of his rigid positions against popular Chinese rites, his refusal to allow Chinese Catholics to attend dramatic performances held at temples, and his inflexible control over native clergy led to angry complaints from local Christians. The Shanxi signatories of a letter sent to Rome in 1848 lamented that Grioglio and his European confreres failed to understand that "what is suitable for foreign countries is not suitable for our land." And they added, "They treat our Chinese priests as slaves and look on the Chinese as insects."[40] Bishop Grioglio's conflicts with his Chinese priests reached such a point that Rome recalled him to Europe in 1862.[41] He died in 1891, having played important roles both in the construction of the institutional prestige of the Catholic community in Shanxi and in the deliberations of the Vatican Council.

After Grioglio, the Shanxi mission's second influential administrator was the apostolic vicar Bishop Aloysius Moccogatta, OFM, born in Castellazzo Bormida, Italy, the same place as Gregorio Grassi, who was also later a bishop at Taiyuan. Moccogatta entered the Franciscan order in 1826, was ordained a priest in 1832, and by 1844 was serving in the China mission. Father Aloysius became Bishop Aloysius in Shandong on 11 May 1845, where he was consecrated to the episcopate and received his crosier and miter. In 1863 he was transferred to Taiyuan and appointed to assist Grioglio in rebuilding the Shanxi mission. In 1876 Moccogatta was sent to Hebei, where he participated in the consecration of his nephew, Gregorio, who later joined him at Shanxi.[42] Regional and ecclesial connections that were formed in Europe (Moccogatta and Grassi were both from the same place in Italy, were related, and were members of the same order) were often transplanted to the Chinese landscape, where friars were sometimes transferred and promoted based on familiarity. When Moccogatta made the trip to Hebei in 1876, he was already quite frail. Nonetheless, he managed to stir disagreement between the foreign and native clergy of Shanxi.

After he settled at Shanxi in 1863, Moccogatta discovered a province that was essentially overseen by native priests, which, it appears, he found untidy. Liu Anrong recounts, "After Luigi Moccogatta had arrived at Shanxi, [he found that] the Chinese clergy were still managing the Catholic affairs themselves. Moccogatta protested this and issued a decree removing all of the Chinese priests from their posts without exception. His action occasioned the immediate and forceful protests of the Catholic community, but Moccogatta still refused to emerge from his delusion."[43] Other sources, however, provide a more nuanced story.

Li Yuzhang and Li Yuming report that Moccogatta was less interested in suppressing the work of native priests than in employing more of them. In their history they state, "While he was in charge, Bishop Aloysius Moccogatta had six Chinese priests ordained, and personally performed the rites of three ordinations."[44] Whatever the situation was, conflicts and accommodations were inevitable as foreign bishops, who understood the situation in China far less clearly than the native clergy, arrived on the scene and began dispensing orders with an air of privileged authority. After six years of blindness and physical frailty, Bishop Moccogatta died at Taiyuan on 6 September 1891 while Bishop Grassi remained nearby.[45] His death was only a decade after the entire province had suffered what Shanxi natives still call the Great Famine of 1877–1878 (*dingwu qihuang*).[46] It had been a bitter and wearying mission for Aloysius, whose physical and mental anguish in his final years were assuaged only slightly by the presence of his nephew, Gregorio, the son of his sister Paola.

THE BISHOPS OF 1900

Bishop Luigi Moccogatta's successor was Gregorio Grassi, celebrated today as a martyr saint—canonized in 2000 by Pope John Paul II (r. 1978–2005)—who was executed during the Boxer Uprising in Governor Yuxian's yamen courtyard at Taiyuan. Gregorio Grassi's parents were extremely poor. He took the Franciscan habit at the early age of fifteen and was fully professed—having taken final vows of obedience, chastity, and poverty—soon after, in 1849; he was ordained a priest in 1856 after completing his philosophical and theological studies at Our Lady of the Annunciation in Bologna. Until 1860, the year he was sent to China, Father Gregorio prepared for mission work at the famous Franciscan church in Rome, Saint Bartholomew-on-the-Tiber.[47] Grassi's first appointment in China was in Shandong, where he learned Chinese and acclimated to his new cultural context and, soon after, was transferred to Shanxi to assist his uncle in Taiyuan. Grassi was made a bishop in 1876, and since his uncle, Bishop Moccogatta, was too infirm to manage the demanding diurnal affairs that occupy episcopal chanceries, Gregorio became the de facto leader of the Shanxi mission.

Moccogatta's physical collapse from overwork was not surprising, for Shanxi had long been plagued with epidemics, natural disasters, and political upheavals, all of which affected the Catholic community. For three years after Grassi's consecration to bishop, a merciless epidemic swept through the province. Pacifique-Marie Chardin, OFM, poignantly, if somewhat hagiographically, describes Grassi's involvement in relief efforts:

> Three years after Grassi's coronation an epidemic ravaged the mission, and he courageously assisted the sick, providing them with food and administering the sacraments. He breathed pestilential air that carried the putrid smell of the dead bodies kept in the cave homes of the native servants, which had a harmful effect on him. After a month of living among these unfortunate Christians he too became ill with typhus. He received Extreme Unction and fell into a delirium that lasted sixteen days. Everything was already prepared for his funeral when he regained consciousness and recovered. For the duration of this double curse, famine and epidemic, the vicariate lost 3,000 Christians to typhus and 1,000 to starvation.[48]

Ordeals such as this were commonplace, and this one was only the beginning of a rash of natural calamities that left northern China's countryside desolate and teeming with starving peasants until violence erupted in 1900.

Besides the incessant natural disasters that kept Bishop Grassi busy with relief efforts, feeding and housing the poor and undernourished, he managed to concentrate also on the brick-and-mortar expansion of the diocese for the spiritual life of Shanxi's Christians. He oversaw the construction of more than sixty new churches, the rebuilding of a local Marian shrine, the expansion of the Franciscan seminary at Dongergou, and the enlargement of the Catholic hospital and orphanages under his jurisdiction.[49] What perhaps most occupied him during his tenure as Shanxi's bishop were the constant local conflicts he encountered between the Catholic community and the local government. These antagonisms would culminate in his arrest and trial in 1900.

FIGURE 1.1. Bishop Francesco Fogolla, OFM (*second from right*), and Chinese seminarians at the Franciscan Convento dell'Annunziata, in Parma, Italy, during their trip to Europe in 1898. Source: Provincia di Cristo Re dei Frati Minori dell'Emilia Romagna, Parma.

Owing to Moccogatta's infirmity, which rendered him bedridden during many of his final years in Shanxi, all diocesan management fell to the severely overtaxed Gregorio Grassi. Without the eventual help of his auxiliary, Bishop Francesco Fogolla, OFM (1839–1900), Gregorio would likely have collapsed from his responsibilities, as his uncle had.

Few players in the Shanxi mission were more prominent than the portly friar from Parma, Francesco Fogolla (fig. 1.1), who was born in the small village of Montereggio, known in Italy for its fine wine and book trade. After his family moved to Parma, he often visited the Franciscan Church of the Annunciation, where he served as an altar boy at daily Mass; his acquaintance with the friars led to his admission to the order on 11 November 1856 at the seminary in Montiano, Forli County.[50] Fogolla was ordained a priest on 4 October 1863, the feast of Saint Francis, and shortly afterward he entered the Pontificia Athenaeum (now Università) Antonianum in Rome and Saint Bartholomew-on-the-Tiber.[51] He did not remain long at the famed Antonianum, for in 1866, at the age of twenty-six, he boarded a ship for the East to join his confreres in China.

After a pilgrimage stop at the Holy Land, Fogolla at last arrived in Tianjin, where the French Vincentians welcomed him and briefed him on the then fairly stable situation of the mission in China.[52] Bishop Moccogatta met Father Francesco in Taiyuan on 11 February 1868 and, soon after, dispatched him to mission posts in northern Shanxi, near ancient spans of the Great Wall (which so moved him that he later wrote a book on the subject).[53] In 1877 Fogolla was obliged to visit the county magistrate, because some of his parishioners were involved in an acrimonious dispute that had come to blows between Catholics and their non-Christian neighbors. The conflict became so severe that he traveled four times to Beijing to appeal to Zongli officials before a resolution could be found. The stout friar apparently was not above imposing his physical size on the Chinese authorities while discoursing with them. As Chardin writes, with some West-centric gravitas, after Fogolla had successfully put an end to the conflicts "the enemies of the Christian name were prompted by his insistence, and a healthy fear, which allowed him to spread even more effectively our holy religion."[54]

It would be exaggeration, however, to suggest that Fogolla was disposed to bullying the natives. Everyone in Shanxi was on edge in 1877 as the entire province began to suffer from widespread famine and starvation, and Fogolla's interventions were no doubt motivated more by a desire for reconciliation between Christians and non-Christians than by a desire for empowerment. R. J. Forrest, chairman of the China Famine Relief Committee, described northern China at that time: "Fugitives, beggars, and thieves absolutely swarmed. The officials were powerless to create any sort of order among the mountains. . . . Broken carts, scattered grain-bags, dying men and animals, so frequently stopped the way [in Shanxi], that it was often necessary to prevent for days together the entry of convoys on the one side, in order to let the trains from the other to come over."[55] Under such circumstances, tensions easily grew into physical hostility. While Fogolla was mediating disputes between Christians and non-Christians, he was also sending catechists to other provinces to seek alms and so was able to relieve several thousand starving Chinese.[56] Among the characteristics that distinguish Francesco Fogolla's time in Shanxi was his reported mastery of Chinese, which he profited from on several critical occasions. He was made a bishop during a brief trip back to Europe in 1898, and he was among those who encountered Boxer conflicts in 1900.

RECONSTRUCTION AND TRANSITION, 1901–1951

After the dreadful summer of 1900, when thousands were killed in Shanxi, the apostolic vicariate of Taiyuan underwent an uncertain period of negotiation and reconstruction. The post-Boxer-era missionary enterprise in Shanxi was no different from that in any other northern province; surviving priests and bishops—Chinese and foreign—were scattered and anxious during the first months of 1901. In the aftermath the northern Shanxi vicariate had only twenty-two priests left, fourteen of whom were Chinese (and better able to obscure their priestly identity and evade persecution).[57] In the interim, while the friars regrouped and awaited Rome's appointment of a replacement bishop, two priests were assigned to supervise and restore northern Shanxi—Fathers Barnabas Nanetti da Cologna, OFM (1867–1911), and Francesco Saccani, OFM (1865–1944). Both Nanetti and Saccani had taught at the Franciscan seminary in Dongergou, and both had eluded capture by absconding to secluded areas. Nanetti, for example, fled to Mongolia and then to Beijing via circuitous and remote roads.[58]

After two years of waiting, Taiyuan at last welcomed, as an independent vicariate, its second prelate, on 6 July 1902.[59] Bishop Agapito Fiorentini, OFM (1866–1941), was confronted with a mission in shambles, but there remained a sizeable Catholic presence in Shanxi's Taiyuan vicariate: 15,412 faithful and 3,671 catechists. Fiorentini, who was born in Palestrina, Italy, the imagined home of Ulysses and the confirmed home of the wealthy Barberini family, indefatigably labored to restore the mission and its prestige. After only eight years in Taiyuan he had increased the vicariate's Catholic population to more than 21,000 faithful and over 10,000 catechists.[60] He had taken the Franciscan habit in 1882, been ordained a priest in 1890, been assigned to the mission at Hubei in 1895, and been consecrated to the episcopacy on 15 June 1902 in the foreign-controlled port city of Hankou.[61]

When Fiorentini arrived in Taiyuan in the wake of the Boxer chaos, he found that the Catholic clergy had installed themselves in the facilities of Shanxi's premiere institute of higher learning, the Lingde Academy, which precipitated a scandal among the local literati. The Franciscans had apparently appropriated the buildings with some insensitivity to the school's denizens. Lingde Academy, for the time being, remained the Franciscan center of all mission activities, though Fiorentini was determined to remove his operation to a more suitably Catholic location.[62]

It was left to Bishop Fiorentini to reclaim land and rebuild structures that had been seized or destroyed during the Boxer Uprising. The area at Taiyuan's north gate, near where the previous cathedral church had been, was sparsely populated and largely unoccupied by other buildings; using reparation funds provided by the local magistrate, Fiorentini commissioned the construction of the present cathedral church. Construction began in 1903, and the completed church was consecrated on 31 December 1905.[63] Few bishops have invested more time in overseeing the construction of so many buildings; including churches, rectories, a chancery, new convents for the Franciscan Missionaries of Mary (FMM), an orphanage, and the spacious Saint Joseph's Hospital, Fiorentini constructed sixty-seven imposing new edifices. Exhausted no doubt from his unceasing enterprise, he resigned from his duties in 1909, shortly before consecrating his successor, Bishop Eugenio Massi, OFM (1875–1944), in 1910. Fiorentini was reassigned to Shanxi in 1916, was granted permanent retirement in 1938, and died at his Taiyuan residence in 1941 after witnessing wave after wave of political conflict on the northern Chinese landscape.

Eugenio Massi functioned as the mission's bishop of the Taiyuan vicariate during Agapito Fiorentini's six-year respite from pastoral duties, and he set himself at once to continuing his predecessor's ambitious construction agenda.[64] Massi had been ordained in 1892 and taught philosophy for four years before being appointed to the Franciscan mission in China.[65] He had arrived in Shanxi in 1903 and been assigned to mission posts in the north, where he devoted a large portion of his time to helping local farmers dig irrigation canals for their fields. Once he became a bishop, Massi, following in his predecessor's footsteps, ordered the construction of two schools, a press, an additional floor to the cathedral rectory, and a building for the Franciscan Missionaries of Mary to use as a charitable hospital.[66] In order to conform to Chinese architectural custom, he had a wall erected around the cathedral complex. Among his more lasting marks on the history of Shanxi Catholicism was Massi's effort to popularize the veneration of a deceased Franciscan Missionary of Mary sister, Maria Assunta Pallotta, FMM (1875–1905), who remains today the object of pious and scholarly attention in China and the West. Bishop Massi was so convinced of the young woman's holiness, and of the litany of miracles ascribed to her, that he invited a famed European physician to Shanxi to perform an autopsy and kept meticulous notes of the doctor's examination of her exhumed body.[67] Massi was transferred to Shaanxi in 1916, moved to Hankou in 1925, and died from a stray bullet in 1944 during the fierce fighting of the Sino-Japanese War.

The last non-Chinese prelate in the Taiyuan vicariate was the spirited friar Bishop Domenico Luca Capozi, OFM (1899–1991) (fig. 1.2). Capozi entered China during an era of particular challenges, both for the native residents in Taiyuan and for the Franciscan friars who lived there. He had already been in Shanxi for nearly a decade when, in 1937, Japanese troops attacked Taiyuan. In the 9 November 1937 edition of the *Canberra Times*, a feature article appeared with the headline "Taiyuan Falls to Japanese, Fierce Fighting." The article recounts that "Japanese forces launched a general attack" on the city, "assisted by artillery and war planes." The account continues: "A jubilant communiqué from the headquarters of the Japanese Army says that the capital fell after fierce hand-to-hand fighting. Reports have been received from London that anxiety is felt for the safety of the 12 British missionaries who are trapped in the city. Before the capture, Japanese planes flew over dropping leaflets calling upon all foreigners to depart; otherwise they would be regarded as combatants."[68] While the Franciscans were not, in the end, required to depart, they lived in fear for their lives, and underground tunnels were installed beneath the Dongergou seminary, where the seminarians sought safety during Japanese bombing raids.[69] By the time Domenico Capozi was made Taiyuan's new bishop in 1940, the members of the Franciscan mission had endured debilitating hardships alongside the native Chinese when Japanese attacks fractured Shanxi's government and diminished its population.

After serving in pastoral appointments outside of Taiyuan, Capozi moved to the capital following his consecration on 14 April 1940; Fiorentini was the principal celebrant of the ordination Mass. Fiorentini retreated from leadership of the growing mission, while demands on Capozi's time grew more intense as Shanxi's reputation increased in Rome, since it boasted the largest number of martyrs of the Boxer Uprising. Capozi was thus entrusted with the onerous duty of overseeing the collection and chronicling of testimonies regarding those who had died, a daunting responsibility given the large number of victims and the wide geographic sweep of anti-Christian Boxer incidents in Shanxi. This was an urgent task, as requiem Masses were swiftly ushering the last living witnesses of that era to their eternal rest. The Vatican Archives are replete with Capozi's notes, annotated and sealed by the advocator of the cause, Father Giovanni Ricci, OFM (1875–1941) (fig. 1.3). Capozi's labors came to satisfactory fruition when, in 1946, he and two of his

FIGURE 1.2. Bishop Agapito Fiorentini, OFM (*right*), and Bishop
Domenico Luca Capozi, OFM, prelates of the Catholic vicariate of Taiyuan,
Shanxi, after the Boxer Uprising. These two bishops were assigned the task
of rebuilding the Franciscan mission in Shanxi after the Boxer indemnity
agreement was signed in 1901. Source: Archivio Curia Generalizia Ordo
Fratrum Minorum, Rome.

FIGURE 1.3. Father Giovanni Ricci, OFM, Shanxi missionary and advocate of the cause for the beatification and canonization of the Franciscans who died in Shanxi during the Boxer Uprising. Most of the available records related to the Boxer incidents in Shanxi were collected and recorded by Father Barnabas Nanetti da Cologna, OFM, and Ricci. Source: Archivio Curia Generalizia Ordo Fratrum Minorum, Rome.

confreres went to the Vatican, where the martyrs of Taiyuan were beatified by Pope Pius XII (r. 1939–1958) under lavish paintings of the beati hung above the famous cathedra in Saint Peter's Basilica.[70]

The revelries in Rome were somewhat muted, however, since a large contingent of the Chinese clergy back in Shanxi requested that Taiyuan be administered by a more indigenous hierarchy. When Bishop Capozi returned to Shanxi in February 1948, he was compelled to appoint Father Joseph Hao Nai (1914–1970) as the new vicar general and Father Paul Zhang Xin, OFM (1911–1999), as the new rector of the vicariate seminary.[71] There was an unwillingness to release the vicariate's financial management from foreign control; all matters of money were placed in the charge of a foreign priest.[72] The contest between native and foreign clergy for positions in the hierarchy was soon resolved. After the victory of the Communist Party in 1949, tensions between the church and the government flared into open hostilities, and Capozi was arrested in February 1951. After seventeen months of imprisonment and relentless interrogations, the bishop and all the other remaining non-Chinese Franciscans in Shanxi were expelled from China.[73] According to some, Capozi had never fully acclimated to life in China, and while in prison he had been forced to request a spoon, since he had never learned to use chopsticks.[74] The Franciscan mission in Shanxi was decisively brought to a conclusion; despite later attempts to return to Shanxi to visit his old friends, Domenico Luca Capozi was never able to reenter China.

Fortunately, Capozi had foreseen the need to increase the number of native Chinese priests, and by 1946 Taiyuan had become an autonomous diocesan territory with a comparatively large local clergy. This allowed the newly established archdiocese of Taiyuan to survive the decades following his expulsion. During Eugenio Massi's six-year reign as Taiyuan's bishop, 9,572 persons had become Catholic, and Domenico Capozi's efforts attracted nearly 3,000 additional faithful to the church in Shanxi.[75] Overall this was an era of tremendous Catholic growth, and once Taiyuan had become an archdiocese it boasted a quickly rising number of native priests, many of whom were ordained under the encouragement of Bishop Capozi. Foreign missionaries cultivated the conditions for the growth of native priests, and the efforts of the friars advanced the process of Roman Catholic indigenization in Shanxi. Shanxi's missionaries promoted a national clergy, which also facilitated the formation of a national episcopate.[76] After 1949 Shanxi's Catholics endured decades of uncertainty and discrimination, but because of planning by the Franciscan friars the archdiocese of Taiyuan was equipped with a sufficient number of Chinese priests to not only survive the Maoist era but also, surprisingly, emerge from that time of insecurity with even more Catholics than when the trials began.

THE FRANCISCAN MISSIONARIES OF MARY IN SHANXI

The friars were not the only Franciscans in Shanxi after the last Jesuits had left their churches empty in the eighteenth century as a result of the Jesuit suppression in 1773; the Franciscan Missionaries of Mary made their own footprints in Shanxi's wide plains, arriving there in 1899, and leaving along with male religious during the transitional years after 1949. Reams of descriptive letters and memoirs by these Franciscan women have remained largely untouched in the Franciscan Missionaries of Mary archive in Rome. The friar bishops were the principal decision makers regarding Franciscan activities in Shanxi, but they were, for the most part, busily monitoring the mission while installed within their chancery edifice in Taiyuan. Rank-and-file mission priests were necessarily occupied with pastoral duties—only they could administer the sacraments of the Holy Mass, penance, extreme unction, and matrimony. The sisters, however, were tirelessly at work among the people of Shanxi. It was they who cared for the sick, looked after the orphans, and were assigned to countless tasks around the Franciscan mission. It is through the accounts of these extraordinary women that we are able to discern a more polychromatic and personal vision of the living conditions and relationships the Franciscans encountered in Shanxi. One sister, for example, described her first meeting with the people of Taiyuan in evocative terms: "I cannot describe to you the warmth of the welcome these poor souls gave us. . . . Women and children would not be satisfied till they had touched our hands, our habits, even our feet, so surprisingly long to them."[77] The women of the mission, Western and Chinese, contributed to and participated in both the positive and the negative aspects of the events surrounding the battles of Shanxi at the turn of the century, from 1899 until 1901, and the missionary sisters who followed the Boxer Uprising also played a significant role in shaping Shanxi's Catholic history.

Seven Franciscan women figure most prominently in this narrative, all of whom arrived in Taiyuan before the Boxer incidents began. After dying in 1905, Maria Assunta Pallotta became an icon of sanctity in Shanxi and precipitated an ongoing public cult of veneration in both China and the West. Pallotta was the eighth of the Franciscan sisters in Shanxi to be beatified at Saint Peter's. Most important to apprehending the particular emphasis of the Franciscan sisters of Shanxi is an understanding of their founder's motivations. When Mother Mary of the Passion (Hélène Marie Philippine de Chappotin de Neuville, 1839–1904) first learned that the Vatican had ratified her new missionary order, she wrote of her ardent wish to "give the world the reign of charity and truth."[78] Works of charity, whether through teaching, caring for orphans, or treating the injured and infirm, were perhaps the most notable characteristic of the sisters who lived in Shanxi. In a promotional booklet published by the Franciscan Missionaries of Mary in 1926, the sisters affirm their Franciscan identity, describing the order as "imbued with the distinctive characteristics which Saint Francis wished to see in his children: abandonment to Divine Providence, apostolic zeal and complete detachment, in order to attain that perfect love which alone can say in truth, 'My God and my All [Meus Deus et Omnia].'"[79] Outlining the requisite qualities of a young woman considering a vocation to the order, the booklet emphasized that FMM sisters are all "united by the bonds of common charity."[80]

The only Franciscan sister serving in Shanxi who may have garnered more international attention than Sister Maria Assunta is the French mother superior of the Taiyuan convent, Marie-Hermine de Jesus, FMM (Irma Grivot, 1866–1900).[81] When Bishop Fogolla was in Europe in 1897, he petitioned Mother Mary of the Passion to send missionary sisters from her new order to accompany him back to Shanxi. Grassi had earlier appealed to Fogolla to bring sisters back who could assist the friars, especially in developing a Catholic orphanage and medical clinic. Marie-Hermine and six *consoeurs* were selected for the long journey (fig. 1.4), and at their ceremony of departure the seven Franciscan Missionaries of Mary received a final Benediction of the Blessed Sacrament at Saint Raphael's convent in the port city of Marseille. Having been blessed and commissioned with the intonation of a Marian hymn, the sisters left their native Europe on 12 March 1899, and as Louis Nazaire Bégin (1840–1925) recounts, "stormy weather gave them a rough sea, and all were sea-sick"; as the waves lashed their boat, "they were tossed to and fro in their berths."[82] Fogolla had asked for twelve missionary women; he had been given only seven, and by the time their turbulent sea voyage had ended in April, when the sisters first gazed over the lush panorama of Hong Kong, northern China was growing more agitated by natural misfortunes and cultural misunderstandings.

While the friars in Shanxi had already acculturated to China's social patterns—they had been well prepared for this process before leaving their

SEPT FRANCISCAINES MISSIONNAIRES DE MARIE
MASSACRÉES AU CHAN-SI (CHINE). JUILLET 1900.

FIGURE 1.4. The seven Franciscan Missionaries of Mary sisters who were
executed at Yuxian's prefectural yamen in Taiyuan on 9 July 1900. This photograph
of the sisters was taken in France near the time of their departure ceremony.
Source: Archivio Curia Generalizia Ordo Fratrum Minorum, Rome.

native Europe—the seven sisters were less equipped for what they encountered in China, since they had undergone little advanced formal preparation. Their correspondence to their families and fellow religious in Europe reveals tension between the Chinese and European women and even conflict among the sisters. It is easy to forget just how divergent their European childhoods were from the society of turn-of-the-century China.

Marie-Hermine de Jesus, born in Baune, France, in Burgundy, did not have the support of her parents as she entered the novitiate of the Franciscan Missionaries of Mary, though she nevertheless moved to Vanves in 1894 to become a missionary sister. In his heavily hagiographic work on the Franciscan Missionaries of Mary who traveled to China, *Gigli e rose* (Lilies and roses), Giovanni Ricci describes Marie-Hermine's religious devotion: "Hermine was most devoted to the Child Jesus and the Blessed Sacrament, the little Jesus inflamed her love for holy humility and the Blessed Sacrament made her melt from the desire to sacrifice for souls."[83] Such pious prose was not uncommon in Marie-Hermine's own writing, and it was perhaps due to both her distinguished piety and her particular aptitude for organization that she was made mother superior of the new convent at Taiyuan, which Mother Mary of the Passion named after the Franciscan saint of the Eucharist, Saint Paschal Baylon, OFM (1540–1592).[84]

While Marie-Hermine's six companions were, by and large, also inclined toward pious devotions and the missionary charge to convert souls, Bishop Fogolla envisioned more diurnal tasks for the sisters. When outlining the expected duties of the Franciscan Missionaries of Mary, Fogolla informed their founder that the sisters in China should be skilled in needlework, photography, painting, basic surgery, and general nursing.[85] Fogolla's band of Franciscan sisters was indeed proficient in these skills, and even more, they represented a number of European countries and possessed skills far beyond the bishop's expectations.

Maria Amandina, FMM (Pauline Jueris, 1872–1900), from Belgium, had lost her mother at the age of seven and had been obliged to raise six girls and a boy, since her father could find work only in a neighboring village. Her personal history contributed to her independence and aptitude with children, skills that proved useful in Shanxi. Marie de Sainte Nathalie, FMM (Jeanne-Marie Kerguin, 1864–1900), was the daughter of poor French peasants and was responsible for the care of the family's farm animals. Having received only an elementary education, Marie de Sainte Nathalie was apportioned some of the more menial responsibilities at Saint Paschal's Convent in Shanxi—laundering, farmwork, and milking cows. She referred to herself meekly as "Saint Francis' little donkey."[86] Maria della Pace, FMM (Marianna Giuliani, 1875–1900), was born in Aquila, Italy; her father was adamantly antichurch and had abandoned Maria, her mother, and her sisters. Anticlericalism was prevalent in Italy during the nineteenth century; and for many of the Franciscan missioners in China, being in a foreign country was a relief from the tensions they encountered at home in Europe. Maria della Pace was the youngest member of the Franciscan convent in Shanxi on the eve of the Boxer troubles in 1900.

Maria Chiara, FMM (Clelia Nanetti, 1872–1900), was born on the Venetian bank of the River Po in Ponte Maddelena and named after the celebrated companion to Saint Francis, Chiara Offreduccio (1194–1253), better known as Saint Clare, the founder of the Poor Clares. Like Maria della Pace's father, Chiara's parents did not support their daughter's entrance into religious life, but Chiara's brother was already a Franciscan and persuaded them to allow her to enter the Franciscan Missionaries of Mary novitiate in 1892.[87] She made her perpetual vows in 1898, just one year before leaving for China along with Bishop Fogolla and the other Franciscans under his direction.

Of the Franciscan sisters who were involved in Boxer violence at Taiyuan, Marie de Saint Just, FMM (Anne Moreau, 1866–1900), was perhaps the most advantaged, having been born into an affluent family in La Faye, France. Several histories have centered on Marie's internal struggles; as one account relates, "Darkness clouded her soul, plunging her into doubts of all kinds."[88] Once in the order, Marie de Saint Just grew gradually more distant and apathetic, apparently reexamining the soundness of her decision to become a sister. She had quietly hidden herself away from her mother—her father had died while she was young—and secretly entered the Franciscan Missionaries of Mary at Les Châtalets, severing ties with her family when she took the white habit. While living with the Franciscan community at Vanves, Marie was taught skills thought useful for future work at the mission, such as shoemaking and the maintenance and operation of the printing press.[89] By the time she was settled in Shanxi, as her letters indicate, Marie de Saint Just's "dark night of the soul" had apparently given way to a recommitment to her beliefs and commitment to religious life.

The final member of the first Franciscan Missionaries of Mary mission to Shanxi was a Dutch woman from Ossendrecht, Marie Adolphine, FMM (Anna Dierkx, 1866–1900), who was not only born into a needy family of six children but also had been orphaned when young. Charitable neighbors, not much better off than her own family, took Marie Adolphine and her siblings into their care.[90] After several years of tiring work as a housemaid and factory worker, she entered the Franciscan Missionaries of Mary in 1892 at the age of twenty-seven. Having come from humble origins, Marie Adolphine was assigned to modest tasks in her community of sisters, such as laundry and attending to kitchen duties.[91]

The seven sisters of Shanxi's Convent of Saint Paschal Baylon were not the first Roman Catholic women to serve as missionaries in China—the Daughters of Charity and other orders had already blazed the trail—but following the Poor Clare sisters, who had first entered China in 1634, they constituted the next large wave of Franciscan women to serve in China.[92] Mother Marie-Hermine de Jesus and her consoeurs had hoped that their principal work in Shanxi would be at a hospital, but they quickly discovered that their time would be spent almost entirely with the care and education of orphaned children who flooded into their orphanage, especially as economic and natural hardships affected the lives of poorer peasants without means to feed their children.[93] In an anonymous Chinese history of the Franciscans of Shanxi, published by the Diocese of Taiyuan in 1946, the brief undertaking of the sisters is summarized well, though in language common to the mission: "In the spring of 1899, seven sisters peacefully arrived at Taiyuan and began their works of compassion, such as organizing the mission orphanage and establishing a hospital. Step by step they set themselves to their tasks in order to assist the missionary enterprise of saving many souls. But the Lord of Heaven had an even better plan."[94] According to this account, the "better plan" was the suffering they encountered during the Boxer Uprising. The letters written by the sisters during the Boxer conflicts are much more raw and anxious than the ornamented official church publications that followed.

These seven Franciscan Missionaries of Mary are most often discussed in hagiographical writings related to the anti-Christian violence of 1900, though such works tend to describe them in melodramatic terms that portray them as one-dimensional paragons of Catholic holiness. They were followed by other Franciscan Missionaries of Mary, all of whom were inculcated with an expectation of, even desire for, martyrdom. Imagined martyrdom was an unremitting fancy in the minds of all these women as they prepared for their voyage to Shanxi; and shortly before the sisters left Europe they were shown a photograph of the recently martyred Franciscan friar Victorin Delbroucq, OFM (1870–1898), "his body covered with wounds," suggestive perhaps of what awaited them in China.[95] Shanxi's Franciscan mission eventually had two orders of Catholic sisters: European women known as "White Habit Sisters" (Baiyi) and Chinese women known as "Black Habit Sisters" (Heiyi).

A second wave of Franciscan Missionaries of Mary voyaged to China at the request of Bishop Agapito Fiorentini after the Boxer Uprising, arriving at Taiyuan in 1902; these European women were, despite their best intentions, at times culturally at odds with the local Chinese women who likewise wished to serve as celibate religious.[96] Some Chinese women were accepted into the "White Habits" (Franciscan Missionaries of Mary), but for the most part the European Franciscans in Shanxi were distinguishable from Chinese sisters by their distinctive white attire. An equally recognizable difference existed in hierarchy. There was no question that the European women were the spiritual and temporal mentors of the Chinese sisters, even though the Chinese sisters more seamlessly fit into the fabric of Shanxi culture. This does not mean, however, that these two groups were always antagonistic; indeed, they were held together by religious bonds that, for the most part, repaired the inevitable cultural tensions that occasionally arose between them.

EARTHLY PARADOXES AND HEAVENLY BATTLES

The famous Legalist philosopher Han Feizi (c. 280–c. 233 BCE) coined the most common Chinese term for "paradox," maodun, which literally means "spear and shield." The term appears in Han Feizi's story of a street peddler selling both a "spear that can pierce anything" and a "shield that cannot be pierced." Thus, maodun alludes to any two points that appear irreconcilable. Han Feizi's spear-and-shield describes well the situation of the Franciscan mission in Shanxi. On the one hand the Franciscans there were well accepted by the native Chinese whom they befriended, especially as they became more "Sinified" (Hanhua)—that is, as they accommodated to Chinese cultural mores and grew more linguistically fluent. On the other hand, no matter how acculturated the Franciscans became, they remained foreigners in China. The real paradox in their situation revolves around the concept of "indigenization" (Zhongguo fengsuhua). From the historiographical point of view, the fate of the Franciscans was not unlike that of the Manchus who had entered China in 1644. In the historical Chinese treatment of the Manchus, certain contradictions had been accepted; like the Franciscans in China, they were tolerated once they became suitably indigenized. But when things in the province took a turn for the worse, they were blamed, partly because, after all, they were not Chinese.[97]

FIGURE 1.5. A Red Lantern girl during the Boxer Uprising, in a photograph taken at an unknown location, possibly Tianjin. The Red Lantern in this image has bound feet. Source: Archivio Curia Generalizia Ordo Fratrum Minorum, Rome.

Although many have assumed that the tensions of the late Qing were mainly antiforeign, most of the victims who were attacked and killed during the summer months of 1900 were Chinese. And although late-Qing tensions between China and the West have been characterized as predominantly economic and political, most of those who were attacked and killed during that time were poor native Christians, not foreign merchants or diplomats. More accurately, the tensions and conflicts between the European Franciscans and local Chinese in Shanxi from the late nineteenth century to 1900 centered on religious and cultural misunderstandings. The earthly battles that ensued from 1898 to 1900 began in the minds of both Chinese and Westerners largely driven by their respective religious visions of heavenly battles raging above in an ethereal realm of gods, angels, and immortals. The history of the Franciscans in Shanxi during the late Qing, like the history of the Boxers, includes two distinct though enmeshed narratives, a *maodun*, that involve gods and immortals at war with each other, and living women and men who, once friends on the plains of Shanxi, had by 1900 become enemies.

Not long after her arrival in Shanxi, the Franciscan mother superior, Marie-Hermine de Jesus, wrote a letter home that presciently described the paradoxical nature of the Shanxi mission. "The people in Shanxi," she wrote, "are the most peace-loving people in China," but in the same letter, the French sister anxiously announced that "China must have victims."[98] When the diarist Liu Dapeng sat at his desk to record the local events of his native Shanxi, his writing brush naturally chronicled the sudden appearance of an eccentric group of fanatically anti-Christian and antiforeign men and women who identified themselves as the Yihetuan, most often referred to as the "Boxers" or "Fists of Righteous Harmony" in Western histories, and the *hongdengzhao*, or "Red Lantern" women (fig. 1.5). In his *Jinci Temple Gazetteer* (Jinci zhi), Liu wrote, "By the beginning of the sixth month in summer of the Gengzi reign year [1900], the Yihequan [Fists of Righteous Harmony] arose in great numbers, and by fall of the seventh month they were repeatedly congregating at Jinci Temple."[99] Jinci Temple was a short distance from Taiyuan, where the Franciscan friars and sisters lived at their mission, and as the Boxers and Red Lanterns performed rites of possession there, asking their gods to empower them in their campaign against foreign demons and foreign religion, the Franciscans intoned prayers of intercession, asking God and his Mother to strengthen them for the martyrdom they had prepared for. By the time Boxers appeared near Taiyuan, the seeds of conflict had emerged.

CHAPTER 2

Boxers and Local Gods

Just looking at them, they were frightful!   —LIU DAPENG

B Y early July 1900, everyone—commoners, Catholics, and officials—
could see that something had changed around Taiyuan. The "peace
loving" people of Shanxi described by Mother Marie-Hermine de Jesus had
adopted quite another attitude, one that seemed menacing not only to foreign missionaries and Chinese Christians but also to anyone who did not
support this new trend toward hostility, even to those at the highest level
of the Qing bureaucracy. A peculiar event transpired in July 1900, one that
would have been unimaginable only three months earlier. A large troupe
of Boxers under the leadership of a Shanxi man nicknamed "Old Master
Immortality" and his two female cohorts, collectively called the "Three
Teachers," approached the north gate of Taiyuan. Flummoxed perhaps by
their brazen display of confidence, not to mention the shimmer of a hundred
glistening weapons in the hands of their fellow Boxers, the county official,
He Zongxun, accompanied by a retinue of minor officials and local gentry,
rushed out of the city gate to welcome the oncoming Fists of Righteous
Harmony and the Red Lantern women.

Liu Dapeng colorfully narrates what happened after the Boxers had been
politely escorted into the city: "The Three Teachers settled themselves high
on the dais of the Great Hall, and Old Master Immortality was waited on

as the other Boxers arrayed themselves to his left and right. The officials stood below in deference. The Three Teachers hurled insults on the officials while Old Master Immortality indignantly spat onto the face of one official. He accused them of committing crimes against the people."[1] How could a ruffian from a backwater village terrorize Taiyuan's officials, arrogate the magistrate's dais, and launch invective against the Qing authorities? What precipitated such popular unrest at the ground level, and what was the official response?

Featured in an anonymously published pictorial book of the late nineteenth century are several woodblock prints of famine in China. One image by humanitarians Xie Jiafu (fl. 1880) and his colleagues from the Taohuawu Association, an assembly of men dedicated to charitable service, depicts a gruesome image of famine in northern China.[2] Featured in the small booklet *Peculiar Pictorial Depictions of Famine in Henan to Invoke Tears from Iron* (Henan qihuang tieleitu) is a print of six emaciated famine victims; two of them squat, knife in the hand of one, over the skeletal body of someone who has died of starvation.[3] The caption reads, "Contending to carve up a corpse on the road of one who has died from starvation."[4] Similarly distressing themes are depicted in Xie Jiafu's other images: orphans being lured to their deaths to become food, wives being sold for food money, and people committing suicide to escape hunger.

It is not an exaggeration to describe Shanxi's misery as it is depicted in these images as a Great Famine of the 1870s, and a similar famine struck again in the years just before the Boxer violence of 1898–1900.[5] In fact, if we are looking for a catalyst for the changes that prompted this outrageous challenge to Qing authority, we might turn to the effects of the severe droughts of the mid- to late nineteenth century. It was not merely the ensuing famines that caused these changes, however, but the admixture of human misery and religious accusations based on fanatical beliefs in a heavenly battle, that eventually culminated in the Boxer violence in 1900 Shanxi.

SHANXI'S DROUGHT

The widespread view of who caused Shanxi's recurring droughts drove anti-Christian and antiforeign thought in Shanxi, building on religious tensions between Chinese and foreigners, non-Christians and Christians. Economic and political complaints were conspicuously absent from the popular rhetoric of the Boxers, and mostly absent from the rhetoric of the imperial officials at both the local and national levels. The spiritual and earthly dimensions of Shanxi's famine were the principal topics of discussion. Today, the people of Shanxi still associate "the third year of emperor Guangxu's reign" (1877) with the famine and recount local memories that have taken on the aura of legend:

> In Guangxu 3 it didn't rain and the harvest failed. The people were starving. In one family there were only two brothers left; their parents had already perished. The elder brother knew that one of them had to survive to carry on the family line, so he decided it was necessary to kill his younger brother and eat him. He began to sharpen his knife on a stone, and ordered his younger brother to boil some water. His younger brother asked, "Elder brother [*gege*], why are you sharpening the knife?" The elder brother glared at him and answered, "To kill a man with!" So the younger brother began to boil the water. But while doing so, he found one red bean [*hongdou*] at the bottom of the pot that somehow had been overlooked before. Instead of eating the bean himself, he brought it to his elder brother and said: "*Gege*, you eat this. You're not strong enough to kill a man!" When his elder brother saw this, he realized his brother's goodness and did not kill him. So one red bean saved his life.[6]

Shanxi was not the only province afflicted by drought and starvation; greater China, too, suffered a string of famines from 1877 until 1900. An 1897 correspondence recorded in the *North China Herald* notes that "the roads are usually filled with refugees going South, but this year the movement is reversed, and hundreds of wretched families are to be met making their way northward."[7] By the advent of the Boxer Uprising in 1898, foreigners in Jiangsu, to the southeast of Shanxi, recorded that "elm trees were stripped of their bark, the lower branches of the willows stripped of their leaves, and caterpillars and snails were eaten when they could be gotten."[8] European and American foreigners in China could record the droughts in China as bystanders, as most of them lived in mission enclaves with sufficient food supplies, but to the poorer population in Shanxi these calamities meant their own suffering and, often, death. The foreign onlookers, though active participants in relief efforts, were increasingly blamed for the dry, unremittingly fruitless plains of Shanxi, cracked from sun and lack of rainfall.

After the Franciscan Missionaries of Mary had arrived in Taiyuan and begun attempting to alleviate the human suffering caused by the drought,

Boxer placards began to appear in Shanxi that accused the foreigners and their religion of causing the famine. One such message read: "The gods help the fighters, the Fists of Righteous Harmony, as the foreign devils have disturbed the central plains. They force their religion and only believe in Heaven [viz., the Lord of Heaven]. They don't believe in the gods or the Buddha, and they neglect their ancestors. Their men are improper and their women immoral. . . . The heavens won't rain and the earth is scorched, and all because of the foreign devils, the skies are blocked."[9] Thus the claim spread that the gods in their irritation were withholding the rain until foreigners and their heterodox religion were eradicated.[10]

Foreign missionaries stationed in Shanxi during the mid- to late nineteenth century wrote much about the conditions on the central plains at that time. One of the friars serving the Shanxi mission at Taiyuan, Father Théodoric Balat, OFM (1858–1900) wrote in a letter dated 5 December 1899: "Already meals are restricted in many families, even those who are comfortably off. For the rest they are fortunate if they can get a kind of thin watery soup, made from a little millet boiled in water. Others mix husks with the millet to make it go further. . . . I have seen children quarrelling over waste cabbage leaves which the gardener had thrown away when picking the cabbages."[11] Doctor Ebenezer Henry Edwards, a Protestant medical missionary in Shanxi for eighteen years, included this passage in his hagiographical record of Protestants who died in Shanxi during the peak months of the Boxer Uprising: "So great was the terror spread by these reports that numberless persons were killed who had no connection with Christianity whatsoever, for, in consequence of the long-existing drought, many people were wandering about picking up a precarious living; and not a few of them were accused of being in the pay of foreigners, and killed at sight."[12] The late nineteenth-century drought in Shanxi had stirred the people—quite understandably after the devastating famine of 1877. Protestant missionary Jennie Clapp (1845–1900) wrote from Shanxi: "We never watched the clouds and direction of the wind so closely before."[13]

The storm clouds foreseen by the Franciscan mission were metaphorical. The droughts had not only put Shanxi's agrarian population out of work with no fields to harvest but also left them wandering about the province hungry and homeless. To them, the missionaries appeared well fed in their grand foreign edifices, staffed with cooks, janitors, and groundskeepers. These were historically based perceptions; since the treaty settlements in 1842 following the Opium War, China's cities and inland areas seemed overrun with foreign Christians, who were converting large numbers of Chinese to their alien religion. Gossip about Europeans abounded: in the imagination of northern China's poorer inhabitants, foreigners were laden with body hair; they were popularly referred to as *maozi*, or "hairies." Chinese Christians were thus called *ermaozi*, or "secondhand hairies," by affiliation. Left without employment, Shanxi's displaced population had ample time to entertain such rumors and add to them a patina of superstitious new myths. Like the "insidious" Doctor Fu Manchu, an Orientalized creation by Sax Rohmer (Arthur Henry Sarsfield Ward, 1883–1959), foreign missionaries were mythologized into sinister conjurers-cum-colonialists, whose gods were likewise poised to destroy the native lands and native beliefs of Chinese.

THE RISE OF THE BOXERS

More Christians—Chinese and foreigners—died at the hands of Boxers in Shanxi than in any other province; even today the "Boxer Movement" (*Yihetuan yundong*), as it is presently called in China, figures notoriously in the identity of Shanxi Catholics.[14] The diocesan cathedral in Taiyuan now features a marble frieze of the Catholic martyrs of 1900 on the main altar in the large church.[15]

The first reports of a martial arts band determined to attack Christians and destroy churches emerged in the spring of 1898 in the unassuming town of Liyuantun, in Shandong. In February 1900, the Roman Catholic newspaper *Huibao* (Church newspaper) described China's first Boxers in Shandong: "The society has five names: Plum Flower Boxers, Boxers United in Righteousness, the Red Lantern Shining, the Armor of the Golden Bell and the general name, Big Swords. . . . It began with the Eighteen Chiefs of Guan county, who had repeatedly destroyed the church in Liyuantun. In recent years it has spread further and further to encompass now almost all of Shandong with the object of quelling the foreigners and eradicating their religion."[16] The China missionary Giovanni Ricci wrote more about the Shanxi incidents of the Boxer era than anyone else, and in several of his works he succinctly outlined the formation of the Boxer campaign before its entrance into Shanxi.

In his *Franciscan Martyrs of the Boxer Rising*, Ricci, who had been assigned the task of collecting information in Shanxi about the movement, locates the first ripples of Boxer activity in 1898, "when the German Government demanded a large strip of territory in reparation for the murder of two German missionaries."[17] He describes additional insults to China by foreign powers: the construction of a Catholic church on what had been the site of a non-Christian temple, the occupation of Port Arthur (Lüshun Port, Dalian) by Russia, along with the "persistent rumor that the Great Powers aimed at nothing less than the dismemberment of China." The immediate result, Ricci suggests, was the formation of the Boxers, who viewed Christian missionaries as the "vanguard of the destroying armies," whose religion was "merely the sword in disguise."[18] Once the movement had taken root, its branches crept quickly through Shandong and Zhili (modern Hebei). Near the end of the century, Boxer fraternities carried banners with the slogan "Fu Qing mieyang" (Support the Qing, exterminate foreigners).[19] Once this popular uprising began to openly parade its support for the reigning Manchu rulers, the anti-Christian, antiforeign impulse driving the movement was more readily co-opted by the Qing Court. Even before the Boxers appeared on the plains of Shanxi, they had gained the political and military assistance of many ruling elites.

We may better understand why the Shanxi campaign was so effective if we bear in mind how collaborative the Boxers and Qing troops had become before they first entered the province. Several key officials had by 1899 grown as fanatically anti-Christian and antiforeign as the Boxers and Red Lanterns. While not always as immersed in popular superstition as the Boxers, many Qing officials shared their disdain for foreign missionaries and Christianity, and Boxer appeals to "exterminate foreigners" found ready support in powerful court factions. Beijing's influential general Dong Fuxiang (1839–1908) announced that his special skill was "to kill foreigners."[20] In June of 1900 Xu Tong (1818–1900) and Chong Qi (1829–1900), two high court officials in Beijing, submitted a memorial to the court unambiguously demanding the killing of all Chinese Christians and foreigners in China.[21] Xu Tong, a Hanlin scholar and intransigent champion of neo-Confucian orthodoxy, made his views unmistakably clear to the central authorities, asserting that he "abhorred Western studies [and regarded them] as a deadly foe"; once Boxer violence against Christians had begun, Xu declared, "China will become strong beginning now!"[22]

A catalogue of anti-Christian and antiforeign officials during the late Qing, which included even members of the imperial family, would be too long to reproduce here, but few officials were as fierce as Yuxian, who, after serving as a prefect in Caozhou, Shandong, was transferred to Taiyuan, where his "extreme xenophobia" compelled him to collaborate with the Boxers in killing more Chinese and foreigners than were killed in any other area of China during the violence of 1900.[23] Germany's excessive, and perhaps aggressive, demands on Yuxian after the Boxer killing of two German missionaries contributed to his enmity toward foreigners, but this does not explain the brutality with which he dealt with the several thousand native Chinese who had converted to Christianity.

Yuxian was a Manchu member of the Yellow Banner, a military unit under the Manchu court distinguished by a yellow flag, and he was enrolled in the illustrious Guozijian Academy in Beijing. There he studied the classics near the very courtyard where a commemorative stele stood that honored the official famously converted to Christianity by Matteo Ricci, Xu Guangqi (1562–1633). When Yuxian was appointed to Caozhou in 1899, he distinguished himself as an efficient force against banditry in the county, executing approximately fifteen hundred persons in the frame of three months.[24]

While some Qing officials continued to recommend prudence in the court's interaction with foreigners and relationship with the Boxers, which many viewed as superstitious bullies, Yuxian's antiforeignism and sponsorship of the Boxers was well known. In 1899, Yuxian was elevated to the position of Shandong's provincial governor, holding the opinion that "the will of the people can be used." He favored employing the Fists of Righteous Harmony and enlisted them as an association, granting them legal status. The Boxers even received a banner with Yuxian's surname, "Yu," on it.[25] When Yuxian had settled into his new yamen accommodations at Taiyuan after his transfer to Shanxi on 15 March 1900, the Boxer movement was flourishing in northern China and, with his support, was "spreading over the plains like a wildfire."[26] When the Shanxi missionaries submitted to Yuxian a plea for protection, he responded that their request was "unreasonable."[27]

Shanxi's Franciscan community perceived Yuxian's arrival as an inauspicious sign, and in a letter posted in May 1900, the Franciscan friar André Bauer, OFM (1866–1900), wrote, "He has come to Taiyuanfu, the notorious persecutor of Christians in Shandong. What can we expect of him at any time now except persecutions?"[28] After Yuxian arrived in Shanxi he summoned Chinese who had complaints against foreigners to visit his yamen to lodge their grievances; his first act as governor was to amass "evidence" against the Christian mission.[29] While Yuxian made official arrangements for aggression against the Franciscan mission, Boxers assembled in temple courtyards to drill with sabers, spears, and hook-ended swords. Shanxi's Boxer training was conducted in the presence of the gods, who were, they believed, already battling foreign gods on their behalf in the numinous realm above.

SHANXI'S BOXERS: LEADERS AND POSSESSION RITES

Owing largely to the provincial musings of Liu Dapeng, the careful archival protection of materials at Shanxi's archives in Taiyuan, and the remaining documents of the archive at the Catholic Diocese of Taiyuan, we can reconstruct a fairly comprehensive history of Shanxi's Society of Righteous Harmony. The distinctive features of Shanxi's Boxer culture were its relational infrastructure, in which units collaborated with each other and with the local Qing authorities, and its relationship to local temples.

Ebenezer Edwards recounts that, by April 1900, "Boxer placards were posted up and sold in different cities," and that soon after, "Boxer leaders brought by the governor [Yuxian] from Shantung appeared in several towns in central Shansi."[30] Liu Dapeng notes that by the beginning of the seventh lunar month, three large Boxer militias had formed in Taiyuan county villages: one at Nanchengjiao, one at Beige, and another at Xiaodian.[31] It was in these three centers that Boxer activities around Taiyuan were chiefly planned, prepared for, and launched; the heart of Boxer rituals and training, however, remained at the famous Jinci Temple, which was conveniently near Taiyuan and a number of Franciscan mission churches.

That Boxer women and men trained at Jinci Temple not only was a matter of convenience but also made sense in light of Boxer religious practice. While Jinci Temple contains several individual shrines dedicated to various popular gods, it is chiefly dedicated to a "Holy Mother" (Shengmu)—ironically the same name in Chinese as that used for the Virgin Mary—whose principal appeal to Shanxi natives is her role as a rain goddess. This goddess was associated with the Jin River, which supplied the surrounding agricultural region with much-needed water.[32] During times of drought Taiyuan's governors routinely made ceremonial offerings at the temple, imploring the Holy Mother to send rain; these rites sometimes included the ritual execution of "drought dragons," which were held responsible for obstructing the skies. The Boxers gathered at the temple to prepare for the execution of foreigners and Christian converts, who were understood to be another manifestation of the "drought dragons."

Reflecting on the origins of the Shanxi Boxers, Liu Dapeng wrote that, by the summer of 1900, Jinci Temple was teeming with Boxer religious activities.

Again and again they gathered at Jinci Temple, each carrying some sort of weapon. They wore a red scarf on their head, a red belt around their waist, and red leggings around their shins. They came in threes and fives, shoulder to shoulder, and entering the temple of ancestors (Haotian) they worshipped the heavenly spirits, lit fireworks, and paid homage to their chief. There were the young as well as those who had been ceremonially "capped" [i.e., after the age of twenty to mark adulthood], in all equaling several hundred people. They were as if in a drunken frenzy. Once gathered they formed lines and set out, the leaders bearing red flags with slogans on each side: "Protect the Qing and exterminate foreigners" and "Carry out the work of Heaven."[33]

Shanxi's Boxers, like those in other areas, concentrated on spiritual practices and the ideal of supporting the Qing's efforts against foreigners.

The Boxers at Nanchengjiao village organized under the leadership of three people, mentioned previously, one man and two women, though they were guided principally by a villager from Xiaozhan named Hu Xingyuan, who went by the nom du guerre "Old Master Immortality." Hu shared the leadership of his militia with a woman more than thirty years old, "Goddess Yang," and a young girl of ten, "Red Lantern Shining."[34] Of these three, popularly called the "Three Teachers," Liu Dapeng observed, "They slaughter Christians."[35] According to Liu, the Three Teachers led a Boxer unit of some one hundred persons, though Zhang and Jia state that their group numbered as many as five hundred to six hundred.[36]

Hu Xingyuan, who was described as "so strong that he was able to lift up a milling stone in a wheat field," directed most of the martial arts training at the local Erlang Temple, though they assembled three times at Jinci Temple. It was their practice to suspend a banner from a nearby tree as they drilled, advertising, "The Society of Righteous Harmony in every village supports the Qing and exterminates foreigners."[37] Under the command of the Three Teachers, the Nanchengjiao Boxers attacked and destroyed several Catholic villages and killed large numbers of Christians.

The second Shanxi center of Boxer instruction was at the small village of Beige, which was under the leadership of a man known as "Old Master Guan," aptly named since he led his followers in martial arts training at Lord Guan Temple. Such temples functioned as communal settlements for local Chinese and lodged powerful deities and legendary heroes who provided protective services, often communicated through their martial arts skill.[38] The most

popular such hero-deity, known especially for his martial and apotropaic efficacy, was Lord Guan, the historic general of the late Eastern Han (25–220),
who was also commonly invoked to possess the bodies of spirit mediums
all over China. Features of spirit possession involving Lord Guan included
"martial arts displays, often with sword, spear, or halberd," and such a possession was convincing to temple audiences when a person's entire bearing was
altered by it.[39] The possession rites of Shanxi's Boxers at Lord Guan Temple
followed the pattern typical of spirit possession ceremonies, including the
veneration and procession of Guan's statue on an ornamented litter.[40]

Old Master Guan's disciples derived from villages surrounding Beige,
where four hundred to five hundred Boxers "trained day and night" to prepare for their attacks against churches, Christians, and foreigners.[41] The
Beige Boxers massacred some of the largest numbers of Chinese Christians
in Shanxi and encountered some of the most determined Catholic resistance. As in the tragic attacks against Zhujiahe, a Jesuit mission village in
Zhili that unsuccessfully resisted a siege by Boxers and Qing imperial troops,
several Shanxi Catholic villages attempted to oppose the Boxers.[42] At Zhujiahe roughly three thousand Chinese Christians were killed, while Shanxi
Catholic villages lost several hundred Chinese Catholics.[43]

Shanxi's third Boxer center was at Xiaodian village under the leadership
of Guo Qizi, who, like Hu Xingyuan, took the nickname "Old Man Immortality."[44] Guo allowed another Boxer leader from Qingyuan village, known as
Zhou Cang, to train his group in Xiaodian. Together they drilled a collective
assembly of three hundred to four hundred people at the popular Baolian
Temple.[45]

Boxer religious rites were common to all of China's northern provinces,
though there were regional differences. Shanxi's Society of Righteous Harmony, for example, was partial to the gods worshipped at Jinci Temple, as
well as to the ubiquitous Shanxi veneration of the divinity Old Man Heaven.[46]
Previous studies of China's Boxers have focused on their rites of invulnerability, wherein the practitioner was, in the language of the Boxers, made
"invincible to swords and bullets" (*dao qiang bu ru*) after the performance
of a prescribed ritual.

Descriptions of Shanxi Boxer rituals in contrast to those of other regions,
emphasize rites of spirit possession rather than invincibility, and it appears
that Boxers in Shanxi were more concerned with how their gods might collaborate with their efforts against Christianity and missionaries than with the
gods' ability to render them invulnerable to swords and guns. The notion of

spiritual assistance, indeed instruction, in the process of cultivating martial arts competency was not new to the Boxer era. Martial arts practice, often when attached to a rebellious faction such as the White Lotus sect, a sectarian Buddhist militia, was believed to be enhanced when taught under the patronage of a popular deity. A group near Beijing, for example, who called themselves the Red Sun Society, trained in the martial arts only after entreating the Ten Patriarchs of Daoism to appear and teach them pugilism.[47] Shanxi Boxer rites similarly summoned spirits who derived largely from heroic figures exalted in popular Chinese literature and legend.

One Shanxi Boxer announcement transmitted to Beijing from Shandong provides a general sketch of the expectation behind the Boxer possession rite: "Raise the charm paper and venerate with incense. Make invitations to all the precincts [lit., "caves"] with their spirits and immortals. The immortals leave their caves and the spirits descend from their mountains to possess our bodies. They complete our training in the arts of fists and weapons [so] that we may quell the demons."[48] Spirit possession and martial arts training under the tutorship of the gods were clearly understood to be the result of such ceremonies.

Shanxi Boxer rites stipulated precise compass points to which offerings must be made; the rites also included actions to be performed by those who lived in cities and villages in order to be spared undesirable magical after-effects. In one announcement disseminated throughout the province, the specific dates that the Boxers and Red Lanterns would arrive were carefully outlined, as were the ritual ceremonies that households were to perform to be spared from injurious spells before their arrival. "At midnight burn incense toward the southeast and present an auspicious offering," the announcement suggested, and "in every street and alley, home, and place of business, draw a red blood circle or a cross on the door."[49] Those who did not perform this ritual of protection were warned that they "will go insane after several days."[50] Curiously, other Boxer announcements accused Christians of a similar rite, which was said to harm rather than protect the non-Christian population. This announcement included directions on how to recognize the distinctive attire of the Red Lantern women, who performed the protective magical spells and invoked the assistance of the gods on their behalf.

Shanxi's Boxers were commonly attached to Buddhist figures and to the legendary characters of the famous novel *Journey to the West* (Xiyouji). In one Boxer oath taken during the rite of spirit possession, deities such as the founder of Chan Buddhism, Damo (better known in the West as Bodhidharma), were invoked just before mentioning the recipient's name. After appealing to Damo, the rite stated: "I, the disciple _____ [name], piously beseech Tripitika, Sandy, Pigsy, and Monkey with kowtows to depart from their dwellings and descend to possess my body and protect it. Facing southeast this disciple makes this entreaty."[51]

The ceremony continued, instructing the recipient to "wash your hands with pure water, cough, and make a reverential bow with hands clasped," after which the practitioner was advised: "Close your eyes with faith and in a short while the spirits will come."[52] Westerners witnessing these rituals, who were mostly Christian and prepared to view them as "demonic," often wrote descriptive reports. For example, the *Shanghai Mercury*, a periodical that published long narrative descriptions of the Boxers during the uprising, described Boxer militias in this way: "Each band was conducted by a 'demonized' leader, who by the selection of an epileptic or by the patient aid of hypnotism, caused a 'medium' to display wild and strange speech, this serving as a basis for the claim of this Society to spiritual power. Every follower was assured immunity from death or physical injury—their bodies being spiritually protected from sword cuts and bullets."[53] While Shanxi's Boxers conducted rites at local temples to invoke the spiritual patronage of Chinese gods, Western onlookers grew increasingly fearful of these ceremonies.

BOXER MYTHOLOGIES:
RAINLESS SKIES AND POISONED WELLS

Describing the mythologies disseminated by Shanxi Boxers in 1900, Ebenezer Edwards wrote of an "old fable of foreigners and Christians cutting out and scattering the figure of a man in paper, which in a few days came to life and then had the power of doing much harm."[54] There were other rumors in Shanxi, such as a report that Christians hired poor beggars to poison village wells and mark the doors of non-Christian homes with a red substance that cursed the inhabitants with illness or death—though marking the doors of homes with blood was more commonly a Boxer spell intended to protect Chinese against "foreign magic." Edwards also notes an "anti-foreign pamphlet" circulated through Shanxi that described "foreign vessels seized at the coast" containing "large quantities of human blood, eyes, and the nipples of women's breasts."[55] The former housekeeper of the Franciscan residence in Taiyuan, Joseph Leu, described the city's rumors in a 1910 interview: "The non-Christians . . . had strong words to say about the priests, and especially

about the so-called depravity of the women [sisters], that they remove people's eyes and carve out the hearts of children."[56] A large number of Boxer
announcements propagated such mythologies, soliciting popular support for
the Boxer cause by accusing foreign gods of corroborating with foreigners to
caste nefarious spells on non-Christian Chinese and to initiate the droughts
and famines that plagued Shanxi.

In one Shanxi announcement the Boxer myth that the foreign god had
caused China's calamities was made explicit. The placard related that the Jade
Emperor, the highest deity in the Daoist pantheon, had appeared in a dream
to Lord Qing and "charged him to set straight the Lord of Heaven [affair],
and restore the Great Qing to its appropriate way."[57] In more assertive terms,
the declaration continues: "If you don't correct this you shall later regret it,
because the Lord of Heaven and Jesus show no respect for the law of the
Buddha, and these [foreign] gods destroy what is holy."[58] The foreign god
was thus believed to have provoked "the rage of Heaven and Earth to shun
away the snow and rain and send down a spiritual army . . . and [so Heaven]
has transmitted an assembly of gods to the Fists of Righteous Harmony to
borrow from the strength of men and protect China."[59] The spiritual causes
of China's natural calamities necessitated intervention by the Chinese gods
and the Boxers.

In another Shanxi notice, Heaven's ten grievances were enumerated,
among them "drought," that "half of the people everywhere have died," and
that "there are clothes that can no longer be worn" because of emaciation.
Like other notices, this one encouraged Shanxi's commoners to assuage the
anger of the gods and solicit their support, by "burning incense toward the
southeast and to present an auspicious offering."[60] Readers of the announcement were urged to produce extra copies, usually five to ten, and distribute
them. Some Boxer notices even alerted the reader that to neglect making
copies would bring additional misfortunes upon him or her.

Yuxian appears to have supported, if not openly encouraged, the proliferation of Boxer propaganda around Taiyuan. Rumors were epidemic as the
court vacillated in its response to Boxer activities of 1900. When the court
sided with the Boxers it created a perception of having absolved the Boxers
of wrongdoing, legitimizing their actions. Rumor and antiforeignism increasingly flourished and were supported particularly in Shanxi.[61] Paul Cohen
suggests that on the north China plain during that time, the "menace of inop-
portune death was everywhere," which triggered the people "to give credence
to the most spectacular religious and magical claims of the Boxers."[62]

Public hysteria in Shanxi precipitated by Boxer tales of ominous foreign gods and foreign magic included the belief in widespread reports that foreigners were dropping poison into their water supplies, spoiling water that was already precariously scarce. One short notice consists only of an antidote to be administered if one had consumed poisoned water. Titled "Prescription Antidote against Poison Dropped into Wells by Demons," the placard lists such ingredients as dried tangerine peel, fresh black beans, and calamus root, noting that "the amount doesn't matter; just wrap the ingredients into a cloth and put it into the container." Other notices included generic recipes of herbal formulas to protect against magic in general, such as "demon white lantern beams of light" produced by foreigners.[63]

The proliferation of Shanxi Boxer announcements can be summarized in a single example: "Disciples unite and be diligent; everywhere form militias . . . and wipe out all foreigners from the face of the earth."[64] The Boxers envisioned themselves as a messianic militia summoned by the most eminent pantheon of gods to do away with the "hairies" and their religion and to either compel Chinese Christians to apostatize or die as "secondhand hairies." On the Double Ninth Festival, foreigners would be attacked with the help of the gods, one announcement stated; and, the Boxers promised, after their victory "the immortals and gods will return to their precincts, and all under heaven will be at peace." Furthermore, this notice assured readers that the following year would produce "a rich harvest," once the Christians and foreigners were gone.[65]

A steady stream of Society of Righteous Harmony propaganda, laden with admonitions and tales of magic, helped to convey the organization's message and alert people in advance of the arrival of the Boxers, who would be recognizable by their distinctive uniforms, such as the "red belt they will wear."[66] As seen in Liu Dapeng's description, each Boxer held a weapon, wore a red scarf on his head, a red belt around his waist, and red leggings; but what Liu found most extraordinary was not their clothing but the rituals they performed.

The Boxer rites were described almost precisely the same way in Liu's firsthand accounts as they were by foreign observers in the *Shanghai Mercury*, though without the Christianized rhetoric of the missionaries. In *Casual Notes from within the Garden* (Qianyuan suoji), Liu included a reflection on what he viewed as the bizarre ceremonies of the Boxers in Shanxi. After invoking the gods—characters taken largely from the novel *Journey to the West*—the Boxers became entranced. "Suddenly they raised their gaze and then dropped to the ground as if in a sound sleep. Before long their hands and feet began to undulate. They stood erect and danced around with a fierce expression, their eyes shut so tightly they could not be opened. Then they made fists and claw shapes with their hands, leaping and rushing around."[67] These rites were largely inspired by popular drama. Inviting spirits to descend to the earthly plain was common in performances at venues such as the famous opera stage at Jinci Temple near Taiyuan, where the central Shanxi Boxers routinely met to train, worship the gods, and watch productions. In the custom known as *yingshen saihui*, or "inviting the spirits to the performance," empty chairs were routinely left in front of the stage so the gods would have front-row seating during the acts. Often the characters of the performance represented the very gods invited to the opera.

THE HEAVENS SEND WAR, NOT RAIN

As the arid ground continued to fissure, and as crops withered or failed to appear, Shanxi's temples and market streets saw a rising number of Boxer notices and a growing number of young, displaced, mostly illiterate Boxers and Red Lantern women wearing red sashes, head coverings, and leggings gathered together. As Shandong Boxers streamed into Shanxi to enlist local peasants in their ranks, Shandong's popular gods were combined with Shanxi's to produce an even larger pantheon of spirits, all purported to be enraged at the presence of foreign missionaries and foreign gods. As the Boxers prepared to confront their enemies, they marshaled spells, curses, charms, and a multitude of other magical forces against the magic of the "Western gods."

Shanxi's popular religious practices were perhaps even more animated than were the spiritual rites in Shandong, where the Boxers first emerged. Commonly posted on the principal wall of Shanxi homes was a placard dedicated to the Family Hall Gods (*jiatangye*), sometimes accompanied on an ancillary wall by a placard dedicated to the god of heaven and earth. The Family Hall Gods could thus be understood as a kind of singular deity, inclusive of all gods and all of one's ancestors. Shanxi villagers also frequently worshipped bodhisattvas in their households and displayed an image of the popular Shanxi deity Lucky Auntie in their daughters' rooms; many venerated a representation of the God of Wells near their courtyard water well and, if they kept horses, worshipped the Horse King God. In some households, especially those of the literati elite, Confucius was venerated.[68]

Shanxi residents had the singular notion that the gods and ancestors could be worshipped in one, comprehensive god; the preservation of images of this god, and their regular veneration, was a distinguishing cultural mark of Shanxi.[69] When families converted to Christianity they discontinued this practice, which was interpreted by their neighbors as a rejection of their identity as people from Shanxi and, even worse, as Chinese. Catholics, for example, did not sweep graves on Tomb Sweeping Day, and so were rebuked by many non-Christians, who accused them of lacking respect for their ancestors; Shanxi's Christians were viewed as having deserted their family lineage and were called "those who cut clan lines."[70] These impressions of Christians, which were latent in Shanxi long before the Boxer Uprising, dovetailed with the message of the Boxers; the broad misgivings in Shanxi about the religious practices of Christianity and foreign missionaries were co-opted by the zealous Boxers.

Practically speaking, however, Shanxi's Christians and non-Christians had, overall, coexisted peacefully since the eighteenth century, until the widespread drought and Sino-Western conflicts of the nineteenth century engendered new, more open tensions between the two communities. News of conflicts and rising antiforeignism spread rapidly through the well-connected Franciscan network of communication. In a letter to the vicar general and the Franciscan father general in Rome, dated 1 February 1900, Bishop Francesco Fogolla conveyed his anxieties about the events in distant Shandong: "There is sad news of the persecution and the massacres in Shandong. Since the Prussians occupied one of the territories of the province the population there is irritated and swears never to forgive. Bands of rebels rise everywhere. Not daring to come to blows with the Germans who are well armed, they prey on the missionaries and the Christians; the province is all fire and blood."[71] By May 1900, Father André Bauer lamented that Yuxian, the putative official sponsor of Shandong's Boxer movement, had arrived at Taiyuan. Yuxian would make quick work of his objective to mobilize the Boxers in Shanxi. And as Giovanni Ricci recalled, "Already in Taiyuanfu and other places in the province[,] the Boxers by the end of June had made fire and mayhem in churches and homes of Christians."[72] Within the span of a single month, the rumors of Boxer activities in Shandong had become a reality in Shanxi.

The Franciscans, like the Boxers, had their ideas about spiritual warfare, and nearly all the Boxer beliefs had some form of religious analog within Shanxi's Christian mission. The militant Boxers were staging themselves against the Roman Catholic "Church Militant," for the missionaries in Shanxi viewed themselves as the vanguard of a spiritual Christian militia that struggled against devils. Saint Paul, they claimed, had referred to this battle in his letter to the Ephesians, where he alluded to spiritual warfare against "the rulers of the darkness of this world, and against spiritual wickedness in high places."[73]

CHAPTER 3

Catholics and Foreign Gods

Friends, farewell, and may God speed you, and to holy combat lead you.
In the far off heathen land, where in darkness most repelling, teeming
millions still are dwelling, who await your noble band.

— CATHOLIC MISSIONARY HYMN OF DEPARTURE

THE Jingxian Boxers in Hebei chanted the following song in preparation
for the spiritual and earthly warfare to come:

All foreigners must be killed, and peace shall be attained.
Kill even their converts, and spare not a single one.
Wear a red hat, belt, and pants, and carry a big sword.
Kill the devils and seize their converts, terrify them, leaving them no
    place run. . . .
Offer incense to the immortal precincts, and they shall descend their
    mountains. . . .
Raid the churches, overthrow their people, and dig up railroads to block
    their trains.[1]

Whereas Shanxi's Society of Righteous Harmony was publicizing its belief in
a battle between local and foreign gods, the Catholic missionaries had been
inculcated with a similar theology of spiritual warfare. Franciscans, Jesu-

its, Dominicans, and other missionary orders that sent members to China employed comparable anthems to embolden missioners for "holy battle," as exemplified in the late-nineteenth-century departure hymn of the Society of the Divine Word:

Friends, farewell, and may God speed you,
And to holy combat lead you
In the far off heathen land,
Where in darkness most repelling
Teeming millions still are dwelling
Who await your noble band. . . .
Shall he [Satan] longer yet enslave them?
Hasten, brethren, forth to save them. . . .
though the hosts of hell impede you,
God will His angels lead you.[2]

When the Franciscans left Europe, commissioned by such words, they were given a "missioner's crucifix" to remind them of the sacrifice of the cross and the sacrifices they too should expect to make on the spiritual battlefield.

The role of exorcism in the Catholic mission tells us much about the standard contemporary missionary view of Chinese deities, with whom God's army was doing battle. As early as the beginning of the eighteenth century, Chinese folk gods were viewed as demonic forces. In a 1701 letter written in Fuzhou, the Jesuit Emeric Langlois de Chavagnac (1670–1717), reported that a Chinese family contacted the priests after unsuccessful attempts to relieve the entire household of evil spirits using conventional Chinese methods. The Jesuit intervention included, foremost, the destruction of all household images of local gods, personal charms, and Daoist books and talismans; after this they administered holy water, invoked the name of Jesus, and made the sign of the cross.[3] Another Jesuit, François Noël (1651–1729), wrote in 1703 of the efficacy of holy water and the sign of the cross in combating evil spirits.[4] Mendicant orders such as Dominicans and Franciscans were even more active in exorcising China's gods, readily accepting these roles and viewing folk deities as embodiments of evil.[5]

Of the Franciscans who traveled to Mongol-ruled China in the fourteenth century, Anselm Romb, OFM, Conv., recalled that "the holiness of their work and, more fundamentally, the need of their work, was the exorcisms performed by the Franciscans of Tartary." In language resonant with that of the

Church Militant, Romb added: "The exorcisms were the symbols of the victory over the powers of darkness by these crusaders of light"; and for these Franciscans confronted with the "powers of darkness" in China, "casting out devils was as common and ordinary there as putting the dog out of the house anywhere else." Already in the first Franciscan mission to China during the Yuan dynasty, we see evidence of a presumed battle between the God of the West and the gods of China that influenced the Franciscans' impressions of the Chinese and their Mongolian rulers: "Like Boniface of Germany, the friars scorned the national deities [of China]."[6] As Romb wrote of this early encounter between European missionaries and the East, "God was bending out of heaven, making plans of His own to vanquish Tartar souls and to tame their stubborn hearts for Himself."[7]

Protestants were equally convinced that China's myriad gods, spirits, and immortals were demonic forces that often possessed non-Christian Chinese. John Livingston Nevius (1829–1893), in his book *Demon Possession and Allied Themes*, discusses possessions in Shandong at some length.[8] Nevius, a forty-year missionary in China, recounts that in 1878 he was informed of a Chinese man named "Mr. Kwo" who was "suffering all sorts of inflictions from an evil spirit."[9] When Nevius at last met the possessed man, the Chinese peasant pointed to "the shrine where he worshipped the demon," after which the missionary "told him the first thing to do was to tear away this shrine."[10] The afflicted man was then taught about Jesus, given some Christian books, and exhorted to convert. Despite their ecclesial and theological dissonances, both the Catholic and Protestant missions equally agreed that China's local gods were "diabolical."

CHURCH MILITANT AND CHURCH TRIUMPHANT

If spiritual warfare was viewed as a supernatural reality, and if missionaries were to enter non-Christian countries where local gods must be evacuated and exorcised, then the missionary was, to use a term coined by Peter Fleming, SJ, "Christ's soldier hero"; in the language of Robert Streit, "the Catholic missionary army was set in motion with the first preaching of the apostles."[11] Reflecting on the spiritual teachings of Saint Ignatius of Loyola, SJ (1491–1556), Fleming points out that in his famous *Spiritual Exercises*, Ignatius "depicted the world as a battleground with the forces of Satan on the one side and the forces of Christ on the other," and the exertant was exhorted to choose either the "standard of Christ" or the "standard of Satan."[12]

Just as the Catholic mission to China in the early eighteenth century envisioned such a heavenly battle, so too was the missionary enterprise imagined in the twentieth century. From the pulpit of Saint Patrick's cathedral in New York City in 1945, Cardinal Francis Spellman (1889–1967) announced to two thousand American members of the Catholic Students Mission Crusade that missionaries are "gallant soldiers of Christ. . . . For them no gold stars glisten in the windows. But there are shrines burning in the hearts and homes that they left, and in the houses of those to whom they brought the starlight of faith in the world's remotest regions."[13] The language of spiritual battle was deeply embedded in Catholic thought during the eighteenth, nineteenth, and early twentieth centuries, and the task of the missionary was described and discussed in the vocabulary of military activities.

The Roman Catholic analogue to China's Lord Guan, the patron deity of justice and heroism, was Saint Michael, the sword-bearing archangel given charge over the "Army of God."[14] The eighteenth-century English hagiographer Father Alban Butler (1710–1773) describes Michael in this way: "'Who is like God?' was the cry of Archangel Michael when he smote the rebel Lucifer in the conflict of the heavenly hosts. And when Antichrist shall have set up his kingdom on earth, it is Saint Michael who will unfurl once more the standard of the cross, sound the last trumpet, bind together the false prophet and the beast and hurl them for all eternity into the burning pool."[15] Michael, like Lord Guan, represents the fight against evil; he is the angelic model of the heavenly warrior. Saint Michael's merits as God's general are also expounded in the book of the Apocalypse, which was commonly read by missionaries in their predeparture formation: "Then war broke out in heaven. Michael and his angels fought against the dragon, and the dragon and his angels fought back. . . . The great dragon was hurled down—that ancient serpent called the devil, or Satan, who leads the whole world astray. He was hurled to the earth, and his angels with him."[16] For Catholic missionaries of the late nineteenth century, Saint Michael personified the spiritual confrontation against Satan's forces that awaited them in China. European clergy and religious—including Franciscans—left their native shores to "conquer the forces of Satan."

One might suggest also that any eschatological religion or ideology—Judeo-Christian, Buddhist, or Marxist—intrinsically espouses the view of an eventual "victory" fought for and won by the martyrs of its cause in a form of righteous battle. This was true as early as the time of Emperor Constantine (272–337), who was able to defeat his enemies after observing an illuminated cross suspended in the sky. Christians who followed him would advance under the same standard as an Ecclesia Militans, or Church Militant. The early Christian Church, after the victory of Constantine, began to employ the Christogram IHS, which stood both for the first three letters in the Latinized Greek word for Jesus (IHSOVS) and first three letters of the phrase *in hoc signo vinces*, "by this sign you will conquer." By the nineteenth century, images of a globe crowned by a cross were common in Roman Catholic mission iconography, and the decades between 1815 and 1914 were witness to insatiable colonial growth imbued with tremendous energy that was largely driven under the banner of this image.[17] This was an era of unmatched colonial expansion and intellectual refutation of the claims of Christianity and the authority of the church; as the hierarchy in the Vatican observed this development, it responded with a renewal of its own rhetoric of militancy. Society worldwide—which was in part aided by expansion of the church and nation—was increasingly secular and hostile to Christianity.[18]

It complicated matters that the nineteenth-century Roman Catholic mission enterprise followed in the footsteps of European colonialism and was indeed often facilitated and protected by conationalists. In 1900, the year his cathedral in Beijing was besieged by a large force of Boxers, lamas, and Qing troops, the proudly French Lazarist bishop of the city's famous North Church, Pierre-Marie-Alphonse Favier, CM (1837–1905), wrote of the French protectorate in China's capital and its relationship to the Catholic mission: "Once more this incident has proved the necessity of the French protectorate of the Catholic missions, a protectorate which France has never abandoned and which the Church was never willing to take away from her. You will always see a consulate next to a church, and the tricolor sheltering the Catholic cross! . . . The admirals and officers compete with each other for the glory of the religion and the fatherland."[19] As early as the Protestant Reformation, during which the Catholic Church lost large portions of the Catholic population to Protestantism, it had grown increasingly eager to enter the foreign mission-fields opened by colonial powers to supplement its diminishing numbers.[20]

Beyond this alliance between missions and their European national protectorates in China, another factor in the mission politics of the late nineteenth century was the privileged position of the papacy in both temporal and spiritual matters, which had been threatened by political and intellectual secularization. Wishing to empower the state over the papacy, the French National Assembly had stripped away much of the church's authority by enacting the Civil Constitution of the Clergy in 1790.[21] Then in 1802, Napoleon Bonaparte (1769–1821) further reduced the church's authority when he added his Organic Articles to the 1801 concordat agreement between France and Pope Pius VII (r. 1880–1823). The concordat had stipulated that Catholicism was France's official religion of the majority, but Napoleon's addendum proclaimed that all significant papal declarations were subject to the approval of the French government. Napoleon's militia transferred the pontiff out of Rome, effectively making him a prisoner of France, and he did not return to his Vatican apartments for five years. Later popes of the nineteenth century witnessed what they viewed as dangerous threats to the supreme authority of the church; the church reacted politically by more visibly emphasizing its role as Church Militant and by blurring the lines between the temporal and spiritual authority of the Holy See.[22]

Even before the historical factors of the nineteenth century agitated the papacy and caused it to retrench its forces and renew church identity as an Ecclesia Militans, Franciscan and Dominican missionaries were known for their language of spiritual conquest. This was particularly evident in an early memorial by the Dominican chronicler Diego Aduarte (1570–1636), who wrote, "In the spiritual conquest (*conquista espiritual*) of this powerful kingdom [China], God takes up the Gospel as the battering ram that gradually approaches and finally breaks those great walls of resistance."[23] Despite their intention to avoid political or armed conflict with the Chinese, the rhetoric of the Ecclesia Militans remained common during the Boxer struggles of 1900; the Franciscans were at war, as were other orders in China, even if their weapons were assumed to be spiritual. Before their executions in the local official's courtyard, the Franciscan bishop Gregorio Grassi (fig. 3.1) announced to the gathered Franciscan Missionaries of Mary, "The hour of combat is here," but clarified that this "combat" involved martyrdom rather than violent resistance.[24]

The Catholic idea of a Church Militant, which represents the spiritual and earthly battle between the forces of God and the "rulers of darkness of this world," is part of a tripartite conceptualization of the "one holy catholic and apostolic Church." In addition to the Ecclesia Militans, the church is also constituted by two other groups: the Ecclesia Penitens, or Church Suffering, made up of those Christians whose souls are in purgatory, where they await the Beatific Vision after a period of atonement; and the Ecclesia Triumphans, or Church Triumphant, consisting of those souls who already enjoy the Beatific Vision of God in heaven. While the Church Triumphant is typically envisioned as those who are in heaven, a "triumphalistic" aesthetic,

FIGURE 3.1. Bishop Gregorio Grassi, OFM, a Shanxi missionary who was executed at Yuxian's yamen on 9 July 1900. This photograph was probably taken at the Taiyuan cathedral shortly before the Boxer Uprising. Source: Provincia di Cristo Re dei Frati Minori dell'Emilia Romagna, Parma.

even attitude, has been manifest on earth at times in the Catholic Church's long history and is often interpreted as an example of earthly victories of the Church Militant's contest against its enemies.

One triumphalistic expression of the church's "battle" in China was its practice of replacing formerly non-Christian structures with ecclesial edifices, a pattern set by post-Nicea Christianity with Roman and Greek temples.[25] Beginning in 1860, three principal Catholic cathedrals—in Canton, Tianjin, and Beijing—were constructed. The Canton cathedral was erected on the former yamen of Viceroy Ye Mingchen, opponent of the English at the time of the siege of 1856. The Tianjin cathedral stood on the site of a Confucian temple that had been razed and then placed under the protection of Our Lady of Victories. And the Beijing cathedral, with its towers looming over the imperial palaces of the Forbidden City, was a sign of extreme incivility according to Chinese sensibilities.[26]

Such triumphalism, while perhaps more often intended as an expression of spiritual rather than political victory, did not help the reputation of the missionaries, who were after all foreign guests. That the missionaries imagined these churches as symbols of triumph is evident in the dedication of the church in Tianjin to "Our Lady of Victories." Not all European missionaries, however, envisaged their mission in such nationalistic terms as did Bishop Favier, who, as noted earlier, expressed his gratefulness for "the tricolor [French flag] sheltering the Catholic cross." Indeed, Shanxi's Franciscan mission inclined itself more toward the values of humility and charity, esteemed from the beginning as the salient virtues taught by Saint Francis himself. Nonetheless, the Franciscan mission in Shanxi built churches in a grand, perhaps even triumphalistic style. The Catholic church in the small Shanxi village of Guchengying stood directly across a narrow alley from the much older Nine Dragons Temple, and the cathedral complex in Taiyuan city towered over its surrounding buildings.

Franciscan missionaries also brought both the culture and the conflicts of their homeland with them when they entered Shanxi. The European battle between altar and throne for social influence had been largely transplanted onto Chinese soil, though the Franciscans in China lived as a religious minority in a land filled with temples dedicated to non-Christian gods. Both the Chinese Boxers and the Western missionaries had formulated "imagined spiritualities," to reformulate Benedict Anderson's "imagined communities,"[27] in which an understood war between gods, or angels, existed in a preternatural realm. These imagined battles, and the rhetoric used to describe them, manifest as actual conflicts in cities, villages, churches, and fields. Imagined spiritualities materialized into physical confrontations.

THE FRANCISCAN MANNER OF HOLY BATTLE

Although the rhetoric of the Church Militant and its accompanying belief in a spiritual battle was present in the Franciscan mission—it was at some level present in all Catholic missionary ventures of the early modern era— the Franciscans, like the Jesuits in China, had learned from the success- ful methods of such illustrious early fathers of the mission as Matteo Ricci, Adam Schall von Bell, SJ (1591–1666), and Ferdinand Verbiest, SJ (1623–1688). These pioneers belonged to the era of what George Dunne, SJ (1905–1989), has termed the "generation of giants"—missionaries who were able to con- struct bridges of friendship that attracted more interested ears to the Chris- tian message. Dunne describes that "generation" in terms that could also be applied to a large number of the friars and sisters who served in Shanxi dur- ing the closing years of the Qing: "by their readiness to put aside European prejudices, by their adaptability, their innocence of snobbery and smugness, their alertness to discover the good and reluctance to note the bad, by the sympathy and understanding they brought to their contact with China."[28] The Franciscans occupied a position between the ideal of Sino-missionary accord and the Church Militant theology emphasized in the late nineteenth century.

Many Franciscans, as well as members of other orders, believed that spiri- tual victory over the enemies of the church could be accomplished by mar- tyrdom, because, as Tertullian (an early Christian writer, ca. 160–225) said, "the blood of the martyrs is the seed of the Church."[29] The Franciscans were educated within a theological paradigm that held, as Saint Paul wrote, that the Christian "battle is not against human forces but against the principalities and powers, the rulers of this world of darkness, the evil spirits in regions above."[30] Martyrs are defined as such by the fact that they are killed *in odium fidei*, "in hatred of the faith." To be killed *in odium fidei* is, in other words, to be killed by an enemy, even if the enemy is merely a participant in a larger spiritual battle between "Christ's soldier heroes" and human manifestations of "principalities," "powers," and "the rulers of this world of darkness."

The archetypes of spiritual warfare and victory by martyrdom were recalled each evening in Franciscan communities after recitation of the eve- ning Office and the Martyrologium Romanum Seraphicum, or the Franciscan version of the Roman Martyrology, which detailed accounts of anti-Christian persecution, arranged according to the feast days of Franciscan martyr saints and beati. They were also routinely told about Franciscans who had already been martyred on the mission. During the late nineteenth century the Franciscan friar Hugolin de Doullens (1852–1897), who had served as the novice master at the Shanxi seminary in Dongergou,[31] was visiting Europe and had given Mother Mary of the Passion a positive report of the mission at Shanxi. She was not persuaded, however, and reportedly believed that she was in fact sending her sisters to the victory of martyrdom.[32] As the Franciscan sisters prepared for their mission in Shanxi, they played a game in which they would "draw slips of paper to see which will be the first to obtain the coveted palm [of martyrdom]."[33]

Perhaps viewed as an alternative form of martyrdom, a "dry martyrdom" since it did not include blood, was the Franciscan practice of bodily mortification, which was a manner of spiritual battle with oneself and a form of reparation for the offenses of others. Personal piety and self-denial were emblematic of the Franciscan mission in Shanxi and were considered indispensable components of spiritual warfare, especially in a non-Christian land such as China. Jesuits, Dominicans, Lazarists, and others practiced mortification as well; disciplines such as flagellation were in fact expected of some tertiaries and sodalities of other orders.

In the realm of spiritual warfare, however, the Franciscans attributed more weight to personal piety and mortification than to other modes of triumphalism ascribed to the church's supernatural battle. Gregorio Grassi was known for his self-denials, humility, and pious practices. One of Grassi's contemporaries described the bishop's asceticism: "Bishop Grassi had a lean, austere-looking figure, a long beard and a dry, dry voice. I'd say that he was like a repentant hermit who had restrained his character . . . by means of mortification and patience."[34] Odoric of Pordenone (Odorico Mattiussi, ca. 1286–1331), a famous Franciscan who traveled to China in the fourteenth century, also was known for self-mortification, including such disciplines as wearing "small plates of cold metal linked about his waist next to his skin and an iron chain bound tightly around each arm."[35] When Gregorio offered Mass, his habit was to spend a very long time in prayer beforehand and then again afterward in thanksgiving. Even though he was a bishop with an extraordinarily crowded itinerary, "Grassi intoned the daily Canonical Hours in choir with his confreres, unless he was ill, extended his daily visits to the sanctuary Tabernacle," and "was assiduous in blessing the sisters in the chapel for the Franciscan Missionaries of Mary."[36]

Not only was personal holiness perceived as an effective agent in spiritual warfare, but also the exposition of the Blessed Sacrament—understood by Catholics to be the actual body of Christ—in grand processions through the streets and lanes of Shanxi was used in the battle against pagan gods. Gregorio Grassi employed this method of "warfare," too, and in one of the rare photograph we have of him, the bishop of Taiyuan is seen in one of his organized Corpus Christi processions, during which he and an impressive assembly of clergy, acolytes, and faithful weave through the streets of Taiyuan with the Blessed Sacrament displayed in its golden monstrance beneath an extravagant canopy.[37] One of the patent aims of these processions was to pass along avenues with local temples—the real presence of God confronting, in a sense, the non-Christian gods of China.

One of the most passionately debated issues of the Catholic missionary enterprise in China around the time of the Boxer Uprising was the question of indigenous clergy: should more Chinese be enlisted in the clergy to serve in the Church Militant? Through the late nineteenth century and into the twentieth, the question of whether native Chinese should be ordained, how many, and whether they were even able to learn the required Latin, stymied church growth and indigenization. Even more acerbic were deliberations regarding the intentional indigenization of China's hierarchy; up until the closing years of China's imperial era, most orders, with the notable exception of the Franciscans, Dominicans, Lazarists, and Marists, dragged their feet on this issue.[38] The Franciscans felt that training Chinese seminarians in Europe would perhaps inculcate in them a sense of the global church, as well as provide them with a more thorough priestly formation. The Friars Minor established the Holy Family College for Chinese seminarians in 1732 in Naples, Italy, and at least ten Chinese priests in Shaanxi and Shanxi had completed their studies at this school.[39] One of these priests was Wang Tingrong, OFM (d. 1891), who went to Naples in 1840, and who is today celebrated in China for his defiance of Italian missionary dominance in Shanxi.[40] Wang's resistance to what amounted to Western clerical discrimination against Chinese priests made him a hero of Chinese nationalism.[41] The Franciscan friars from Italy supported the training and ordination of Chinese clergy but did not as readily recognize their equality in positions of administrative power.

Only seventeen years after the Boxer movement, the Belgian Lazarist Father Frédéric-Vincent Lebbe, CM (1877–1940), wrote an impassioned apologia to his bishop in favor of a more aggressive policy of ordaining, consecrating, and empowering a native Chinese church:[42]

The time has come to found a living, fertile, national Church, to be the leaven in the lump, flesh of the people's flesh, blood of the people's blood sanctified *in Christo*, the only Church with a hope of survival, the only Church to contain the embryo of promise of the future. Preparations for this Church belong no more to the distant view, they have become immediate, crucial and concrete. If we have the will to found this Church, the means are at hand to do it, discreetly, smoothly, by degrees: all that is needed is to will it.[43]

This letter likely found its way to the desk of Pope Benedict XV (r. 1914–1922), who appears to have been influenced by Lebbe's petition when drafting his apostolic letter *Maximum Illud*, in which he encouraged the development of local clergy in Catholic mission areas. Who better to convert and pastor the Chinese than Chinese themselves? If the goal of the Ecclesia Militans was to win China for God—the "foreign god," according to most Chinese—then it would have to be accomplished with the help, or better, leadership, of a Chinese hierarchy. As Catholic leaders, they would understand and appeal to native Chinese far more effectively than a legion of foreign prelates whose understanding of the Chinese language only slightly mitigated the fact that they were not Chinese.

The Franciscans in Shanxi understood long before Lebbe wrote his letter that for a "foreign god" to be accepted in China the church must shed its status as foreign.[44] As early as the first decade of the nineteenth century, the Franciscans of northern China were actively recruiting and training native Chinese for the priesthood, and from the time of Bishop Antonio Luigi Landi, OFM (1749–1814), who served in China from 1802 to 1814, Chinese priests prepared for their ordination at the seminary at Shanxi. Cipriano Silvestri writes, "When Bishop Grassi arrived . . . he located the seminary at Dongergou, where he spent the early years of his missionary life busily applying himself to the spiritual and scientific training of young men in preparation for the ecclesiastical life. He drew higher-level students from Taiyuan to go to Dongergou . . . and required the aspirants to the priesthood to live a life of earnestness and irreproachable conduct."[45]

As if to allay the suspicions of detractors who would object to the training of native clergy—who by simply being non-European were regarded by some as harboring deceitful intentions or of being "rice Christians"—Silvestri recounts that "dubious vocations were tested, and aspirants who lacked the requisite qualities were not accepted."[46] The Franciscan seminary for the training of Shanxi's priests opened in 1810, a century before Lebbe's petition for a native Chinese clergy and episcopacy reached Europe. By the time of the Boxer Uprising in 1900 more than seventy of these priests had died from persecution, which was naturally heralded as a spiritual victory won by native priests. Churches and monuments later rose above the places of their sacrifice.

The spiritual battle envisioned by the Franciscans in Shanxi was perhaps less visually triumphalistic than at other mission areas. But while Franciscans anticipated that spiritual warfare would be conducted more in the realms of mortification, personal piety, and the expansion of an indigenous clergy and hierarchy, the expectation of victory through martyrdom, common also in other orders, remained a vigorous component of China's Franciscan culture. After 1900, Western friars requested the installation of monuments to recall the thousands of Chinese Catholics killed by Boxers and Qing troops. Commemorative stelae recounting the sacrifices were installed, largely at the local government's expense, at such Shanxi village churches as Guchengying, where four large stone monuments were engraved early on, and where, in 2010, a hall and pavilion were erected in honor of the victims who died there in 1900. Pavilions and stelae have been erected in and around Taiyuan, too, to celebrate the mission's spiritual conquests.[47] Shanxi's heavenly battle was commemorated not only in China, however; large celebrations were hosted in Europe as well.

In 1947 the missionary journal of the Franciscan Missionaries of Mary published a number of special features highlighting the martyrdoms of the seven sisters who died in Shanxi during the Boxer Uprising. One article describes an extraordinary liturgical tribute to the sisters' 1900 "triumph" in Shanxi. The succession of three days of liturgical ceremonies was, significantly, held at two chapels dedicated to warrior saints, Michael the Archangel and Joan of Arc. The opening rites consisted of a Solemn Mass of the martyrs offered by the Franciscan priest Father Léon Paschal Leveugle, OFM, minister of the province of France, who was joined by a host of other Franciscans and "friends of the [Franciscan] Institutions and the parents of those distant missionaries."[48] Subsequent events included homilies by eminent bishops, cardinals, and the superior general of the Paris Société des Missions Étrangères, France's high-profile foreign missionary society.

These events culminated in the intonation of the "antiphon for the Vespers of Martyrs," in which the martyrs were entreated to pray for the living—*Orate pro nobis beatae Martyrs*—and which invoked "each of the seven [Franciscan Missionaries of Mary] martyrs." The article continues:

> Emotion reached its peak when everyone rose under the floodlit nave
>   and sang the great song of Rue du Bac:
> O God, thy soldiers, crowned with glory,
> God, by which our Martyrs have won the victory,
> Deign to listen to our wishes on this solemn day![49]

And in the liturgical finale:

> One felt the desire and yearning with each refrain:
> Our martyrs' Mother, Queen, and Patroness,
> Teach us to pray, to suffer.
> All we want is to win this crown,
> For Jesus Christ, we all want to die![50]

An important distinction between spiritual warfare imagined by Shanxi's Boxers and by Shanxi's Franciscans is that in the minds of the Boxers the battle was to be won by killing, and in the minds of the Franciscans, by dying. In both cases, however, the images of such a battle influenced personal behaviors. Even though the Franciscans in Shanxi were perhaps less nationalistically triumphalist than their co-missioners of other orders, they nonetheless envisioned themselves as participants in the Ecclesia Militans.

THE "TRIUMPH" OF THE FRANCISCAN BATTLE

The confrontational rhetoric of battle was softened somewhat by the notable Franciscan attention to charity, and one of the unique marks of the Franciscan method of missionizing China was the urgent call to serve the "poorest of the poor," the unwanted children, and the infirm. Saint Francis himself had flown in the face of social taboos to care for lepers and be "the hands and feet of Christ." The Shanxi Franciscans carried out their work amid tension between the imperatives of spiritual warfare and the demand to succor the afflicted without regard for whether they were Christian.

While the conversion of souls was undoubtedly the principal aim of the Franciscan mission in Shanxi, the daily work of the friars and sisters was largely occupied with the more diurnal tasks of caring for those in need. This included especially the streams of orphans who were either collected during rounds throughout the city by those looking for abandoned children—these were predominantly girls—or dropped off in baskets at the orphanage, which functioned much like the foundling hospitals in Europe. In her correspondence back to Europe, Mother Marie-Hermine de Jesus described the household and occupational skills the sisters taught the orphans in preparation for their future. Saint Paschal's Convent and the orphans' residence in Taiyuan bustled with activities: "Today not one of them is idle. Some make clothing for the rest, others do mending, they turn out shoes of all sizes. In another room they are hairdressing; further along is a laundry opened three weeks ago which is doing very well. Lastly, weaving has been started in a newly built house. At the moment they are spinning cotton. Nine spinning wheels, worked by the girls, the eldest fourteen, the youngest only ten, are humming all day long."

Their charitable work at the orphanage had to compete, however, with the increasing demands of both Christians and non-Christians who flowed into the infirmary. Exasperated by the almost unmanageable volume of orphans and the infirm, Marie-Hermine wrote, "Four more sisters would be very welcome here, two for the sick and two for the orphanage."[51] During the last two years of the nineteenth century, attention shifted to the growing need to treat those suffering from the drought and an outbreak of typhoid that plagued central Shanxi. In one letter, Théodoric Balat lamented that since there were so many "visits of pagans to the dispensary," there was scant time "for any spiritual work to be performed."[52]

Vicariate statistics prepared by Bishop Grassi before his death in 1900 reveal that despite the weight of the mission's charitable enterprise it was still able to accomplish its evangelical objectives. In a detailed handwritten report submitted to the Franciscan (OFM) Curia in 1896, Grassi reported on the state of the mission in Shanxi. By 1896 the Taiyuan vicariate had registered 15,510 Christians, 18 Chinese priests, only 6 European priests, and 1,200 recent adult conversions. Figures involving children are highly informative: the Franciscan mission had received 596 orphaned children into their care, 546 of whom were abandoned females, and of the 9,120 infant baptisms performed by priests and lay associates, 8,406 of these children died still in their infancy owing to the fact that children left on their doorstep were often already on the threshold of death.[53] In 1899, when the sisters began their work at Saint Paschal's, the "spiritual work" of the mission advanced; by then the number of Catholics had grown to 17,330, though there were two fewer Chinese priests than three years earlier.[54] Considering the general

Franciscan predisposition to develop an indigenous clergy, it is surprising that Grassi permitted the number of Chinese priests to diminish—though by 1899 there were still thirty-seven seminarians in training, most of whom were Shanxi natives.[55]

By 1899, news of rising anti-Christianism had spread through the order, and letters containing even the most mundane of topics were often punctuated with comments alluding to an expectation of martyrdom. After his arrival at Taiyuan, a new missionary, André Bauer, wrote a letter describing his new setting: "We arrived here on May 4, and my cell consists of four earthen walls, paper for windows, and my bed is a fifty-five centimeter high brick wall. The box spring is replaced by earth, on which rests a mat, and on this mat is a mattress with a blanket stuffed with wool. . . . May I imitate the Child Jesus in His Manger, and I ask Him the grace to die as He did, to emulate the martyrs and shed my blood for His cause."[56] His final remark, which appears as a non sequitur after his inventory of routine descriptions regarding his living conditions, is typical of the Franciscan letters that poured out of Shanxi at this time. Grassi assigned Bauer to look after the lay workers of the mission and to work in the surgery.

Charity was a useful tool in building a bridge of friendship between the Catholic mission and the native population, and in this goal the Franciscans were in some ways similar to the Jesuits, and in other ways slightly different; for the friars and sisters of Shanxi, cultural rapprochement was a by-product of religious charity. Whereas the Jesuits were occupied with the long-term sustainability of the Catholic mission in China on intellectual grounds, the Franciscans were more consciously occupied with the short-term need to feed mouths, clothe the poor, and heal the sick; one might say that the Franciscans appealed to China foremost through the compassion of Christ rather than through the mind of Christ. Both the Jesuits and the Franciscans sought conversions through both the heart and mind, but in different proportions. Gregorio Grassi went to extreme measures to help save the dying in Shanxi from starvation and typhus, contracting the illness himself. While he was tending to the physical needs of the suffering, Grassi still "fought courageously against the persecution of catechumens" in Shanxi that "checked the spread of Catholicism."[57] He also fought against "idol worship" and commissioned the construction of majestic churches to help establish, or assure, the "victory" of the church.

By 1900 the Franciscan mission in Shanxi was flourishing, having nearly sixty priests, fifty-seven seminarians, and 669 churches and oratories; it was a burgeoning Catholic population.[58] Regardless of recent mission growth and stability, the battle between the Boxers and the Franciscan mission ended on 9 July 1900, when the missionaries were captured and confined near the magistrate's court. During the Boxer violence of mid-1900 a large number of the 669 churches and oratories were destroyed, and perhaps more than ten thousand Catholics were killed, including many Franciscans.[59]

When Mother Marie-Hermine appealed to Bishop Fogolla to allow her and her six consoeurs to remain in Shanxi during the Boxer riots, she spoke of potential martyrdom as a form of "conquest" in the supernatural war against non-Christian China.[60] In its assumption of spiritual warfare, the missiological approach of the Shanxi mission was infused somewhat with an assumption that un-Christianized people were somehow less "civilized," an opinion that did not help to moderate the real cultural distance between Chinese and Western culture. Chinese edicts of this time were also decidedly antiforeign. In one Shanxi edict, the Franciscan missionaries are accused of leading native Chinese astray by "seditious language," and it states that Chinese who converted to the foreign religion have "debased themselves."[61]

The "triumph" of the Franciscan sisters who died in Shanxi during the Boxer Uprising is heralded today by Shanxi's clergy and its Catholic population, who are all Chinese. The Red Lantern women Boxers are decried as superstitious magicians, whereas the Franciscan sisters are honored for their charitable works in their orphanage and hospital. Shanxi's Catholics, while no longer employing the rhetoric of the Church Militant, assert that the "sacrifices" of the Franciscan sisters in 1900 resulted in the later renaissance of Shanxi Catholicism. Whereas the Catholic population of Shanxi was around thirty thousand during the Boxer Uprising, the Taiyuan diocese alone boasts a Catholic population today of more than eighty thousand, and it is currently the most influential and the fastest-growing diocese in China.[62]

THE EVE OF CONFLICT

Westerners in general were far from insensitive to the horrible plight of the population of Shanxi, and while the Boxers were convinced that the foreign gods had caused the drought, Western missionaries, both Catholic and Protestant, were busily collecting data as well as resources to combat the human suffering around them. Historical records show that between 1876 and 1879, the massive famine that afflicted China's five northern provinces claimed more than nine and a half million lives.[63] Appeals were sent throughout the

FIGURE 3.2. Father Barnabas Nanetti da Cologna, OFM, Shanxi missionary and brother of Sister Maria Chiara (Nanetti), FMM; the latter was killed on 9 July 1900. Nanetti da Cologna was stationed at the Franciscan seminary at Dongergou during the executions at Yuxian's yamen and managed to escape Shanxi through a remote route. Source: Provincia di Cristo Re dei Frati Minori dell'Emilia Romagna, Parma.

world's Western media for funds, and Roman Catholic contributions from Europe equaled some forty thousand pounds sterling, a significant sum at that time.[64] From the Taiyuan bishop's residence in March 1877, Monsignor Aloysius (Luigi) Moccogatta reported this distressing turn in his vicariate: "The people have begun to kill the living to have them for food; husbands eat their wives, parents eat their sons and daughters, and children eat their parents."[65]

Francesco Fogolla sent petitions abroad asking for foreign aid, and to add to the donations he received in reply, he sold what valuable gifts he had received, such as silver utensils and bronze statues, to raise more capital with which to help feed the hungry.[66] After the worst of the famine had passed, Fogolla used the remaining funds in 1884 to commission the construction of a stately church in Shanxi dedicated to the sacred heart of Jesus, as described in letters sent back to Europe.[67] It is curious that more was not mentioned in Franciscan letters about the Boxer notices disseminated around them in 1900, though some of these notices have been preserved in Franciscan archives. The majority of our sources about Boxer rumors derive from Protestant missionary materials.

The daily diary of one of the Franciscan friars who witnessed the events of 1900 in Shanxi and survived, along with his journal (later published in 1903), has been of particular value. On 26 June 1900, Father Barnabas Nanetti da Cologna (fig. 3.2) wrote, "Edicts against the Christians and Europeans have appeared everywhere, and thousands of subversive leaflets have been circulated among the pagans, including prescriptions by [Buddhist] monks to be used to save oneself from the influence of Europeans. These are disseminated in shops and in marketplaces; some of which are in the hands of Christians, and some of which are in my own hands."[68] Once the Franciscans saw these notices, it was too late to prevent what quickly beset them. On 28 June, Father Barnabas wrote again from his bureau at the Dongergou seminary: "Three seminarians came to the convent from Taiyuan, exhausted from their journey. They said that the situation in the city is turning toward the worse, and the bishop has ordered the seminarians to leave." The entry ends with: "We're told that the soldiers are coming here to the convent, and they're determined to slaughter the Europeans and Christians!"[69]

PART 2

The Deluge and the Earthly Battle

CHAPTER 4

Red Lantern Women and Franciscan Sisters

We are sometimes so surrounded that we nearly suffocate in the crowd,
and the orphans, around two hundred, think that we are heavenly angels.
—SISTER MARIA AMANDINA, FMM

O N 5 July 1900, only four days before his confreres and consoeurs—
including his sister by blood, Maria Chiara Nanetti—were paraded
into the governor's yamen for a hasty trial, Barnabas Nanetti da Cologna
mentioned for the first time in his journal a new development in the Boxer
culture of Shanxi:

> There are women boxers called Red Lanterns, all dressed in red and
> carrying red lanterns everywhere. They're from 11 to 14 years old, are
> unmarried, and like the young men they rage in a hypnotic sleep of evil,
> though even more so than the males. Based on their pagan beliefs they
> believe they are also invulnerable, and what is more important, they
> think they can fly, and destroy and burn with an invincible power. They
> are strictly forbidden to use anything European, or even made in the
> European way, such as canvas, matches, oil, and so forth. Even touch-
> ing them [a Western object] is considered unclean . . . and many such
> things have been vandalized.[1]

The presence of these women and girls added an important, and more curious, dimension to the Boxer activities in Shanxi; in fact the role of women on both the Franciscan and Boxer sides of the incidents of 1900 paints a poly-chromatic tableau of Shanxi's late-imperial Sino-missionary history. While Boxers were burning churches and killing Christians, the Red Lanterns were behind them launching spells, invoking the gods and powers to assist them. And while churches burned and Christians died, the Franciscan women were launching prayers, invoking the Blessed Virgin and angelic hosts to protect those on their side of the conflict. Male-dominant accounts of the Boxer Uprising in recent historiography have given the impression that women played only a minor role in the events of 1900; however, the women in Shanxi were no less involved than the men.

THE NUMINOUS POWER OF YIN

As the Boxers quickly formed into a more definitive structure in Shandong as summer approached in 1900, a female contingent, which called itself the Red Lanterns Shining, began to take shape in Beijing and Tianjin.[2] The presence of women among the ranks of Boxers is particularly important in light of the Boxer idea that women, especially menstruating women, were contaminat-ing. Male Boxer adherents, in an attempt to heighten their martial prowess, eschewed sexual activity, fearing pollution by the female yin element.[3] Red Lantern women were, as Nanetti da Cologna observes in his journal, mainly between the ages of eleven and fourteen, and so they were generally premen-strual. For this reason male Boxers viewed them as comparatively "pure," magical antidotes to the female "poison" of Western women and Chinese Christian women, whose "impurity" was used to their advantage in malicious feminine sorcery. Red Lanterns provided positive and unpolluted yin as a counteragent, as exemplified in the use of these largely preteen and teenage girls during the siege of Beijing's North Church (Beitang).

From 14 June until 16 August 1900, Bishop Alphonse Favier and around thirty-four hundred Christians—mostly Chinese—were besieged by Boxers, Qing troops, and lamas from Yonghegong Temple, while behind them stood a division of Red Lantern women who buoyed the attacks from afar (fig. 4.1), casting spells that were expected to, at least in part, counteract the magical arts of the Christian women.[4] On the Feast of Corpus Christi, 14 June, Favier wrote from within the beleaguered cathedral compound:

At eight o'clock in the morning we saw from the top of the church the constant blaze of Tung-t'ang [Dongtang] and several other fires. We can no longer hold communication with anyone; the gates of the Yellow City [Imperial City] are closed, guarded by the troops of Prince Tuan [Duan]. At half-past eleven o'clock the old cathedral of the Immaculate Conception in Nan-tang [Nantang], the residence, the college, the hospital, the orphanage, all took fire; it is a horrible sight! . . . Cries of death from Boxers all around us. *Cha, Cha,* kill! Kill!!! *Chao, Chao,* burn, burn!!! [*sha sha shao shao*].[5]

After the siege was over, the French prelate reported the severity of the attacks to an American missionary, Arthur Judson Brown (1856–1963). Brown recalls the interview:

He said that of the eighty Europeans and 3,400 [Chinese] Christians with him in the siege, 2,700 were women and children. Four hundred were buried, of whom forty were killed by bullets, twenty-five by one explosion, eighty-one by another and one by another. Of the rest, some died of disease but the greater part of starvation. Twenty-one children were buried at one time in one grave. Beside these 400 who were killed or who died, many more were blown to pieces in explosions so that nothing could be found to bury. Fifty-one children disappeared in this way and not a fragment remained.[6]

Surprisingly, or miraculously, the cathedral and most of its inhabitants survived the siege; it was the only Christian church in Beijing to survive Boxer attack.[7] Throughout the bloodshed, the Red Lanterns remained vigilant participants, and the fact that the attackers could not overcome the cathedral's defenders was attributed to the potency of Christian magic, especially the "female pollution" of the women inside the large church.

At least one Chinese pro-Boxer grand councilor, as Chiang Ying-ho notes, "believed that Pierre-Marie-Alphonse Favier, a bishop in Peking, was invulnerable because he painted women's menses on his forehead."[8] In addition to the imagined apotropaic use of menstrual blood, the Boxers imagined even more elaborate forms of Christian female magic, including hanging a flag woven of pubic hair and displaying "dirty things" as a potent antidote against Boxer spirit possession.[9] The role of the Red Lanterns, then, was to assist the men with magic of their own. And as the Boxers asserted, "The Red

FIGURE 4.1. Illustration of the Boxer siege against Beijing's North Church (Beitang) from 14 June to 16 August 1900. A Red Lantern woman is clearly depicted in the upper section of the image casting protective magic around the attacking male Boxers. She is also seen carrying a red lantern, the identifying feature of the Red Lanterns Shining. Source: Whitworth University History of Christianity in China Archive, Spokane.

Lanterns are all girls and young women, so they do not fear dirty things."[10] Not only was it said that these girls were able to neutralize the black magic of Christian and Western women, but also they were thought capable of causing Christian homes to burst into flames from a distance, thwarting Christian gun and cannon fire, traversing water, and attacking foreign ships; and, as Nanetti da Cologna wrote, they also were believed to fly through the air, the facility for flight being their most well-known ability.

Organizationally the Red Lanterns structured themselves in parallel to the Fists of Righteous Harmony; as male Boxer leaders were called "senior brother," female leaders were referred to as "senior sister," though it appears that the eminence of the Red Lanterns, or at least the popular sense of their preternatural authority, surpassed that of their male associates.[11] Liu Meng-yang (1877–1943), a resident of Tianjin during the turbulence of the Boxer era, rendered a vivid description of Red Lantern prominence: "When they walk through the streets, they avoid women, who are not allowed to gaze upon them. The people all burn incense and kneel in their presence; they call them female immortals and dare not look up at them. Even the Boxer bandits, when they encounter them, fall prostrate on their knees by the side of the road."[12] The very term *Red Lantern* was associated with methods for rendering men impervious to bullets; their magical skills left people in such awe of them that even in artistic depictions of these teenage women they figure as the central supernatural force supporting the Boxer war against Christians. In one contemporary woodblock print (see fig. 4.1) a Red Lantern woman appears above the attackers of Beijing's cathedral; in her right hand is a red lantern, and in her left hand a whip extends above her head, which releases a protective barrier that extends around the attacking Boxers; she appears to be in the process of invoking magical powers of protection between the crossfire of the Christians and Boxers.[13] As the Society of Righteous Harmony made its way to the central plains of Shanxi, the Red Lanterns followed with their daunting command of feminine sorcery.

RED LANTERNS ILLUMINATE THE PLAINS OF SHANXI

The large number and influence of Boxers in Shanxi was largely due to Yuxian welcoming the Society of Righteous Harmony, after which the Taiyuan Boxers swiftly grew more numerous.[14] Liu Dapeng recounted in his *Casual Notes from Within the Garden* (Qianyuan suoji): "At the same time the Boxers emerged, women organized into Red Lantern Shining groups. . . . They all drilled in the women's quarters, as their parents held them in confinement and would not allow them to leave their homes. Even if they could not themselves take to flight into the sky, they mounted high walls as if they were monkeys."[15] Women who could leave their homes and join Boxer activities did, and those who could not remained in their homes and practiced Red Lantern arts in confinement. Even those in captivity "mounted high walls," where they appeared to conduct the undertakings that occurred below them.

Liu Dapeng's interest in the maneuverings of Red Lanterns in his county allows us to reconstruct with some detail the principal actions of Shanxi's Boxer women based on his reflections. Liu's enumeration of Boxer women includes those at fifteen locations, mostly small villages, several of which had prominent Catholic communities. According to Liu, the Red Lantern woman was generally a teenager; when describing such a woman, he often notes that she had "just received the hairpin" (*jizhe*), meaning that she had reached the age of fifteen, when a hairpin was placed in her hair to mark her coming of age.[16] The youngest and oldest Red Lanterns mentioned in Liu Dapeng's brief catalog both derive from the same location, Huangyecun village; the youngest was ten and the oldest was thirty years old.[17] Each village produced only a small number of Red Lanterns; and according to Liu, several villages, such as Shangyingcun and Xijiacun, had only one Boxer woman, while others, such as Tiancun, boasted eight.[18]

Interposed within his careful inventory of villages and their Red Lanterns are Liu's descriptions of their ritual practices, their special ability to fly, and their performance of other mystical skills; he also records a number of other female Boxer groups. In one passage, Liu outlines a typical Red Lantern ceremony in Shanxi: "All of the women drilled facing due south and made an offering of incense. They straightened their lapels to show respect and made their four gestures of obeisance, kowtowing and then standing up. They grasped a fan in their right hand, wore red turbans on their heads, held magic formulae in their left hand, and intoned incantations with their mouths."[19] Red Lantern rites were similar to the ceremonies of male Boxers; both groups made ritual offerings to particular deities—Shanxi Red Lanterns often venerated the Bodhisattva Guanyin and the goddess Nüwa—kowtowed, and wore red turbans. These two deities, both female, were associated with popular Chinese novels, which brought their legends to commoners and literati alike. Guanyin is the most popular female Bodhisattva and appears in the novel *Journey to the West*; Nüwa is known as the sister of one of China's model sages of antiquity, Fuxi, and is connected to several origin myths in ancient China, appearing in scattered mythological texts dating to the era of the Warring States (475–221 BCE), such as the *Classic of Mountains and Seas* (Shanhaijing), and the later, Ming fantasy novel *Investiture of the Gods* (Fengshen yanyi).[20] These once-fictional characters were transformed via perception, becoming elevated to the status of hero-deities. The women Boxers who invoked these female spirits differed, however, in that instead of carrying swords, spears, and other weapons, they carried spell books for intoning curses.

After the women completed their invocations they entered into a trance, "and then they immediately tumbled to the ground. Soon after falling down they rose and began to move about as if in combat." At first they looked as if they were merely frolicking, Liu recounts, and then, "after a while they flew up, higher than the wall." As Nanetti da Cologna remarked in his journal, Shanxi's Red Lanterns were specialists in flight. At Shangyingcun, it was discovered that one Red Lantern "was able to ascend in her room as if in flight," which reportedly so frightened the girl's parents that they locked her in and would not let her out of the house.[21] The roots of the Red Lantern mythology of flight in Shanxi derived from previous examples in other provinces. When the Vincentian church in Tianjin, Notre Dame des Victoires, was earlier attacked and destroyed, Chinese witnesses reported seeing female Red Lanterns circling the church in the air as flames engulfed its towers.[22] The Franciscans, too, observed Red Lantern women in attendance while their churches were razed in Shanxi.

Other skills besides flight were attributed to these young women. In a Yuci village, Nantiancun, the seventeen-year-old Red Lantern nicknamed Goddess Yang was "able to predict in advance what the Christians would do," and "all of the evil Christian actions were thwarted by Goddess Yang." Yang's prophetic and magical skills were such that people in Shanxi "venerated her as a deity."[23] Other Red Lanterns, from Baiyancun village, one fifteen and one twenty-five, were both "able to make fire arise."[24] George Lynch, a journalist who accompanied the multinational forces as they entered China in 1900, wrote of popular rumors that "the red lantern girls could pull down high-storied houses with thin cotton strings, and could," as Liu Dapeng also recorded, "set fire to a house simply by moving a fan."[25]

Perhaps in part owing to their young age, or to the dangers confronted by anyone in proximity to the Boxers as they attacked Christian buildings and killed Christians, it was common for parents to object to their daughters' membership in the Shanxi Red Lanterns. As noted, the Shangyingcun girl's parents locked her in the house after discovering her flying in her room, and in Guojiabao village two Red Lantern girls trained for only three days before their parents began to consider how they might be stopped.[26] In some cases parents confined their Boxer daughters to their rooms for simple reasons of traditional Chinese modesty, in order "to prevent them from being gazed at by men."[27] Shanxi's deeply conservative, and perhaps religiously animated, culture meant that allowing teenage girls to spend time among and collaborate with young men was unconventional, to say the least. In this era of arranged marriages, young betrothed women were expected to remain within the protective confines of their homes until their wedding day. While not unique to Shanxi, the cultural confinement of women may have been more intense there. That these young women were allowed to assist the Fists of Righteous Harmony at all attests to the prestige and influence of the Boxers. After one Tianjin Red Lantern girl returned home after being away for several days, her suspicious parents confronted her. Her excuse was that she had just returned from Russia, where she had flown to demolish the capital; she also warned that she would kill them if they prevented her from her involvement with the Boxers. Her intimidation appears to have worked, as henceforth they presented no further objections.[28]

In addition to Red Lanterns, Shanxi was rumored to have hosted Blue Lanterns Shining and Black Lanterns Shining, but by far the two most shadowy women's groups were the White Lanterns Shining and the Green Hands Shining. Liu Dapeng reports, "The White Lanterns and the Green Hands taught a martial arts [and magical?] practice to women that was said to be able to destroy Red Lanterns and the Fists of Righteous Harmony."[29] Shanxi's White Lanterns appear to have modeled themselves after the powerful Bodhisattva Guanyin, for they emulated common Buddhist depictions of her; they clothed themselves entirely in white and held a white water vase, typically associated with Guanyin's vase of mercy.

Rivalries between male Boxers and White Lanterns emerged, for at least in one case a thirty-year-old White Lantern woman from Yuci county who "wore white, carried a water vase, and could fly through the air" was executed by the Fists of Righteous Harmony. In Taiyuan county, however, two White Lantern women, who were able to fly "like a sparrow," collaborated with the Boxers in their efforts to destroy foreigners and Christians. Green Hands Shining women were more fearsome and enigmatic than the other groups of Shanxi women Boxers. These women were reported to appear high in the sky, shrouded in red and black mists, and in one account a "green hand suddenly appeared in the firmament like a chariot." The most salient characteristic of the history of Shanxi's Boxer women was their use of supernatural skills and rites.[30]

Shanxi's women Boxers inherited much from the Red Lantern culture of China's other northern provinces, and they were active accomplices in the provincial war against foreigners and Christians. Like the Red Lanterns of Beijing and Tianjin, Shanxi's Red Lanterns functioned as agents opposing the negative yin forces of Western women and native female Christians—who were viewed by the Boxers as "polluting" because of their active sexuality (viz., they opposed married Christian women)—and those who had passed puberty and begun menstruation, both married and unmarried. Shanxi's Red Lanterns were perceived to possess, like the other Red Lantern groups, distinctive and efficacious paranormal magical skills, such as the ability to cast spells, to ignite fires with their fans, and, most significantly, to fly. Such popular mythologies provided these mostly teenage Red Lantern women with unprecedented social prestige, which at some levels surpassed even that of the male Boxers. Most important, however, Shanxi's Red Lantern women Boxers functioned as powerful magical collaborators with China's gods in the heavenly battle against the gods of the Franciscan mission.

THE FRANCISCAN MISSIONARIES OF MARY

It is significant that the Franciscan Missionaries of Mary took Mary, the Holy Mother of God, as their patron and protector, for it is Mary who shall, according to Catholic belief, conquer the serpent (Satan). The Roman Catholic view of Mary has been largely influenced by the church's traditional interpretation of Genesis 3:15: "I will put enmity between you and the woman, and between your seed and her seed; he shall bruise your head, and you shall bruise his heel." Theological deliberations regarding Mary's power over the devil were still fresh in ecclesial parlance when the Franciscan Missionaries of Mary were founded in 1882. This followed the official proclamation of the doctrine of the Immaculate Conception on 8 December 1854, which in part highlights the Blessed Virgin's particular power to resist the devil and his subordinates. As recently as 1996, Mary's role in the fight against enemy spirits was discussed by popes, and in his reflection in *L'Osservatore Romano*, Pope John Paul II (r. 1978–2005) asserted, "The same biblical text [Genesis 3:15] also proclaims the enmity between the woman and her offspring on the one hand, and the serpent and his offspring on the other. This is a hostility expressly established by God, which has a unique importance, if we consider the problem of the Virgin's personal holiness. In order to be the irreconcilable enemy of the serpent and his offspring, Mary had to be free from all power of sin, and to be so from the first moment of her existence."[31] By the late nineteenth century, Mary's roles as "mediator," "protector," and "enemy of Satan" were all part of her identity as patron of missionary work in non-Christian countries.

All sisters of the Franciscan Missionaries of Mary took the name *Mary* once they entered religious life, to which was often added the name of a secondary patron saint. This practice can be seen in, for example, the names of Sister Marie de Sainte Nathalie and Marie de Saint Just. Among the Franciscan Missionaries of Mary who entered Shanxi after the seven sisters were martyred in Taiyuan was Maria Assunta Pallotta, who became the center of a cult following that extended to Europe. The Franciscan Missionaries of Mary, who wore long white habits that stood out as they traveled and worked in

China, emulated the example of Saints Francis and Clare of Assisi, seeking to live austere and pious lives as missionaries. During the rite of final profession, these sisters each made a solemn oath "at the moment of Communion before the Sacred Host," which concluded with "I offer myself as a victim for the Church and for souls, and dedicate myself to the adoration of the most Holy Sacrament and to the work of the missions."[32]

The sisters' unique commitment to the practice of perpetual adoration of the Blessed Sacrament was among the more important features of their daily routine in Shanxi, and the presence of Christ in the Sacrament was an essential component of the spiritual encounter between the God of the missionaries and the gods of the non-Christians. Not only did adoration strengthen the spiritual resolve of the sisters, but more important they believed it also brought the presence of God, literally, into a non-Christian culture. Even if the local people were unaware of God's presence in Shanxi, the gods of China's popular religions were, the sisters held, acutely attentive to Shanxi's new spiritual guest.

The seven sisters selected to accompany Bishop Fogolla to Shanxi were all highly aware, even before their departure to China, of the spiritual significance of the Eucharistic presence at their mission in Taiyuan, though Mary's role in "winning souls for Jesus," as Marie-Hermine de Jesus put it, was never forgotten.[33] By February 1899, Sister Marie-Hermine (fig. 4.2) had been informed of her appointment to lead the Shanxi convent, and in a letter to her consoeurs on 26 February 1899, the new mother superior wrote of a special gift they would bring with them to China:

> I write now as I look at Our Lady of the Sacred Heart placed on
> the table in front of my cell. This delightful image of the Blessed Virgin
> . . . was given yesterday to Mother Mary of the Holy Faith by the older
> children of Marie de Saint-Raphaël. A nice sister of one of the girls
> donated a carved wooden pedestal, painted in white and gold, which
> will support our Holy Mother in our future oratory, and a lady offered
> a pair of candelabras with five branches, and another promised flowers
> and secondhand clothes.[34]

In addition to these gifts, the departing Franciscan Missionaries of Mary were given a handmade statue of Saint Paschal, Franciscan patron of the Eucharist and their new convent in Shanxi.[35] These donations were gratefully accepted, the sisters were gathered together, and an emotionally stirring

FIGURE 4.2. Sister Marie-Hermine de Jesus, FMM, the mother superior of the Franciscan Missionaries of Mary convent, Saint Paschal's, in Taiyuan during the Boxer Uprising. Sister Marie-Hermine wrote a large number of letters during her time in Shanxi. Source: Archivio Curia Generalizia Ordo Fratrum Minorum, Rome.

ceremony of departure was orchestrated to see the sisters and the spiritual tools of their mission off to China.

In one of her final letters from France, Marie-Hermine wrote to her friend, Alice, describing her forthcoming departure: "Sunday, March 12, at four in the afternoon we fourteen religious will leave for our mission in China." She notes her "heavy charge as Superior to found a hospital and an orphanage in Taiyuanfu in north Shanxi," and in terms resonant with the mission of the Church Militant, Marie-Hermine continues, "Please pray for me, my dear Alice, that I bring many souls to the Divine Shepherd in that distant land where Satan reigns as master."[36] Before boarding their ship to Asia on 12 March, the Franciscan sisters and friars were sent off in a stirring ceremony conducted in the Chapel of Saint-Raphaël in Marseille. There were fourteen Franciscan sisters in the group; seven would ultimately occupy the Shanxi mission. A friar, Father Dupré, offered the sermon on the topic of the Pater Noster (Our Father); and reflecting on the *adveniat regnum tuum* (thy kingdom come), the homily naturally turned to the subject of sacrifice and then to martyrdom.

The Franciscan missionary sister, the friar suggested, must "die to every-thing she loved—her community, the altar where she was betrothed to Jesus" and—"have no connections, because any strings on the heart or the feet prevents flying away." In his concluding remarks he reminded the departing sisters of the sacrifice of martyrdom, a common refrain among those des-tined for "spiritual combat" in China. "Do not forget those who remain," he urged. "They do not[,] like you[,] have the sweet hope of martyrdom. . . . If you die martyrs, pray, pray, for those who remain!"[37] Sister Marie Adolphine was known particularly for her desire for self-sacrifice, and in an anecdote set in the period before she left for China we are given a sense of the culture of martyrdom shared among the Franciscan sisters as they prepared for their mission in China.

> While looking at a photograph of the martyr Father Victorino, her companions asked her jokingly: "Aren't you afraid they'll [the Chinese] cut you up into little pieces?" And she replied in all simplicity: "No. I think in that case I'll go straight to heaven. And then I'll return to take a walk down this corridor and tell you: 'It is I; don't be afraid.' . . . and I'll give each one of you a piece . . . " "A piece of what?" her sisters asked in trepidation. "Of my palm [of martyrdom]!" she concluded cheerfully.[38]

Six weeks into their journey, Sister Maria Amandina wrote a description of their conveyance from Marseilles to Taiyuan, noting that several weeks still remained of their journey by ship, "followed by two days on a train, after which we set aside our religious habit to dress in Chinese style to begin our donkey caravan" to Shanxi. "We have all suffered from seasickness," she continued, "and Sister Marie Adolphine has often thought that her last hour had come."[39] Between bouts of seasickness, or in spite of them, Bishop Francesco Fogolla met with the sisters twice each day to teach them Chinese, and he continued to be their language instructor after they were settled in Shanxi. The demands of their travels left the sisters lethargic, and Marie de Sainte Nathalie was so exhausted from the voyage that she grew "seriously ill." Amandina wrote, "I sleep beside her and take her temperature, which climbs to 40–44° Celsius [104–111° Fahrenheit] with a pulse of 130."[40] At first their battle was less spiritual than physical: but after their fatigue had begun to subside, Bishop Grassi was eager to put Taiyuan's new Franciscan sisters to work.

THE "WHITE HABIT" SISTERS IN SHANXI

Once the "white habit" sisters had arrived on the yellow plains of northern China, the pragmatic necessities of establishing the mission tempered the spiritual rhetoric of the Ecclesia Militans and concerns for martyrdom; the quotidian burdens of running an orphanage and hospital, and of maintaining the rigorous liturgical obligations of the institute, demanded constant attention and were physically exhausting. When they first arrived at the Franciscan mission in Taiyuan, however, the sisters were gladdened by the church, which was "very attractive and large, has three naves, and is surmounted by a tower with bells and a chiming clock." One letter by Marie-Hermine expressed her glad relief, after arriving in Shanxi, that "China is not a country of savages, as we like to repeat in France."[41] The sisters were not without criticisms, however, and several letters included anecdotes about the poor standard of Chinese hygiene.

One account describes an eight-year-old child who, having been admitted to the Franciscan clinic in Taiyuan with typhoid fever, was discovered to have worn the same trousers for fifty days; neither the girl nor the trousers had been washed. When the trousers were removed, the newly arrived European sisters were appalled as they witnessed "a good handful (I'm not exaggerating) of vermin" being released from each leg. At the time of the sisters' arrival the vicariate cared for eight hundred orphans, and on average twelve or fifteen new children, almost all of them girls, were left at the orphanage each day. As mentioned earlier, the majority of the infants among them were already gravely ill before being entrusted to the Franciscan mission, and so most of them died shortly after their entrance into the orphanage. Marie-Hermine wrote in one letter that even with the food and care they gave the young children, most "fly to a beautiful country where suffering is unknown! Their fate is lovely, better than the expected, which was to be eaten on the road by the unclean beasts, but it is still painful to see the suffering of these poor little creatures!"[42]

Giovanni Ricci recounts that the sisters were sent to work at the hospital immediately: "The news that seven European virgins . . . had reached the Catholic church immediately attracted many sick people to the small clinic," where the mother superior worked alongside her assistant, Sister Maria della Pace, who treated serious and infectious diseases, such as ulcers and scabies, which commonly disappeared "with a simple rinse of water and phenol."[43] The care of patients and orphans had previously been assigned to the Chinese virgins, local Christian women who lived as dedicated, celibate catechists.[44] These virgins had, before the appearance of the European women, fulfilled the principal role of female leadership at the Shanxi mission. As Ricci notes, "Even though the Sisters . . . very delicately tried to avoid offending the sensibilities of the Chinese virgins, they reluctantly witnessed the take over of the management of the orphans," which brought new tensions within the mission.[45] Tensions over water preservation versus bathing also arose, and shouting arguments sometimes erupted between the native and foreign women.

One letter complained, "Every day, ten or fifteen times we are forced to cross the courtyard of the orphanage. . . . And when we go out we see 150 to 200 children, hardly clad, filthy, and covered in vermin—eating, fighting, or crawling in the mud just like puppies. . . . Many times Sister Maria della Pace and I have chastened the Virgins responsible for watching over them, trying to make them understand that we should take care of these children." It was likely that the virgins felt they were indeed caring for them, and while not in the way the European sisters expected, they were caring for the children already at a standard much higher than outside of the orphanage.[46] In another case, an eight-year-old girl fell into a deep well because the virgins were not monitoring where the children were playing. After saving the girl by use of ropes and ladders, the sisters again quarreled with the Chinese caretakers over watching the orphans.[47] It was not merely the issue of bathing or of monitoring the children's safety that exasperated the Franciscan women, however. Even more disconcerting were the austerities women endured under Chinese social mores. Mother Marie-Hermine de Jesus described an incident in Taiyuan involving a sixteen-year-old girl that represents well the kinds of daily cultural antagonism that occupied the lives of the seven sisters:

> Poor little Chinese! Women are truly to be pitied in China, even among Christians, and we cannot completely eliminate old Chinese customs. Bishop Fogolla told me yesterday the story of a girl of sixteen who was obliged to marry. A child adopted by her uncle, named Mary, was ten years old when she was engaged to a young Chinese with parents who poured a good dowry into their future as a token of their commitment. Consulting a woman is a little known thing in the Celestial Empire, and all indications are that little Mary was not asked about her feelings. The thing was done as it is usually done, through intermediaries, men responsible for dealing with marriages between young boys and the parents of young girls. Five years after this resolution, Mary had an opportunity to come to the orphanage to see her cousin who was raised here. Life is peaceful for orphans and Chinese Virgins who largely pray to God, and this pleased the girl who felt an awakening in her heart and a desire to remain a virgin. She wrote to her family at the earliest opportunity and declared that she would not marry. The supplications, prayers, and threats of her parents could not change her feelings. In vain was the representative of the engagement contract, whose assertions that she would disgrace her whole family were useless. The intermediaries, who said that the engagement was required to be carried out successfully, were unhappy. "This is obstinacy," her father said, striking her with such violence that blood flowed, though nothing could shake the child's determination. The groom, having heard of this, came in person to ascertain the facts, and the father confessed the truth and promised to make every effort to change the girl's mind. After renewed attempts by her parents to make her change her resolution, Mary loosened her foot binding and cut her hair, and then throwing her bindings and hair into a fire, the courageous child exclaimed, "Now the boy won't take me!"[48]

The sisters made entreaties to Bishop Fogolla to intervene after the girl had been so roughly handled in this dispute that her clothing was left in shreds, hanging from her shoulders, though nothing more is related about the girl's fate. Scenes such as this one left little time for the sisters to consider the spiritual warfare they had been commissioned to fight during their departure ceremony in France, though such occurrences functioned to reinforce their impression that China was "controlled by Satan." During their first few months in Shanxi the Franciscan Missionaries of Mary were obliged to confront a litany of problems, including the hygiene of vermin-infested children, power struggles between themselves and the Chinese virgins, and domestic disputes over arranged marriages, foot binding, and the potential vocations of those drawn to the celibate religious life.

More lighthearted interactions also marked the sisters' first few months in Shanxi, which were expected as local Chinese first encountered objects unknown to their native culture. Sister Amandina described an experience she had while bringing medicine to a patient in the Franciscan pharmacy: "One day I brought medicine in a glass to a patient, and what astonishment she had! She called all the others to come and touch the glass to see if it was not made of ice." Equally amused were the European women when they discovered that their convent windows consisted of paper rather than glass. Amandina continued: "It may surprise you that here the windows are made of white paper; we have such windows in the dormitory, refectory, and the pharmacy. When the evening comes in our kitchen it is amusing to see the Chinese who are curious wet their fingers and make small holes in the paper, and they are often seen in the light—twenty eyes looking through small holes. Women look with much astonishment at our big feet! Theirs are not more than 10 centimeters!"[49] These more cheerful encounters helped sustain the sisters' spirits as they themselves occupied some of the beds in their overcrowded clinic, recovering from illnesses of their own.

The spiritual dimension of their mission did not disappear under the weight of the more routine problems, however; and as the sisters grew more accustomed to their new context, the question of converting souls was restored to a more dominant position in their minds. While patients treated at the Franciscan hospital in Taiyuan were usually Catholic, a number of non-Christians also sought treatment, and into the medicines administered to patients of all creeds was commonly mixed a little water from Lourdes. Another practice the sisters added to their care of non-Christian patients was their request that the patients "recite the names Jesus and Mary, and make the sign of the cross" when they arrived for treatment.[50] Perhaps the sisters' most adamant desire at the mission in Shanxi, however, was for daily exposition of the Blessed Sacrament, which was understood to be one of the more prevailing armaments in the battle for souls. The patron saint of the convent, Paschal, was a preeminent representative of Eucharistic devotion at the end of the nineteenth century.

THE BODY OF CHRIST IN THE CAPITAL OF SHANXI

Saint Paschal Baylon was a Franciscan contemplative mystic and a "saint of the Eucharist." After Pope Leo XIII initiated the church's response against modernism in his encyclical *Providentissimus Deus*, in 1893, issues such as biblical interpretation began to emerge as arenas of theological and intellectual conflict, and devotion to the Eucharist became one of the church's "weapons" against error and "secular rationalism." The rising significance of Eucharistic devotion in the church's battle against its contenders culminated in Leo XIII's encyclical *Mirae Caritatis*, in which Saint Paschal became known as the "seraph of the Eucharist," the advocate in heaven who would underpin the church's struggle against its enemies. In this encyclical, Leo XIII asserted that the Eucharist "enriches the soul with an abundance of heavenly blessings, and fills it with a sweet joy which far surpasses man's hope and expectations; it sustains him in adversity, strengthens him in the spiritual combat, preserves him for life everlasting, and as a special provision for the journey that accompanies him thither."[51] The convention of bearing the image of a monstrance on the Franciscan habit is generally attributed to Saint Paschal's connection to Eucharistic adoration, signifying devotion to Jesus in the Blessed Sacrament. It made sense according to nineteenth-century sensibilities, therefore, that a Franciscan convent would be placed under the patronage of such a saint, one associated not only with the hallowed Franciscan virtues of poverty and charity but also with the greater church's struggle against its enemies—which were, the church believed, more easily defeated through devotions to the Eucharist. Bringing the Body of Christ to the capital of Shanxi was one of the principal ambitions of the Franciscan sisters at Taiyuan.

Given the growing popularity of Paschal Baylon, who was a Franciscan saint no less, it is not surprising that his patronage and a desire to perpetually adore the Blessed Sacrament figured heavily in the minds of the sisters in Shanxi. Regarding the early weeks of the sisters' lives in China, Giovanni Ricci writes, "There was still one thing that was dear to all, the adoration of the Blessed Sacrament. It has been noted, and it is proved by the fact that the admirable spirit of sacrifice of the Franciscan Missionaries of Mary is drawn from the daily worship [of the Eucharist] that forms the happiness of the Institute."[52] Even before Marie-Hermine left her native Europe, her letters were interposed with invocations of Saint Paschal's protection.[53] In one letter she wrote, "I am not surprised that the foundation stone of our home is Saint Paschal Baylon," and she continued: "His ardent love for Jesus in the Eucharist is all I ask, so that we can win souls for Jesus and console our Mother."[54]

From the moment of their arrival, the Franciscan sisters made regular appeals to the bishop to permit daily exposition of the Blessed Sacrament for devotion, which the two bishops, Gregorio Grassi and Francesco Fogolla, were for some reason reluctant to approve. August 24 was the anniversary of the episcopal consecration of Bishop Fogolla, and the sisters sent him a card they had made with painted flowers, in which they promised to dedicate an entire day of prayer to his private intentions. On the day of his anniversary, the mother superior, Marie-Hermine, and Sister Maria della Pace went into the sacristy after the bishop's Mass of thanksgiving and congratulated him, tenderly thanked him for all of his support, and turned their conversation slowly to the subject of daily adoration. At first he refused, but after some quick banter the bishop at last conceded: the sisters were granted exposition of the Blessed Sacrament every Friday for two hours, from 3:30 to 5:30 PM. The sisters were grateful for at least one day of adoration per week, which was, as Mother Marie-Hermine wrote in a letter about her victory in the sacristy, "a consolation that helps me to forget all the troubles that abound in Shanxi and elsewhere."[55] This final remark was among the first mentions by any of the seven European sisters of "troubles" in Shanxi; rumors of social unrest on the northern plains had penetrated the Franciscan mission. Frightening reports were beginning to arrive at "our little world" (*notre monde*), Marie-Hermine's term for their Franciscan mission in Taiyuan, of increasing threats to human lives because of famine and civil discontent among the starving and displaced. These people were beginning to place the blame for China's natural calamities on the Christian God and the ill effects of foreign presence.

FINAL LETTERS

The inauguration of 1900 was inauspicious. On 24 January 1900, Sister Maria Amandina (fig. 4.3) wrote to her older sister, a member of Daughters of Charity back in her native Europe: "Since we have been here it has only rained twice, so the Chinese can neither sow nor plant; famine has begun to be felt very strongly."[56] The money that Bishop Fogolla had collected while in Europe had all been spent on the construction of the Franciscan hospital, and so the mission had scant resources left to help the afflicted. As early as September of 1899, rain clouds only timidly made their appearance in the skies of Shanxi. Mother Marie-Hermine de Jesus wrote that "the sun shines brighter than ever! A few drops of water, a simple dew fell in the night on Friday, then nothing! Harvest this year will be nearly zero, and if the drought continues the next year will be compromised. Seeds cannot survive without rain. In the end, all is permitted by divine providence!"[57] As the drought grew more severe in 1900, the sisters continued to write of their concerns, and their final letters are burdened with anxiety and alarm. Marie-Hermine's letters are perhaps the most tragic.

On 6 May 1900, the mother superior of the Taiyuan convent reported that "the drought continues and everywhere despairs. Nothing grows. The wind raises clouds of dust so thick that the sun is obscured and it is diffi- cult to breath." Her language is laden with melancholy: "Sad thing, life! To whatever side we turn our eyes or ears, we see and hear only suffering and groans."[58] And in a letter dated 25 June 1900, the last letter she is known to have written, Marie-Hermine de Jesus recounts the hopelessness she felt as the sisters realized the desperation of their circumstance.

> Drought continues to torment China—from all sides more alarm-
> ing news. Missionaries of the vicariate wrote to the bishop begging
> him to help relieve their Christians, many of whom have already died
> of starvation; . . . every day unfortunate women covered in rags come
> and kneel at our feet, begging us to give them clothes and food for
> themselves and their children. With a heavy heart and tears in my
> eyes, I can only distribute very little. Mission resources are so few,
> and mouths so many! Our orphanage currently has 260, and each day
> brings new recruits—Chinese women to whom have been entrusted
> the care of foster children for up to six, seven or eight years, can no
> longer keep them because of the low wages they receive. The price of
> millet, the ordinary food of the poor, has more than tripled. What shall
> we do if the five or six hundred children who are nursing right now are
> all returned?[59]

FIGURE 4.3. Sister Maria Amandina, FMM, member of the Franciscan Missionaries of Mary convent, Saint Paschal's, in Taiyuan during the Boxer Uprising. Sister Amandina wrote several personal letters while in Shanxi that aptly describe daily life at the Taiyuan mission. Source: Archivio Curia Generalizia Ordo Fratrum Minorum, Rome.

They faced inadequate resources to help even the Christians connected with the mission, and even worse was the daunting question of what could be done with five or six hundred suckling infants without wet nurses.

Added to these concerns was the fact that several of the Franciscan members of the Shanxi mission were dying of typhus. Two European friars at the Dongergou seminary, ages twenty-two and twenty-five, died eight days after contracting the illness; Chinese friars, too, lay on their deathbeds. The only respite the sisters received during this time derived from the circumstance that fewer Chinese dared to seek treatment at their hospital because, as Marie-Hermine describes, non-Christians in the area "utter terrible threats against us and want to kill anyone who is a friend of the Europeans. Patients do not dare to come. . . . Meanwhile," she continues, "the rebels cut the telegraphs, destroy railway tracks, and intercept roads"; the rapidly growing world of Boxers and Red Lantern women was encroaching on the small and isolated world of the Franciscan women.[60] All the Franciscans grew more aware that they, too, might soon face Boxer swords and Red Lantern curses, and in her letter to her sister, Amandina writes, "Before my letter reaches you we may already be expelled or massacred."[61]

Both Protestants and Catholics in Shanxi believed that the arrival of rain in early July of 1900 would cause the departure of the Boxers and their anti-Christian, antiforeign message. As he heard about attacks against his Protestant colleagues in Shanxi, the Reverend C. W. Price wrote in his journal on 1 July 1900: "Oh for copious showers"; perhaps then the violence would abate.[62] On 3 July, Price had cause for optimism: "*Six o'clock.*—A glorious shower of rain. It will do immense good, and many of the people will have work to do, so that their minds will be taken up with something else besides destroying foreigners. While it was raining we sang 'Praise God, from whom all blessings flow.'"[63] Ironically, while Price wrote these lines in his journal, and while the rains fell, the governor of Shanxi, Yuxian, was drafting his edict, which was posted only two days later, on 5 July 1900:[64]

The righteous [non-Christians/Boxers] people will burn and kill, and calamities will come down.

I exhort you who are Christians to reform before it is too late.

Correct your evil and return to what is proper and all shall be benevolent.

If you maintain this distinction [between Christian and non-Christian], you will become a respectable person.[65]

Officials accept this command to protect yourselves.

For those who do not know to change, they will have regrets for no
good reason.

To this end explicit directions are given, and all should revere [this
decree] with trepidation.[66]

Yuxian's decree was clear; apostatize or die. The showers that descended
from welcome rain clouds were followed by a deluge of bloodshed.[67]

Friars, Magistrates, and the Fists of Righteous Harmony

Take away your opium and your missionaries and all will be well.

—PRINCE GONG, ZONGLI YAMEN

MOTHER Mary of the Passion, founder of the Franciscan Missionaries of Mary, sorting through her mail in her Roman bureau, noticed the stamp on a letter: Maison Saint-Paschal Baylon, Taiyuan. Her heart raced as she opened the envelope, which contained a letter by Mother Marie-Hermine dated 20 May 1900. The sisters in Europe had only recently heard of the "holocaust of Taiyuan" (*l'holocauste de Taiyuanfu*); this note was, as one anonymous writer describes it, a "letter from beyond the grave" (*lettre d'outre-tombre*).[1] Something so dreadful had happened to Mother Marie-Hermine and her Franciscan companions that when Mother Mary of the Passion was first informed, she was in such distress that her consoeurs were needed to support her as she walked to notify the other sisters.

The seven Franciscan Missionaries of Mary had been arrested, paraded through the streets of Taiyuan, stripped to the waist, and beheaded one by one in Yuxian's yamen courtyard while they intoned the *Te Deum*, their chorus fading as they died, a story that would be similarly told in the tragic final act of the 1953 French opera *Dialogues des Carmélites*, by François

Poulenc (1899–1963). Mother Mary read the letters, which had seemingly miraculously arrived after an adventure of their own. Bishops, friars, sisters, tertiaries, and lay Catholics had been executed beside English Protestants connected to the China Inland Mission, and Franciscans throughout the world were swift to discuss and commemorate their fallen. The letters they wrote were quickly compiled along with other materials related to the Franciscan mission in Shanxi, and friars were assigned almost immediately to initiate the process of beatification and canonization for the most recent martyrs of the "Seraphic order," or the Franciscans.

TAIYUAN'S BOXER GOVERNOR

Shanxi had never been known as an especially antiforeign or anti-Christian province, and from the start foreign Catholic missionaries had lived, with few exceptions, peaceably with Shanxi's officials. The ability of the Jesuit Alphonse Vagnone to amalgamate Christianity with the hallowed tenets of Confucianism earned the Shanxi missionaries the respect, or at least the tacit toleration, of native literati, and the earliest official Chinese document to discuss the Catholic mission in Shanxi mentions Vagnone in complimentary terms. In an edict by the prefect of Jiangzhou published in 1635, the magistrate censured the emergence of "heterodox doctrines" that had spread throughout the county. After criticizing Buddhism and Daoism for "causing men's minds to become befuddled and disordered," he applauded the Jesuit missionary.[2]

The edict praises the teachings and behavior of Father Vagnone, and after critical remarks about other religions, the decree notes, "We are fortunate to have Mr. Gao [Vagnone], a Western Confucian, who cultivates virtue, serves Heaven, and loves others as himself. Because he imparts loyalty and filial piety as his principal teaching, he is given honor from our sagely Son of Heaven [emperor] and worthy ministers. Even the learned, officials, and all gentlemen revere him as their teacher and love him as a brother. The common people who follow his teachings are all transformed into virtuous persons."[3] There are no complaints in this early document regarding Western foreigners or their religious teachings; it is Vagnone's apparent Confucianism that is most favored, and he is admiringly called a "Western Confucian." Yuxian's appointment to Shanxi in 1900 marks a decided shift in public opinion; the province's new governor applied every means to encourage antiforeignism and anti-Christianity, largely employing the same methods that had been effective in Shandong, his previous post.

From the moment Yuxian (fig. 5.1) first arrived at Taiyuan the Franciscans had apprehensions regarding his ability, or desire, to protect them from the Boxers, of whom they had heard rumors. Once Yuxian was in Taiyuan, Bishop Francesco Fogolla requested an audience, during which he reportedly "asked about the Boxer incidents at Shandong."[4] There is little doubt that Fogolla's question intentionally provoked the governor, and Yuxian's "expression turned furious"; the governor ignored Fogolla as the bishop was unceremoniously dismissed from the room.

One of the most detailed accounts we have regarding Yuxian's first activities in Shanxi is found in the *Quanhuoji* (Record of Boxer calamities), an exhaustive collection of records and testimonies related to the Boxer violence of 1900. This source is valuable because it was compiled and written by the Shanghai Jesuit Li Di (also known as Li Wenyu, 1840–1911) immediately after the events took place. Li recounts that as soon as Yuxian had moved into his governor's yamen in Taiyuan, "he invited all the common people to come to his office and register any grievances they had [against foreigners]. They would not have to feel at all awkward, and one could even provide a written report to an official, because Yuxian felt that the people of Shanxi were fearful and had long been beguiled by foreigners."[5] His apparent strategy was to collect enough grievances—actual or contrived—to use as a pretext for action against the Franciscan and Protestant missions in Shanxi. Two months later, Yuxian confronted two exasperating problems; his yamen had not received a single complaint about foreigners or Christians, and Shanxi's famine was growing more severe. Li Di writes that Yuxian "stamped his feet [in frustration] and then went himself into his court to make an offering of incense [for rain]."[6]

Perhaps aware that Shanxi was not as antiforeign as the coastal provinces, such as Zhili and Shandong, where foreigners were more common, Yuxian brought with him a number of men who were "supporters of his faction," and he enacted policies that secured the assistance of his new provincial subordinates. As Li Di puts it, "There were some [officials] who were like him [Yuxian] and some who were not; those who agreed were promoted, while those who did not were discharged."[7] Not only did Yuxian surround himself with a coterie of likeminded officials, but he also supported the use of the Boxers, legalized them in his province, and even conferred on them a banner with his own name on it.[8] Yuxian offered his yamen courtyard as

FIGURE 5.1. Governor Yuxian, prefectural magistrate of Shanxi during the Boxer Uprising who ordered and participated in the executions of missionaries and native Christians during the summer months of 1900. Afterward, Yuxian was perhaps the most vilified person in Western publications. Source: Archivio Curia Generalizia Ordo Fratrum Minorum, Rome.

a martial arts training area for Boxers and allowed them to erect an altar to use for offerings and possession rites. After Bishop Francesco Fogolla had attempted, and failed, to gain a second audience with Governor Yuxian, the friar was met with large numbers of troops and Boxers as he departed from the prefectural yamen.[9]

Yuxian also commissioned the production of Boxer weapons. He ordered a local workshop to hurriedly produce two hundred swords for Shanxi's Fists of Righteous Harmony, which "he distributed to the Boxer units in his county."[10] To the Franciscans, the governor's observable support of the Boxers was mystifying in light of the support and protection previous magistrates had provided to the foreigners, but Yuxian was not acting alone. After the 21 June 1900 imperial declaration by the Empress Dowager Cixi (1835–1908) of hostilities against all Western powers, Yuxian was not only empowered but also directed to wage war against the missionaries. Soon after Cixi's declaration arrived, Yuxian began orchestrating strategies to comply, and he posted official edicts exhorting Shanxi's Christians to "reform" (zixin); his announcements exposed his own sensibilities regarding foreigners. The text of his edict of 5 July 1900, quoted earlier, is typical of his other postings. On 12 July 1900, three days after executing Catholic and Protestant missionaries at his yamen courtyard along with a number of native Christians, Governor Yuxian issued another decree:

Proclamation by Governor Yuxian
The religious teaching of the foreigners employs wicked arts to con-
found the people, and poisons and harms the land of China.
They utterly destroy proper relationships between humans and have
dared to plot rebellion, so I myself have seized them.
I have executed these criminals according to their list of names in order
to extinguish calamities at their root and also all Christians.
It is urgent to make a new beginning; Christians, renounce your religion
and the people will be pacified.
12 July 1900[11]

Yuxian's sense of urgency to act against missionaries stemmed, it seems, from a fear of Christian rebellion. Liu Dapeng writes, "The court ordered a military expedition, concerned that foreigners would gather their Christian forces in collaboration," noting that the court had decreed that "all of the foreigner barbarians from the hinterlands must be securely constrained."

The imperial rescript, Liu continues, declared that "anyone [Christian] who seizes the opportunity to rebel or collaborate in forming plots should be executed on the spot." Liu added that Yuxian was so gratified when he heard the court's edict to suppress foreigners and Christians that "he was moved to tears of appreciation." Liu himself believed these dubious reports and elaborated in tedious detail how the foreign missionaries of Shanxi had, by that time, "already entered into deliberations with the Christians regarding how to initiate a rebellion in the province and take its cities and towns by force, and have summoned the militaries of their respective countries to march into Shanxi."[12] There is no evidence, however, in Franciscan correspondences, diocesan records, or in any available Western archival materials that the friars and sisters in Shanxi had conceived any intention of rebellion.

Catholics and Protestants seldom interacted with each other in late-imperial China; instead they indulged most often in denominational battles over theological questions and missionary territories. Had they been better allied, the Franciscans of Shanxi might have been more usefully informed about Yuxian's anti-Christian policies in Shandong. As it was, the friars and sisters were already somewhat aware of his extreme antiforeignism and were anxious about his arrival, but it was unlikely that they knew of the Protestant charges that had been lodged against him while he governed Shandong. Two Protestant missionaries, Arthur H. Smith (1845–1932) and D. H. Porter, had drafted a memorandum, submitted on 22 January 1900, outlining what they knew of Yuxian's activities in Shandong. In their list of indictments, Smith and Porter mention a conflict between Boxers and Qing troops in which one hundred Boxers were killed; Yuxian obtained the demotion of the prefect in charge, dismissed the military official in command of the skirmish, and "encouraged the Boxers by releasing the prisoners taken in that action."[13] The memorandum also accused Yuxian of killing a missionary "with his own hand" and submitting a surreptitious memorial to the throne advocating "the employment of the I Ho Ch'uan [Yihequan, Boxers] as an agency for driving foreigners out of the province [Shandong]."[14] Yuxian's proclivities were known by Protestants several months before his appointment to Shanxi. The Franciscan mission, however, appears to have operated under overoptimistic pretenses; their overtures, which were repeatedly abnegated, continued to be conciliatory, even after their arrests in early July 1900.

Reflecting on the Christian presence in China during the end of the nineteenth century, Paul Cohen remarks, "Traders came to China in the nineteenth century to extract profits. Diplomats and soldiers came to extract

privileges and concessions. Alone among the foreigners, Christian missionaries came not to take but to give, not to further their own interests but, at
least ostensibly, to serve the interests of the Chinese. Why, then, of all those
who ventured into China in the last century, was it the missionaries who
inspired the greatest fear and hatred?"[15] This is a very good question, one
with several possible answers. In Shanxi, at least, there was little antagonism
between Christians and the native population until famines aggravated the
situation, and even then we do not see much evidence of serious conflict until
after the arrival of Yuxian in 1900.

A CHANGE OF COURSE

Catholic missionaries such as those at Shanxi's Franciscan residence at Taiyuan had been conditioned for self-sacrifice. Their mealtime routine, like that
of Jesuits and other orders, included the reading of select passages from the
Martyrologium that were intended to prepare future missionaries for "spiritual warfare." After the *Roman Martyrology* first appeared in 1583 it became
so popular that by its third printing Pope Gregory XIII (r. 1572–1585) made
it an obligatory element of the Liturgy of the Hours in the Latin Church. A
typical reading might include: "At Rome, the martyrdom of the saintly virgin
Bibiana, under the sacrilegious Emperor Julian. For the sake of our Lord she
was scourged with leaded whips until she expired. . . . In Sancian, an island
of China, the birthday of Saint Francis Xavier, priest of the Society of Jesus,
confessor and Apostle of the Indies. He was renowned for his conversion of
the heathen, his gifts and miracles, and he was filled with merits and good
works when he fell asleep in the Lord."[16] Passages such as this, replete with
harrowing accounts of torture and accolades for virtuous acts of holiness,
inspired large numbers of European Franciscans to travel to Asia and aroused
in them an expectation of, if not zeal for, martyrdom.

News reached Bishop Grassi at his residence in Taiyuan in June 1900
that a Shanxi church had been destroyed and a Christian killed in neighboring Yuci county, and since Fogolla was away at the seminary at Dongergou,
Grassi went alone to visit Yuxian. Li Di recounts, "He went to the magistrate's enclosure and solemnly entreated his protection, but Yuxian refused
even to reply."[17] Knowing that the Franciscan mission was vulnerable, Grassi
summoned Fogolla to return for an urgent meeting. The foreign missionaries and the native clergy met to decide upon a policy. Catholic missions
in other locations were convening at the same time to confront this press-

ing problem. The French Lazarist, Bishop Favier, had unambiguously supported armed resistance during the Boxer siege against his cathedral in Beijing's Xishiku area. The cathedral's thirty-four hundred refugees were to be protected by guns, cannon, or whatever other weapons were available. Resistance was fierce, and the bishop reported a "violent explosion" from an underground Boxer mine: "seven yards deep and forty in diameter." Five of the Italian marines enlisted to fight against attackers were lost in the explosion, and "more than eighty Christians, including fifty-one children in the cradle, have been buried forever under this ruin."[18] A Daughter of Charity sister who was inside the cathedral during the resistance, Sister Hélène de Jaurias (1824–1900), wrote that the battle reached such intensity that "a gunner was killed beside his canon; a woman cut in two by a shell; bombs and torches fell on every side."[19]

The decision to resist the Boxers included more than an earthly battle. In one of her letters, Sister de Jaurias disclosed another dimension of her understanding of the warfare raging around the Catholic cathedral in Beijing: "We often hear Satan speaking by the mouths of possessed people. A holy missionary, who has been here for twenty-two years, told me that he heard him declaring through a woman who was possessed that China was his chosen Empire, and that there was not a single spot of this country where he was not worshipped!"[20] If China was, as she puts it, the devil's "chosen empire," then the battle between the West (God's "chosen empire"?) and China during the summer months of 1900 represented for some the convergence of the heavenly and earthly battles. Beijing was not the only area of Catholic resistance against Qing and Boxer forces; the small Catholic village of Zhujiahe, connected to the Jesuit Zhili mission, also decided to prepare itself for an armed conflict with Boxers. Including the fortress built at Zhujiahe, the Jesuit mission in Zhili prepared six Christian defensive fortresses, and all but Zhujiahe successfully safeguarded themselves against attacks.[21]

Pierre-Xavier Mertens, SJ, who was assigned the task of collecting Chinese testimonies and materials on the Zhujiahe incident, writes, "In the month of May the Christians began to make preparations for their defense. Ramparts were built around larger Christian villages, which were provisioned with grains, arms, and gunpowder."[22] Two foreign Jesuits helped coordinate Zhujiahe's resistance as Boxers attacked the village. But once the Boxers were joined by the much larger and better-armed Qing militia, under the command of Li Bingheng (1830–1900), they mounted a collaborative attack and the village quickly fell. In southern Shanxi, Dutch Franciscans assembled

FIGURE 5.2. Chinese Catholic virgins (referred to as "God's little daughters," *xiaoshennü*) from the Franciscan mission in Taiyuan who survived the violence of the Boxer Uprising. Father Giovanni Ricci and his confreres interviewed several of these women after the Boxer incidents, and their testimonies were among those used to produce the Vatican's copious records of the Shanxi Christian martyrs. Source: Archivio Curia Generalizia Ordo Fratrum Minorum, Rome.

centers of resistance, but most of Shanxi's Catholic mission, which was under the auspices of the Italian Vicariate of Taiyuan, chose another course.[23]

After Francesco Fogolla had returned from Dongergou, Chinese and foreign friars assembled at the Taiyuan cathedral in an air of exigent anxiety. One priest advised "assembling several tens of sentinels who would patrol with swords and staffs," and another advocated "purchasing guns to resist their enemies." Bishop Fogolla's response was determined: "Catholic churches are not military bases, and cannot contain swords and guns," to which he added that if God desired him to give his life it would be sweet indeed. Li Di informs us, "When everyone heard his words all discussion of resistance against the Boxers was abandoned."[24] Fogolla's terse reply set the tone for the response of the Franciscan mission of Shanxi to anti-Christian attacks: no resistance. The sisters, friars, virgins (fig. 5.2), and lay Catholics surrendered willingly to both Mandarins and Boxers, and as the church in the small village of Guchengying was attacked and burned, the Catholic community remained in their pews and perished in the flames.[25]

Bishop Fogolla had ruled out resistance, but he had not ruled out escape. Some Franciscans had decided to remain at the mission with the native Christians, who were certain to encounter persecution, and who would undoubtedly be induced to apostatize. Others, however, viewed escape as yet another possible course; otherwise, who would remain to recount what had happened? When the Vatican's advocate for the cause of sainthood, Giovanni Ricci, had begun the long process of gathering materials and testimonies, much of his information derived from survivors who had escaped the July massacres in Shanxi.[26] One such survivor, a Chinese priest identified as Father Antonio Fou, managed to visit the imprisoned Franciscans in Taiyuan immediately before their executions, and in a letter to Ricci recounting this final meeting, Fou recalled a dialogue he had had with Bishop Gregorio Grassi. "After lunch Bishop Grassi called me to the side and said, 'I don't know where Father Francesco is, and perhaps Father Barnabas has escaped for Shaanxi.'"[27] The "Father Barnabas" in this dialogue is Barnabas Nanetti da Cologna, the brother of Sister Maria Chiara. Nanetti da Cologna survived to publish an account of what transpired in Shanxi in 1900, and the details of his escape are particularly dramatic, especially since the normal routes of escape, by railroad, had all been destroyed by Boxers. In fact, the matter of railroads figured largely in the history of Sino-missionary conflicts during the Boxer incidents. The fate of the Italian Franciscans was largely connected to the fate of the railroads that circulated through China. As the tracks were cut, so was the Shanxi mission's connection to the outside world.

RAILROADS

The Shanxi mission had relied largely on the railroad to connect and communicate with other Catholic communities, and the political vacillations at court often related to this network of railways. When Western imperial powers began their "Great Game" to divide and exploit China's land and people, they brought railroads with them, which at first seemed advantageous even to the Chinese. When Ma Jianzhong (1845–1900), a famous member of the secretariat of Li Hongzhang (1823–1901) and a member of a prominent Catholic family, returned from his studies in France, Ma was convinced that China needed railroads to compete with the West. In one of his writings Ma informed readers that "trains travel as fast as lightning or a whirlwind.

They can transport huge amounts of material to distant places and cover thousands of *li* as if it were next door."[28] He argues, "There is no other way to establish the basis for wealth and strength than to build railways."[29] But China's railways benefited mainly the foreign powers that funded, installed, and managed them; the common people paid a high price for this "improvement" to China's "wealth and strength."

An American correspondent for the *New York Sun*, Wilbur Chamberlain, wrote from Shanghai in 1900:

> Everything in China has been done by hand. All the carrying has been so done, as well as all the manufacturing. Now, the foreigners come in and introduce railroads. Every pound of freight that these railroads carry was formerly carried by the Chinese coolies. One railroad takes the place of a thousand or ten thousand coolies, who have, like their ancestors for generations, been carrying freight for a living. These coolies are thrown out of employment. Every railroad is carrying passengers and every passenger carried had formerly to ride in hand-drawn contrivances or was carried by coolies. So the railroads drive out of business all the Chinese in the passenger or freight carrying business.[30]

Western "progress," which many Chinese nobles supported, in reality meant the loss of income for tens of thousands of Chinese, many of whom enrolled in the Fists of Righteous Harmony, who sabotaged the railroads and destroyed railway cars.

There was another, more religiously motivated reason for Boxer animosity toward the railroads that networked through China's northern landscape: traditional geomancy (feng shui). For millennia Chinese geomancers had been employed to survey the curvatures of the land, the ratio and interplay between water and earth, and the channels in the terrain through which vital energy, or qi, was believed to flow. Most often geomancers were consulted to discern the most auspicious area for cemeteries; but qi was believed to occupy all locations, and one of the common rumors disseminated by Boxers was that railroads, built and used principally by foreigners, had dissected important currents of qi, which was among the myriad reasons the gods had become angry and had inflicted drought on northern China. As a result, Boxers uprooted railroad tracks and nearby telegraph wires throughout northern China, especially between Tianjin and Beijing, beginning in June of 1900, for they were both foreign and inauspicious. The immediate effect was the complete isolation of Christian missions. Shanxi's Franciscan community had depended on the railroad to transport supplies and mail, and after its disruption the European friars and sisters grew anxious, especially as alarming reports proliferated, reports that could not be verified for lack of communication with other missions.

In one of Sister Marie-Hermine de Jesus's final letters, which she wrote only two days after the Feast of Pentecost, when twenty-six children received First Holy Communion, she expresses her mounting concerns over the sudden turn of events: "It has been so long—the post from Rome has not arrived. Why? Is this due to the scarcity of letters, or are there difficulties with correspondence? . . . This last assumption could be true because we were told that it takes three days from Tianjin to Taiyuan, and the rebels burn churches and cut the telegraphs and railroads recently built. We don't know what is true in these rumors."[31] Soon after this remark, Marie-Hermine notes, "We storm heaven to obtain the end of this drought. . . . The earth has not had water for ten months!"[32] On 25 June, Marie-Hermine again mentioned the railroads. "The rebels cut the telegraphs, destroy the railroad tracks, and intercept the roads," she writes, and "we are absolutely isolated from the rest of the world."[33] She no longer wrote as if these were rumors; she and everyone else understood that Boxers, and not trains, were coming to Shanxi, and observing developments from her convent window, the mother superior of Saint Paschal's remarked, "They promenade their hideous idols for rain that never comes."[34]

THE ARREST

On the afternoon of 5 July 1900, Yuxian dispatched the subprefect to the Franciscan residence, where he, "with the most beautiful manners," invited the bishops, priests, sisters, and others attached to the community to remove to a smaller facility where "they could be better looked after" by the governor.[35] The Franciscan residence, the subprefect argued, was too large to be easily protected from the growing numbers of Boxers beginning to riot in Taiyuan. In order to "avoid trouble on the streets and the hostility of the people," they were instructed to prepare for relocation at midnight, under the cover of darkness.[36] The Franciscans may have sensed the dubiousness of Yuxian's invitation, yet they nonetheless prepared in earnest for their removal, packing provisions of food, clothing, and even the liturgical vessels and vestments required for the celebration of Mass. Around midnight the promised entourage arrived, which consisted of transport wagons and twenty soldiers; and having passed through the dark streets, they finally arrived at "what was really their prison" at 2A M; they were lodged near the provincial yamen in an alley popularly referred to as "Pig-Head Alley" (Zhutouxiang).[37] In addition to the bishops, priests, seminarians, and sisters, thirteen orphans and several Chinese Catholic servants were confined for "protection." Their provisional dwelling was the former railway bureau, then transformed into a residence for visiting officials.

Before their departure from the Franciscan residence, the question of what to do with the orphans agonized the friars and sisters. Li Di notes that a representative arrived at the residence "with cash and a mandate from Yuxian regarding the 220 female orphans at the sisters' orphanage." The orphans were ordered to be transferred to the Bureau of Silk and Cotton, and the Franciscans were assured that "after two or three days they would be returned"; the bishops, Li writes, "had no choice," and as the girls were taken away, "the wail of their cries was heard."[38] What happened to some of the female orphans after the trial of the foreign missionaries is unclear, but of the orphans who remained with the Franciscans and were imprisoned at Pig-Head Alley, one, Maria Gu, survived to provide firsthand descriptions of their internment.

While the Europeans were not allowed to leave their "temporary residence," native Christians were given access to the Franciscan missionaries, and the priests were able to write brief notes that were taken out by Chinese carriers. In one note by Bishop Gregorio Grassi, he reorganized—somewhat optimistically—the provisional administrative positions of the diocesan clergy, making, for example, Father Barnabas his pro-vicar-general, granting him all leadership privileges excluding those reserved for the rank of a bishop.[39] In a postscript to this note, Grassi asked for a "Solemn Pontifical Mass for rain." There are no records noting that the Mass was ever offered—the priests to whom his letter was addressed were either inaccessible or already in flight out of Shanxi—but shortly after Grassi inscribed his signature, rain began to fall in such profusion that the Protestants in Taiyuan requested the postponement of their transfer to the residence at Pig-Head Alley.[40] Even though the hoped-for rain had at last arrived, there remained an intuitive sense of what Yuxian's intentions were; one message to the Christians outside notes, "Protestants held elsewhere were brought to the house today, the prison of the bishops, to the adjoining courtyard, and so they join us for the carnage."[41]

Among the curious lacunae in surviving sources regarding the Taiyuan incident, in both Catholic and Protestant documents, is a more complete record of the interactions between the Catholic and Protestant missionaries while they were interned together. In one short passage we are told of only a brief dialogue between the two groups that predictably turned to the question of denominational difference: "Monsignor Grassi discussed questions of religion several times with the Protestants, and concluded with, 'How nice it would be if, as we sit here today, we will later be in heaven together!'"[42] The housekeeper of the Franciscan residence, Joseph Leu, who was with them at that time, stated, "Our bishops encouraged the Protestants to die as Catholics."[43] The results of Bishop Gregorio Grassi's attempt at converting the Protestant missionaries are unrecorded, though their meeting could not have lasted long, for the next day they were collectively ushered to their "trial."

Based on several testimonies gathered by Barnabas Nanetti da Cologna and Giovanni Ricci, we can reconstruct a detailed picture of the final days spent in the small residence.[44] A survivor, identified as Father Basilio Van, provided one of the statements now recorded in the Franciscan and Vatican archives. Van noted in his deposition that Bishop Fogolla wrote a letter outlining his belief that whoever was responsible for the coming events was certainly "a Mandarin," and Bishop Grassi requested "a blanket and his robe" and warned the carrier to be careful when transporting their correspondence, as one Christian had already been killed after he was discovered carrying a letter in a Western language.[45] Letters were written in Latin to better obscure their contents from the authorities, but no matter what the letters actually contained, whether it was the reassignment of diocesan duties or a simple request for a blanket, they were interpreted as seditious. "Letters," Van recalled, were claimed, "to be secret correspondence with European soldiers, called to invade the province," and "at that time I observed that people exclaimed in an injudicious and malicious voice, 'The British are coming to the city!'"[46]

According to Franciscan sources, Yuxian had already received an "order from Beijing to suspend the execution of the Europeans because the situation had gone awry and the armies of the powers were about to arrive." It appears that Yuxian may have momentarily reconsidered his plans to seize the foreigners, but once he had been informed of the intercepted letter from Grassi to Father Barnabas Nanetti da Cologna, the governor used this discovery as the pretext to hasten an official trial, believing, as Giovanni Ricci speculates, "that he would be praised after the fact."[47] Whether Grassi's letter actually

was the pretext on which Yuxian hurried his plans, the fact rem
normative process of Qing jurisprudence was overlooked. Tl
interrogations, nor did Yuxian remain at his usual place upon his dais au₁...ᵤ
the legal process; extant sources suggest that he stood with the executioners,
who were stationed near the missionaries.[48]

After only a day the subprefect arrived, around noon on 9 July, to record
the names of the foreign missionaries and Chinese held in the temporary
residence. The record of what happened during those final hours in the compound varies according to source. According to Nat Brandt, "At about two
o'clock, Yü Hsien, dressed in official robes with all the signs of rank, appeared
at the *kong kuan* [accommodation] accompanied by a number of officers and
soldiers."[49] Franciscan sources offer a different version. According to Ricci's
account, Yuxian mounted his horse at around four o'clock in the afternoon
and "with a squad of soldiers proceeded towards the West Gate pretending to
inspect the walls and an arms factory," which he did for fear of an organized
and armed Christian resistance if he more obviously went directly to the former railway bureau. Yuxian and his military escort abruptly changed course
and hastened in the direction of the prison, where he ordered the seizure of
the inhabitants. Ricci writes that the Protestants resisted: "When the soldiers
took the Protestants they resisted the brutal assault against them, firing shots
from their revolver, and only after a bitter struggle between them were the
crying women tied with a rope. The [Franciscan] sisters in the adjoining
courtyard heard the unusual noises and rushed to warn Bishop Grassi, who,
sensing the last hour, summoned Bishop Fogolla, the sisters, the seminarians, and the servants to kneel and receive their final absolution."[50] After the
dramatic resistance of the Protestants, the soldiers became more agitated
and showered blows on the two bishops as they tied the Catholics together
to be marched to the yamen courtyard.[51]

One of the notable details of this arrest is that Yuxian, throughout the
incident, remained anxious in anticipation of militarized Christian resistance. In addition to making an attempt to mask his route to the prison residence, the governor called in advance for reinforcement cavalry and ground
troops from Datong and Pingyang.[52] Boxers and official soldiers were stationed along the route to the yamen and around the courtyard gate where
the Christians were assembled. In Liu Dapeng's version of the arrest, Yuxian
had become aware of foreign plans of rebellion, and, "hearing of this[,] he
urgently commanded the central army [*zhongjun*], leading them himself, to
detain the foreigners in the guesthouse at Pig-Head Alley, which he did on

the pretext that he was protecting them from being harmed by the Boxers. He was covering up the fact that he was arresting them for trial, as the foreigners [missionaries] were plotting rebellion."[53] There can be little doubt that foreign insurrection was a genuine fear in Shanxi, as Yuxian's precautionary maneuvers confirm. As the Franciscan friars and sisters faced Yuxian and his train of red-turbaned Boxers, prayers and supplications were undoubtedly being submitted to heaven. The "battle" on 9 July did not last long, however. Dapeng describes the final moments of Sino-missionary conflict in Taiyuan: "Yuxian donned his military regalia. . . . Everyone was arranged outside the West Gate of his yamen, and one after another was slain."[54]

WITNESSES OF THE "TAIYUAN INCIDENT"

News of the Taiyuan massacre spread quickly in northern China. The telegraph lines had been cut, but Christians fleeing from other incidents in several northern provinces exchanged reports of the violent events that by late July were widespread. In the private papers of a Protestant medical missionary, Doctor Charles F. Johnson (b. 1857), which are now preserved in the Special Collections at the University of Oregon, there is an appended passage, inserted between correspondence dated 11 and 14 September 1900, titled "Story of the Shansi Massacre." The description begins: "The following account was given by Rev. H. D. Porter, M.D. [Henry D. Porter], who received it from an English speaking Chinese teacher who had been employed as teacher in the boys' school in Fenchowfu, and who escaped from the massacre bringing the news to Tientsin."[55] Having arrived through several channels, over such a long distance, and in an atmosphere suffused with apprehension and feelings of vulnerability, it is natural that some of the particulars had become blurred by the time the account reached Tianjin.

The narrative in Doctor Johnson's papers includes several missionary massacres in Shanxi that describe the circumstances of the Protestant mission there; the account of the Taiyuan incident provides the basic outline of what happened, though not without a few mistaken details.

On July 7th the governor, Yü Hsien, sent for a complete list of the names of the foreigners. On the 9th he ordered them all to come to his yamen ostensibly that he might escort them safely to the coast. On entering the first gate of the yamen they were surrounded by a guard of soldiers. About 21 Boxers, then, with drawn swords, were allowed, or told, to enter the circle, and the foreigners were deliberately cut to pieces by these fiends. They were all beheaded and their heads, placed in baskets, were hung over the four city gates. About 40 native Christians were killed at the same time. The next day 10 Roman Catholic priests were killed in the same way. The bodies of the 33 foreigners killed were placed in wooden cases and buried in the baptistery, presumably Mr. Farthing's courtyard.[56]

Accounts such as this represent the first wave of reports to extend outside Shanxi, and as more information was gathered, a more accurate version of the incident was formed.

No direct witness of the Taiyuan incident is identified in the Johnson papers, but Barnabas Nanetti da Cologna and Giovanni Ricci were able to locate survivors who could clarify what had occurred at the yamen's west gate. In the melee of the procession to the yamen, articles of clothing were dropped; Maria Gu, an orphan who was with the friars and sisters throughout much of the incident, recounted the spectacle: "The prisoners filed out, first Bishops Grassi and Fogolla, then the Fathers, and secondly the Religious between two rows of soldiers. . . . The sisters were pulled by their veils, and a soldier lost one of the veils. . . . Even Bishop Grassi, between the rush and pressure of the soldiers lost a shoe. This was collected by an orphan, but the veil was forced to be given to a soldier."[57] Based on witness testimonies provided to Li Di, after Gregorio Grassi had given sacramental absolution and once the Protestants had all been tied together, "the troops entered, each holding a staff, and Bishop Fogolla was struck on the head," and after this first blow, "the two bishops were struck with such heavy blows that the skin of half their heads was peeled off, and blood flowed in streams."[58] The prisoners were transferred to the prefectural yamen, where Governor Yuxian awaited them, encompassed by Boxers, troops, runners, and minor officials. A meticulous account of what occurred next at the yamen's west entrance is found in Barnabas Nanetti da Cologna's journal entry, dated 11–12 July 1900, written shortly after the executions.

Nanetti da Cologna, who produced this account while planning his own escape from Shanxi, writes, "[I] provide here an account of the death of the two venerable prelates . . . as I myself heard from two Christian eyewitnesses," which, he hoped, "will correct the many inaccuracies that shall be later retold and printed, and falsely claimed as true."[59] Since Chinese gazetteers and palace documents have omitted, or later removed, details of the massacre, it will serve here to quote Nanetti da Cologna's journal entry and other sources at length, though these sources display an obvious preference for the missionary view.

> To prevent any evasion or escape, three or four thousand Boxers and soldiers were stationed outside the hall, and were shouting feverishly, "Death to the devils! Death to the Christians!" With a tumult they beat their swords against one or another of the victims, and I was told that an angry Boxer struck Bishop Fogolla while being escorted. The Viceroy sat in his Court of justice and inveighed against the Europeans, claiming that they perverted the [minds of the] people, prevented the worship of the gods and ancestors, and were invaders of the empire, encouraging their compatriots to occupy the lands of China by force. And then they were all sentenced to death.[60]

Giovanni Ricci adds, "The viceroy had received an order from Beijing to suspend the executions," because the "foreign powers were about to arrive" at the capital, though there is no evidence in Chinese sources that this suspension was actually decreed.[61] The question of whether or not Yuxian's order of execution was commanded, or even endorsed, by the court in Beijing is impossible to answer without more substantial evidence; but the manner in which the Catholic and Protestant Christians were tried and executed is well documented, and the episode remains among the most violent of the Boxer era.

Perhaps the most graphic, if histrionic, description of the executions is found in Li Di's *Record of Boxer Calamities*, which spares none of the grisly details:

> Yuxian was at his dais in the great hall when he asked the British pastor, "Where do you come from?" The minister replied, "I am from Great Britain [Da Yingguo]." When he heard the words "*Great* Britain" he could not restrain his fury, and bellowed like a tiger, saying, "Kill! Kill! Kill! What is this *Great* Britain?" Then he asked Bishop Fogolla, "How many years have you been harming the people of China?" "I've been in China for more than thirty years," replied Fogolla, "and I know of no harm done to people, but I do know of great help given to them." Yuxian responded: "We are going to kill you foreigners and burn your churches; we're not afraid of you." The bishop replied, "If you kill us

FIGURE 5.3. The west gate of Yuxian's prefectural yamen in Taiyuan, Shanxi. This photograph was taken in 1901, after the incident, to record the location of the trial and execution of Catholic and Protestant Christians. Source: Archivio Curia Generalizia Ordo Fratrum Minorum, Rome.

foreigners, others will come and kill you. . . ." Yuxian heard this and ordered their execution. . . . The Boxers and rank-and-file soldiers competed with each other to be the first to kill at random. Some victims received several tens of hacks from swords, and some lost their heads. . . . Their blood formed channels and countless corpses covered the courtyard.[62]

Ricci recounts that while the massacre took place, "the soldiers fired their rifles into the air to scare away the souls," and after all were dead "the bodies were all stripped of their garments to be distributed between the soldiers, and the corpses were obscenely mutilated; the scattered limbs were thrown into a pile," the sight of which caused a non-Christian observer to collapse to his knees.[63]

Father Elia Facchini, OFM (1839–1900), one of the friars who had been taken to the yamen the previous day for interrogation, apparently unaware of what all the noise meant outside his locked room, was brought to the yamen courtyard (fig. 5.3) to discover the macabre vision of his fellow Franciscans decapitated, stripped, and callously heaped on the ground. Li Di's narrative notes that Elia was struck more than ten times with the executioner's sword before his body failed. Yuxian ordered the heads of the foreign missionaries displayed at the city gate; "their hearts were removed and their bodies were tossed to an open space outside the south gate," where they were "ravaged by birds and dogs."[64] Once the horrible particulars of this massacre were transmitted to other members of the Franciscan order, they were embellished with examples of piety "on the spiritual battlefield," and subsequent hagiographies added a patina of saintliness to the "final hour" of these sons and daughters of Saint Francis.

In his biographical sketch of the Franciscan Missionaries of Mary who died in the Taiyuan incident, Georges Goyau (1869–1939) provides a carefully crafted narrative, intended, it seems, to underscore the requisite characteristics for later beatification and canonization. He writes,

> In a harsh voice Yu-Hsien ordered the yard to be cleared and the prisoners were dragged out to the tribunal, the people hurling insults at them as they passed down the streets. Yu-Hsien did not even pretend to hold a trial. He himself gave the order to kill and dealt the deathblow to the two bishops with his own hand. On their knees the nuns . . . sang the *Te Deum* as they knelt with heads bowed to the executioner. "They were tranquil," some pagan spectators said afterwards. "They lifted up their veils for the death blow," and added, "it is a shame! These European nuns were so good."[65]

The account accumulated even more details from the pen of Louis Nazaire Cardinal Bégin, who added that the sisters "knelt in prayer with eyes lifted to heaven, praying for the martyrs, for the conversion of their persecutors and for the perseverance of Christians," and at last they "embraced each other, intoned the *Te Deum*, and presented their heads to the executioners." The historian today struggles to disinter fact from speculation in such hagiographic prose, but all witnesses agreed that the seven women sang the *Te Deum* as they were beheaded.[66] Bégin's narrative is particularly inflated, noting for example that Facchini "received more that one hundred sword cuts and at each lifted his eyes to heaven saying, 'I go to heaven.'"[67]

A peculiar aspect of our sources on the Taiyuan incident is the narrative disparities that emerge when comparing witness accounts of Catholics and Protestants. Whereas Roman Catholic sources highlight the martyrs' piety, Protestant sources emphasize the last-minute sermonizing of Yuxian's victims. Jonathan Goforth's account of the incident includes a short sermon given to Yuxian delivered by a thirteen-year-old member of the Protestant mission. Just before the executions began, Goforth writes, the teenage girl lectured the governor in Confucian terms, suggesting that Yuxian did not fully apprehend the hallowed tenet of filial piety (*xiaoshun*): "Governor, you talk a lot about filial piety. It is your claim, is it not, that among the hundred virtues filial piety takes the highest place. But you have hundreds of young men in this province who are opium sots and gamblers. Can they exercise filial piety? Can they love their parents and obey their will? Our missionaries have come from foreign lands and have preached Jesus to them . . . [, who] has given them power to live rightly and to love and obey their parents."[68] None of the Catholic sources recall such an exchange between Yuxian and his prisoners, and, likewise, much of what Catholic sources recount is absent from Protestant narratives.

Drawing from his recollection of what he heard from witnesses, Barnabas Nanetti da Cologna notes what happened after the executions. "Having finished the massacre," he writes, "they began to pillage and destroy the [Franciscan] residence." Believing the sacramental wine in the sacristy to be "human blood and poison," they crushed all the wine bottles with swords, and the Franciscan gardens were all upturned in hopes of discovering "rich treasures" hidden there by the Europeans.[69] After the Europeans had been killed and their properties looted and destroyed, however, most of the province's Christian population remained alive as the deluge continued. Catholics in and out of Shanxi were confronted by difficult decisions: apostatize, resist, or surrender to martyrdom as the Christians had at Yuxian's yamen on 9 July. As Liu Dapeng remarks, tensions continued to grow: "The Christians grew more apprehensive and Yuxian was afraid that they would do something reckless out of desperation," so an even wider sweep of "investigations" was ordered and violence continued to reach further away from the provincial capital.[70]

VIOLENCE SPREADS

On 14 July 1900, Governor Yuxian posted another decree in Taiyuan: "All male Catholics who have refused to reject Christianity," he states, "must report to Beimen Street, Dongtoudao Alley," at a large open courtyard located near the cathedral and Franciscan residence. This edict presented the same choice as did his earlier rescript of 5 July: apostasy or execution. In an act of open defiance, more than a hundred Taiyuan Catholics arrived three hours before the appointed time and knelt in the enclosure. In anticipation of the arrival of the executioner they "wrapped their queues around their foreheads and stretched forth their heads to expose their necks." Qin Geping, who derived much of his information from the commemorative stele erected near the location of the incident, recounts, "The commander ordered their execution and thirty-nine people were beheaded as they were kneeling on the ground. Three people knelt beside large rocks so that during the beheadings the stones obstructed the sword, preventing it from passing fully through their necks; these three were seriously wounded, but were not killed. . . . The executioner suddenly stopped [from exhaustion] . . . and the remaining Catholics wept, calling to the executioner to kill them also, but he departed."[71] By and large, all of Shanxi's Catholics had approved of Fogolla's proposal to resist spiritually rather than physically. Thus the physical conflict between the Boxers and the Christians was mainly one-sided; Shanxi's Christians opted for martyrdom rather than open warfare, though as we see in this account, defiance, which promised a victory of its own stripe, had not been ruled out. One of the survivors of this incident, Li Shiheng, whose neck had been partially chopped, was one of the witnesses who later helped to draft the narrative inscribed on the memorial stele at Taiyuan.

The battle continued for three months in Shanxi, claiming more than four thousand Catholics, and in the Taiyuan diocese alone more than three thousand Chinese Catholics attached to the Franciscan mission were killed.[72] Many survived by, as Giovanni Ricci states, fleeing "into mountains," while others "hid themselves in underground cellars and caves."[73] According to Franciscan records, around one-fifth of the Catholic population apostatized or compromised in some way during the violence of 1900, which no doubt engendered tensions between themselves and other Christians after the uprising, when many former apostates sought reintegration into the church.[74] People like Li Shiheng, who had offered himself to martyrdom, were often unsympathetic to others who had yielded to Boxer and soldier demands to apostatize and had sought the official certificate of protection. "As a rule," Ricci notes, "the 'protected' Christians were required to burn at least a few grains of incense before the idols, after which a certificate was given them to be attached to the front door of their houses."[75] Christians who had apostatized could not easily hide this public notice of protection, and many who had received these certificates simply remained non-Christians after peace was restored in Shanxi rather than face the discomfort of reconciliation.

Those who did not abscond, or did not apostatize in order to receive official protection, remained in grave danger, and massacres extended far beyond the walls of Taiyuan. After the violence, numerous surrounding villages erected stelae to preserve the accounts of the Boxer incidents, including the four monuments at Guchengying and the stele at Yangjiabao.[76] The Guchengying monuments principally describe the names of the victims who died there on 13 August 1900; this group of martyrs refused to apostatize and thus was burned alive in the village church while praying.[77] The Yangjiabao stele provides a more extensive narrative of the deaths of seventy-nine Catholics who were killed in that village, beginning with the note that "evil officials and corrupt officials" largely instigated the violence based on "false and poisonous accusations, surrendering to all sorts of inventions."[78] Notably, despite the apparent support of local officials who endorsed anti-Christianism based on either fear or credulity in response to Boxer myths, official troops were less involved in village violence than Boxers were.

It appears that Boxer pressures to apostatize had solicited widespread gestures of Christian defiance similar to the behavior of the Taiyuan Catholics who insolently bared their necks to their executioner. In Yangjiabao, the Christian villagers prepared in advance of the Boxers' arrival by wearing "their best clothes" in anticipation for martyrdom.[79] The Boxers attacked many Catholics in their homes and set the village church aflame while a group of women sang inside. One Chinese woman, identified as Mary Van, was crushed between two millstones for refusing to apostatize.[80] Acts of gruesome violence at Yangjiabao stand out as particularly concentrated; when one sixty-five-year-old women refused to apostatize, for example, Boxers cut off her arms, imprisoned her, and left her in a small cell to die of blood loss.[81] The Franciscan order was eager to memorialize these events, and shortly after the signing of the Boxer Protocol on 7 September 1901, Chinese and Italian friars began actively to chart the human losses according to village: Yangjiabao lost seventy-nine and Guchengying lost 134 Catholics, for example, and on average each of Shanxi's villages lost more Christian lives than the twenty-six who were massacred in the more famous Taiyuan incident of 9 July. Unlike the Protestants, who recorded their martyred missionaries for posterity, the Catholics looked for more than a record of martyrdom connected to the Catholic Franciscan mission. They required the collection of specific information to introduce causes for sainthood, investigations that included only a small portion of those who had died. To facilitate this, accounts that extended beyond the explicable had to be collected. Miracles were needed, and miracles would, they believed, demonstrate the Catholic victory on the spiritual battlefield.

MARTYRDOM AND MIRACLES

Giovanni Ricci's investigations in Shanxi after the summer of violence in 1900 revealed that more than killing and dying had occurred. In his book, *Avec les Boxeurs Chinois*, Ricci recorded that, "by 20 June, strange new rumors were circulating among the people; a man dressed in white was seen at the top of a tower," and more to the point, the white apparition was said to have "dispersed the clouds to stop the rain and sustain the drought for three months, which has desolated the country."[82] Popular mythologies, or miracle accounts, such as this were common among Shanxi's non-Christians, but the Catholic mission, too, produced a rich narrative tapestry. Unlike non-Christian miracle accounts, which villainized Christian gods, Christian miracle accounts depicted the supernatural preeminence of their own spiritual army and underscored the functional efficacy of martyrs as "witnesses."

Testimonial accounts of Catholic miracles during the Boxer Uprising can be productively considered in the context of China's long tradition of preternatural phenomena. The first emperor of the Han dynasty (206 BCE–210 CE), Liu Bang (256–195 BCE), was described in China's official histories as being distinguished by the miracles that accompanied his person. The historian Ban Gu (32–92 CE), for example, recorded that Liu Bang, who "liked wine and women," often lost consciousness at wine-seller Wang's, and during his inebriated slumber "the old lady Wu and the old woman Wang frequently saw wonderful sights above him."[83] The wine seller was so intimidated by these miraculous formations above the sleeping Liu that she "broke up his accounts and forgave his debts."[84] Reports of these same miraculous apparitions so disturbed Qin Shihuangdi (259–210 BCE), the first emperor of the Qin (221–206 BCE), whose dynasty was to be replaced by the Han, that he, as historian Sima Qian (145–186 BCE) relates, "traveled east to suppress the threat of his rule."[85] In the traditional Chinese view, these miracles represented Liu Bang's receipt of heaven's support or "mandate," which is precisely why Qin Shihuangdi was so anxious to locate and eliminate this contender for the imperial prerogative.

As early as 1747, Chinese Catholic accounts began to attribute similar miraculous emanations to the executions of Christian martyrs. A miracle not unlike the apparitions connected to Liu Bang occurred while a group of Dominican friars were in prison awaiting their executions. A fellow prisoner named Ye Chuandao recorded the appearance: "One day while Bishop Sanz, Father Serrano, and Father Royo were reciting their prayers the prison roof opened and rays of light beamed through. A brilliant cloud slowly descended beside their beds, and then it rose up and transformed into a stream of light. I could see the sky, and it was astounding!" Even the prison guards reported seeing "a strange phenomenon [in the sky]."[86] Nearly a century later, the Lazarist missionary Jean-Gabriel Perboyre, CM (1802–1840), was strangled in Wuchang, during which the miracle of an "immense luminous cross," according to reports, appeared in the sky above his execution ground.[87] Among all the Catholic orders that produced materials on the Christian martyrdoms of 1900, I was unable to locate any that had recorded more miracles than the Franciscan investigators of Shanxi.

The most famous reported miracle in Shanxi is the one attached to the executions of Gregorio Grassi and his companions on 9 July. While the twenty-six Catholics were being martyred at the west gate of Yuxian's yamen, a group of two hundred were gathered in prayer at a nearby church. One Chinese Catholic named Jia Luosa reported several dramatic emanations: "On 9 July, at around 4:00 or 5:00 pm, we were reciting our prayers when we suddenly heard a magnificent sound of music that came out of the sky, such that has never before been heard. A pure white beam of light emerged from where the music was heard; it came from the southeast and drifted toward the northwest."[88] According to the testimony, they interpreted the miracle as an indication that the Franciscan missionaries and other Christians had just been martyred, which was, they claimed, confirmed the following day. In another account of the 9 July miracle at Taiyuan, villagers two hundred kilometers away reported to have witnessed "a beautiful globe with a reddish light of supreme beauty coming from its center, as large fireworks burst into smaller globes of light that disappeared high in the sky."[89] A final miracle attached to the Taiyuan incident involved Elia Facchini, who was the last to die on 9 July. An apostate soldier present at the execution, who had renounced Christianity twenty years previously, reported witnessing "two angels carrying his soul to heaven as the head of Father Elia fell to the ground." As can be expected of this hagiography, the soldier was said to be "so moved by the sight, he left the military to reconvert, and going into the mountain in search of priests hidden there, he sought readmittance into the Church."[90]

Another miracle is recorded as having occurred at Sanxian village, where Boxers had massacred sixty-five Christians and then burned their remains in the small church. "The Boxers witnessed a white dove in the middle of the flames," the account reads, "around which were fluttering large butter-flies with wings of gold; the apparition continued through the night." The account also states that the non-Christians who saw the miracle understood the butterflies to be "the souls of the dead rising to paradise."[91] Another vil-lage reported hearing "very sweet voices singing the *Te Deum* above the graves" of thirty-seven Catholic martyrs; and believing the sounds to be "a dream," several villagers went to the graveyard, "where the chant continued for about a quarter of an hour."[92] Collected testimonies include many more reports of similar miracles in Shanxi: four resplendent beings suspended above a group of martyrs after their death, appearances of recently killed family members, and so forth. Shanxi's Catholic culture of the extraordi-nary equaled the mythologies promulgated by the Boxers, and the wealth of miracles described during ecclesial investigations was more than ample to support the causes for sainthood, which resulted in the canonization of nearly thirty Shanxi martyrs of the Boxer Uprising in Rome on 1 October 2000. Massacres and miracles occurred in alternation in Shanxi until late August 1900, when the Eight Allied Armies and the resulting flight of the court from Beijing distracted magistrates and Boxers from their mission to expel foreigners and their menacing gods from China.[93] Beijing was in rubble by the end of the summer, and the Franciscans who remained in China were keen to survey their battered mission in Shanxi.

Farmers returning to their fields passed the ruins of churches and Chris-tian homes and the expanding graveyards of Boxer victims. The toll of the Sino-missionary conflict on the northern plains was extreme: 191 foreign missionaries were massacred, 6,060 native Chinese Christians were killed, 225 churches and mission structures were destroyed, and 20,000 Christian homes were razed.[94] The Boxers and Red Lanterns of Shanxi quickly disap-peared as foreign missionaries were rapidly replaced by foreign militaries, whose sense of vengeance was fueled by the proliferating accounts of Boxer atrocities; high on the foreigners' list of those marked for retribution was Shanxi's governor, Yuxian. Friars, gods, and immortals were largely forgotten as kaisers, presidents, and emperors stepped onto the field of conflict; atrocity was soon repaid with atrocity.

CHAPTER 6

Revenge and Reconstruction

I commend the sincere virtues of the foreign missionaries and deeply grieve the cruelties they encountered.

—CEN CHUNXUAN, GOVERNOR OF SHANXI

THE Empress Dowager Cixi and her cortege fled Beijing in mid-August 1900 as the Eight Allied Armies entered the city. Pausing to rest in Taiyuan on her way west to flee foreign retribution, she was regaled by Governor Yuxian, who had just massacred the Franciscans at his yamen gate. Her visit to Taiyuan was vividly, or perhaps inventively, described in 1910 by J. O. P. Bland and E. Backhouse in their extensive biography *China under the Empress Dowager*. According to Bland and Backhouse, Cixi arrived at Taiyuan on 10 September 1900 and took up residence at Yuxian's yamen, where only six weeks earlier the courtyard had been the scene of gruesome beheadings. Cixi's meeting with Yuxian is staged in the courtyard of execution. She tells him:

"Because the foreign devils are loudly calling for vengeance upon you, I may have to dismiss you from office, as I had to do with Li Pingheng." . . . A few days later she issued the first of the Expiatory Decrees by which Yü Hsien [Yuxian] and the other Boxer leaders were dismissed from office, but not before she had visited the courtyard where the hapless missionaries had met their fate, and cross-examined Yü Hsien on every detail of the butchery. And it is recorded that, while she listened eagerly to this tale of unspeakable cowardice and cruelty, the Heir Apparent was swaggering noisily up and down the courtyard, brandishing the huge sword given him by Yü Hsien, with which his devil's work had been done. No better example could be cited of this woman's primitive instincts and elemental passion for vindictiveness.[1]

An important theme emerges from the narrative. Only six weeks after Yuxian ordered, and participated in, the massacre in his courtyard, China was swiftly entering an era of court reversal and foreign vengeance, and this time the choice of violent reprisal belonged to foreign powers rather than superstitious Boxers.

SHANXI'S TURN AGAINST THE BOXER ARMY

As Cixi's entourage fled from foreign armies entering China's capital, she just as quickly turned her courtesies toward the foreigners from whom she was fleeing. Her allies, the Boxers, and her enemies, the foreigners, were to exchange seats in China's court. Her route to Taiyuan passed through Datong, one of Shanxi's most famous Buddhist landmarks, and somewhere along the way her attitude changed and she issued an official rescript: all Boxers were to be executed.[2] This order took immediate effect in Shanxi. Yuxian had already flown, and to his last day in Shanxi he acclaimed the Boxers and encouraged them to continue battle. As Cixi's volte-face order was received at the Taiyuan yamen by the temporary governor, provincial troops had just been sent to support a group of Boxers who had been unable to defeat the Franciscan church in Liangquandao (now called Liuhe) village, which had, unlike other Catholic villages under Franciscan influence, taken up arms in resistance.

The Chinese Catholics of Liangquandao had amassed an arsenal of guns and cannons and inflicted a great number of casualties on the attacking Fists of Righteous Harmony. Taiyuan's prefect had dispatched his supporting troops under the command of Xu Handu to aid in the siege of the village church, but once he received Cixi's new order he directed an urgent decree to Xu, commanding him to disperse his troops and abandon his mission to help destroy the village church.[3] As they witnessed the supporting troops retreat, the Boxers likewise broke ranks, though a small contingent remained to continue their attack with redoubled determination. With insufficient numbers the Boxers were unable to overcome the church's defenses. Another provincial decree was posted, "forbidding Boxers from carrying weapons and prohibiting them from being seen on public streets."[4] The remaining Boxers at Liangquandao were to be executed, and Taiyuan's newly appointed magistrate dispatched his troops to seize and behead all of Shanxi's more than one hundred local Boxer leaders.[5]

The suppression of Shanxi's Boxers was swift and violent. After one leader was seized, his entire body was so severely beaten that he appeared to have "as many wounds as there are scales on a fish." Huang Zheng recounts that the Boxer chief remained placid while being punished, exclaiming, "Slaughtering Christians is the will of heaven!"[6] The ultimate about-face occurred in early 1901, however, when the court issued an edict ordering the arrest of Shanxi's governor, Yuxian, who had fled to Lanzhou. On 22 February 1901, the formerly valorized official and supporter of the Boxer movement was publically beheaded.[7] Although local Chinese views of the Franciscan mission, and of Christians in general, were radically revised and restated, there remained a popular cult of support for Yuxian, and the court ordered the prompt demolition of a temple that had been constructed in his honor.[8] The heads of Boxer leaders were suspended outside Taiyuan's city gate, replacing those of the foreign missionaries.[9] While the court's suppression of the Boxers was largely motivated by self-preservation as foreign armies descended like storm clouds on China, foreign governments considered it their manifest duty to exact vengeance on China.

REVENGE

Bishop Francesco Fogolla's earlier appeal to his fellow Franciscans in Shanxi to render no resistance to Boxer aggression was far removed from the diplomatic response of the Western governments; on 27 July 1900, Kaiser Wilhelm II (1859–1941) of Germany set the tone for German retribution. Speaking to his gathered troops at Bremerhaven, he instructed his men to avenge the "outrageous injustice" that had been done to the people of Germany: "If you encounter your enemy conquer him. Give no quarter. Take no prisoners. . . . Just as the Huns made a name for themselves under King Attila a thousand years ago, a name that still makes them appear colossal in historical legend, may the name of Germany be confirmed by you in such a way that the Chinese will never again dare to look askance at a German!"[10] Once the Eight

Allied Armies entered the capital on 14 August 1900, an era of foreign looting and killing began on China's northern landscape.

The commander of the British expedition, Sir Alfred Gaselee (1844–1918), was eager to commence a punitive campaign across northwest China, but he and the other commanding officers paused long enough in Beijing to pillage the city's treasures and launch a reprisal against Boxers and officials who had been unable to escape foreign retaliation. Gaselee described the circumstances of the city as the allied forces combed through post-Boxer Beijing; even he recognized the excess of foreign behavior in the capital: "The condition in and about the city and along the line of communication was bad. Looting of the city, unconditional foraging in surrounding country, and seizure by soldiers of everything a Chinaman might have, as vegetables, eggs, chickens, sheep, cattle, etc. . . . [There was also] indiscriminate and generally unprovoked shooting of Chinese."[11] He also noted that for each person actually known to have been a Boxer, "fifty harmless coolies or laborers[,] . . . including not a few women and children, have been slain."[12] Few among the Eight Allied Armies were more fierce than the German soldiers, who had received their directives from the impassioned and highly nationalistic speech by Kaiser Wilhelm II.

The Russians, too, treated the Chinese badly. Amar Singh, a Rajput nobleman and officer in the Indian army, recorded much of what he witnessed of Russian actions in China after their march into Beijing. Singh wrote that they beat Chinese whenever "they could not make them understand" what they were trying to convey; and after a Russian report of an alleged Boxer attack, the Russians killed eight people for being Boxers, six of whom were innocent women.[13] He expressed his suspicion that the Russian report was contrived: "Probably they had been robbed, raped, and then slain to cover up the whole thing."[14] Foreign atrocities were no less vicious than those committed by the Boxers. While Beijing was being plundered, the man who had been assigned to lead the Eight Allied Armies, the German *generalfeldmarschall* Alfred von Waldersee (1832–1904), was still making his way to the capital from Shanghai. He had missed the initial arrival of foreign forces in the capital, but once he reached Beijing he was not to be left out of the frenzy for collective vengeance. Surveying the situation in the capital city, von Waldersee remarked, "One can only win the respect of the Asian through force and its ruthless application," and the Chinese, he asserted, deserved no mercy.[15]

Foreign revenge against Boxer violence was centered on retribution for the deaths of foreigners, and the foreign forces paid little attention to how many Chinese Christians had died during the summer months of 1900; Chinese victims had far outnumbered foreign missionaries. China must, as the allied commanders asserted, pay for foreign blood, and on 31 December 1900 the Manchu soldier En Hai was led to the very spot where the German diplomat Baron Clemens von Ketteler (1853–1900) had been slain on 20 June 1900. En was charged with von Ketteler's killing and was decapitated for killing a foreign dignitary. As David Silbey puts it, "He might have lain there as a symbol of China itself, its guilt perpetually assumed and its punishment always assured."[16]

RECLAIMING, RECONFIGURING, AND RECONSTRUCTING SHANXI

Traditionally used for cooking and household-warming braziers, coal has long been a valuable commodity in China. After the advent of China's coal-operated railway network, the right to Shanxi's rich deposits became contested by local and foreign companies. The Franciscan missionaries were involuntarily implicated in these clashes before and after the Boxer Uprising. Relying on their connections with the Italian friars, an Italian company had made business overtures in 1897 to a Shanxi official named Liu E, who oversaw an area abundant in coal. Liu seized the opportunity to enrich himself by collaborating with the foreign company; he borrowed a million taels of silver from the Italian company to begin a large-scale mining operation in Shanxi, and he applied to the Commercial Affairs Bureau to establish the Jinfeng Company.[17] With his Italian associates, Liu E orchestrated coal-mining operations in Shanxi's Yu county, Pingding and Ze prefectures, and at Luanfu.[18]

This arrangement had exacerbated Sino-foreign relations in Shanxi, especially since Liu E and his foreign partners had extended their mining ventures to areas outside of Liu's jurisdiction. In order to secure his claim on mining operations in Shanxi, Liu had solicited the support of Shanxi's provincial governor, who signed two agreements with the Italian company; and making matters worse, the Italians had been given management rights over all mining operations.[19] When the Zongli Yamen became aware of this arrangement, which violated legal norms for mining rights, Liu E was removed from his position and the agreements with the foreign company were nullified. In the end, however, the court had profited by selling the mineral rights back to the Italian company on 21 May 1898 and depositing the handsome foreign imbursement into the imperial treasury.[20] Foreign-operated mining in Shanxi was discontinued during the Boxer era, but as expected, once settlements were agreed upon after the Boxer indemnity was paid, foreign companies again sent representatives to several areas in Shanxi to "seal off coal pits for foreign mining," thus restoring the former "foreign monopoly" of Shanxi's resources.[21] Throughout these machinations, both native and foreign, the Franciscan mission attempted to remain as disconnected as possible, though the mission could not, despite its best efforts, completely detach itself from the stigma of foreign imperialism by association. Foreign exploitation of Shanxi's natural resources in the post-Boxer era continued briskly, and the missionary incidents in Shanxi during the Boxer violence were used as a pretext to affirm the "fairness" of foreign retribution.[22]

The Shanxi friars directed their attention to the difficult task of rebuilding their battered mission, even as they struggled to distance themselves from the stigma of being "Italian imperialists" who took advantage of national weakness to seize China's valuable resources. Following the wholesale destruction of their churches, orphanages, hospitals, and schools in 1900, Shanxi's Catholics employed three principal tactics of recovery: remembrance, reconstruction, and vigorous proselytization. An organized program of remembrance involved the creation of commemorative stelae at key Catholic sites, as well as publication campaigns to produce tracts and booklets—both communicated stirring accounts of Christian resistance and martyrdom. During the republican era (1912–1949) and reform era (1980s–present), Shanxi's Catholics lobbied aggressively for state and foreign funds to rebuild destroyed churches; many of these new structures were more impressive, perhaps even more imposing, than their predecessors. Finally, proselytization, including public seminars, services, and signage, attracted exceptionally large numbers of Catholic converts to Shanxi's new churches.

"LA MISSION CIVILISATRICE"
AND THE SHANXI ALTERNATIVE

In addition to facing the coal disputes precipitated by their countrymen, the Italian friars and sisters who replaced their martyred confreres and consoeurs were confronted with the question of reconstruction of both mission resources and reputation. And more to the point, the Franciscans could not but have noticed the nationalistic behaviors of other Catholic missions in late-imperial China. The French mission, for example, operated under an assumed need to civilize "backward" China, *la mission civilisatrice*. This

French imperialist approach was viewed as a civilizing enterprise that presumed the West's cultural and ethnic superiority.[23] The returning missionaries in northern China were often inculcated with the colonial views of their national protectorates, considering the ruled unfit to rule themselves.[24]

Imperial France sought to "civilize" China under a semicolonial state, and when Pope Pius XI (r. 1922–1939) wished to consecrate six Chinese priests in 1926, many feared that the consecrating of native clergy would create a schism.[25] This attitude was so common among Catholic missionaries in post-Boxer China that the Italian apostolic delegate to China, Archbishop Celso Costantini (1876–1958), often complained about Western clergy in his personal memoirs, assigning to the mission such phrases as "religious colony" and "anti-Chinese spirit."[26] Hence the European missionary enterprise, especially under the French Jesuit presence, embodied the Roman and Catholic sense of imperial "Romanitas."[27] In the wake of the Boxer Uprising, and within the nearly fanatical milieu of foreign revenge, *la mission civilisatrice* was often appropriated into the worldview of the post-Boxer Catholic mission. While many missionaries appreciated or benefited from colonial protection, most were not participants in aggressive conflict.[28] The question of empowering a native clergy, however, was in many ways the dividing line between those who endorsed the *la mission civilisatrice* ideal and those who viewed imperialism less favorably.

The Franciscan mission of Shanxi had already demonstrated its preference for developing a native clergy and was decidedly less nationalistic than the French Jesuits. Among the Chinese priests who were ordained as bishops in Rome in 1926 was a Franciscan friar from Shanxi, Aloysius Chen Guodi, OFM (1875–1930) (fig. 6.1). Chen joined the Franciscan order at Dongergou on 4 October 1896 and was ordained a priest three years after the Boxer Uprising, in 1903.[29] The Franciscan willingness in Shanxi to endorse the growth of a native hierarchy is well illustrated in Chen's rise to the episcopate: he was secretary for two bishops, a member of the Provincial Board of Education in Shanxi, and a professor of Latin and apologetics in the Franciscan seminary at Taiyuan.[30] Shanxi's Italian mission proudly advertised this new Chinese bishop in 1926 and celebrated the consecration of another Chinese Franciscan, Odoric Cheng Hede, OFM (1873–1928), by the pope in the same year.

The last Italian bishop of Taiyuan, Domenico Luca Capozi, however, became the center of rancorous tensions between the Chinese and foreign clergy. Accounts note Capozi's inability to get along with the local Chinese

FIGURE 6.1. The six Chinese bishops who were ordained as bishops at the Vatican in 1926 by Pope Pius XI. Bishop Aloysius Chen Guodi, OFM *(second from left)*, was a Chinese Franciscan from Shanxi province, and he returned to Shanxi after his consecration. Source: Archivio Curia Generalizia Ordo Fratrum Minorum, Rome.

in Shanxi, including one incident in which Capozi clashed with a Chinese seminarian over his Latin pronunciation, resulting in the young man's permanent departure from the seminary.[31] It appears that the Chinese priests in Taiyuan were so aggravated by Capozi's perceived superciliousness that, while the bishop was at Rome to attend the beatification ceremony of the Taiyuan martyrs, the Chinese clergy "of the Taiyuan Diocese sent the Vatican an adamant request to remove and replace Bishop Capozi," and requested "the appointment of a Chinese bishop." Until Capozi's appointment in Shanxi we have little evidence of cultural conflicts of this magnitude between foreign and indigenous clergy there, and none of Taiyuan's previous bishops seem to have so dramatically provoked Chinese sensitivities to European imperialism. The Vatican did not approve the Chinese clergy's request to have Capozi removed, but "the open disapproval by the Chinese priests struck a heavy blow" against the monopoly of power held by the foreign hierarchy in China.[32]

Tensions between Capozi and the Chinese priests in Shanxi were an exception to the more common culture of comparative equality promoted at the Franciscan mission, and the Italian friars generally agreed with Costantini's complaints that the Catholic mission in post-Boxer China was overcolonialist. This is not to say, however, that Sino-Western tensions were absent between Shanxi's Catholic clergy; racial and cultural clashes did emerge from time to time. By 1926, when Pope Pius XI ordained the six Chinese bishops at Saint Peter's in Rome, the pontiff was reportedly so moved during the ceremony that "his voice failed him and he was unable for a time to proceed."[33] So committed was the pope to promoting a native hierarchy in China that the Vatican's official newspaper, the *Osservatore Romano*, announced, "A new period has been inaugurated in the grand history of the China Mission."[34] Contradicting the truculent rhetoric of Ecclesia Militans and the nationalistic and condescending tenor of *la mission civilisatrice* that permeated Catholic missions around the era of the Boxers, the Jesuit Father Pascal M. D'Elia, SJ, wrote after the pope's consecration of the Chinese bishops: "My missionaries [the Jesuits] from the time of Father Ricci, S.J., nay from the XIII century [during the Franciscan mission], until the present moment, did nothing but prepare the establishment of the Church in China."[35] D'Elia does not note that those missionaries of the "XIII century" were Franciscans, not Jesuits (the Jesuits did not exist until the sixteenth century), nor does he mention that the Chinese clergy imagined by Costantini, the Italian friars, and the pope was a clergy that was culturally, linguistically, and aesthetically Chinese. The Chinese clergy of the French Jesuits was educated in the French language, studied in a Western manner, and was overseen principally by Western administrators. At Shanghai's Jesuit-run Aurora University, a Chinese priest never "held a major university post."[36]

The Shanxi alternative to the post-Boxer imperialist impulse was to build churches and train more Chinese priests; the Franciscans understood that were it not for the high number of native priests in the Taiyuan vicariate, Chinese Catholics would have had no pastors and no recourse to the sacraments during the first few years following the Boxer Uprising. After the initial wave of Western militaries swept through northern China on their so-called punitive expeditions, the Shanxi Franciscans began their own campaign, which involved both the reconstruction of churches—monuments of the Church Militant—and the erection of commemorative stelae, monuments of the Church Triumphant. As Giovanni Ricci wrote in his concluding remarks about the persecutions of the Boxer Uprising in Shanxi: "The children of St.

Francis have a distinct role to play in the gigantic struggle with the enemies of Christ and His Church in that unhappy land."[37] When Bishop Agapito Fiorentini, the first bishop in Taiyuan after Grassi, arrived in Taiyuan in the wake of the Boxer Uprising, all the Catholic buildings had been devastated and the friars had moved into Shanxi's most esteemed school, the Lingde Academy. It was an unsuitable arrangement, and the friars were in desperate need of new buildings of their own, and of altars and orphanages where their spiritual and charitable efforts could continue. In terms of brick and mortar, the Franciscan mission was forced to rebuild from the ground up.

REPARATION AND RECONSTRUCTION

When the Italian friars began negotiations with the local authorities after the Boxer Uprising, they first addressed two matters: the liberation of the female orphans who had been seized by Yuxian and the restoration of the province's Catholic properties. Yuxian had distributed the girls among his associates and sold them to merchants as servants; Giovanni Ricci figures the total number of orphans displaced by the governor to be around a thousand.[38] Fortunately, Yuxian "had obtained receipts from those to whom he had handed them over," and all but a few were traced and returned to the care of the Catholic mission. These orphans were photographed and featured in Franciscan publications in Italy (fig. 6.2).[39] After this matter had been settled, negotiations turned to financial reparations for the destroyed properties under the care of the Franciscan friars. The Protestant missionaries in Shanxi, on the other hand, did not seek recompense for their lost properties, and subsequent Protestant accounts underscored this point.

One account of the negotiations protested that "the satisfaction of the Catholics had been a heavy expense for Shansi," and it reminded readers that, "whereas the number of Catholics massacred had not exceeded 20 in the entire province, of Protestants, English, American, and Swedish, 156 had been slain."[40] In truth, thousands more Catholics died in Shanxi than Protestants. In the view of the friars, since the damage inflicted on Christian persons and properties during the Boxer Uprising was either committed, funded, or supported by a Qing official, it was only fair that the restoration of the mission's charitable and religious properties be at least partially supported by the central court. Ebenezer Edwards, a Protestant medical missionary who visited Shanxi soon after the Boxer incidents, estimated that around 380 Protestants had been killed, compared to around 8,000 Roman Catholic Christians.[41] In

FIGURE 6.2. Chinese orphan children from the Franciscan mission who were seized by Yuxian during the Boxer Uprising and later returned to the care of the Franciscan Missionaries of Mary in Taiyuan. A small number of the orphan girls could not be located. Source: Archivio Curia Generalizia Ordo Fratrum Minorum, Rome.

addition to the churches and other mission structures destroyed by Qing troops and Boxers, several thousand Chinese Catholics had been left without homes, since these had been looted and destroyed during the disturbances. After a semblance of order had been restored to Shanxi in 1901, many of these Catholics, desperate for property or resources in order to restore their lives and care for their families, began to raid the homes of non-Christians, which caused renewed tensions.[42] In the end, the Italian minister to China and Li Hongzhang, the emperor's principal negotiator, agreed that Shanxi's Catholic mission should receive one million taels of silver to begin reconstruction and to subsidize the cost of erecting commemorative monuments.[43] Ricci stated that these funds "ended the cry of hunger, as the subsidies were distributed to the poorest widows and orphans."[44]

The indemnity funds provided to the Franciscan mission were sufficient only to seed the first stages of reconstruction; the remaining funds would be provided by the order and by donations from Europe. Bishop Agapito Fiorentini was welcomed by a motley remnant of clergy at the temporary Franciscan residence in the Lingde Academy.[45] Arthur Sowerby (d. 1934), a British Protestant missionary living in Taiyuan after the Boxer Uprising, wrote in February 1902 of the local discontent caused by the Roman Catholic seizure of the academy:

> The priests belonging to the Italian mission are young men, with but a few years' experience, and have not proved capable of managing such delicate negotiations. The chief difficulty arises from the forcible possession and retention of the large college known as the Ling Teh T'ang. H. E. Shên Taot'ai recently obtained an expression of opinion from a large number of literary graduates on the missionary question. They wholly acquit the Protestant missionaries of any blameworthiness, but they unanimously express great indignation with the Catholics for their possession of the Ling Teh T'ang.[46]

Edwards recalled that when the Catholics occupied the Lingde Academy, "an image of the Virgin Mary was brought from one of their out-stations to be placed in a building of the newly occupied college"; he also described the elaborate procession with which the Catholics took possession of the academy.[47] Denominational rivalries are easily detected in these accounts of the Franciscan occupation of Lingde; Catholic sources, however, complain of the facility's unsuitability and their eagerness to relocate. Fiorentini's first activity after arriving at Taiyuan on 2 July 1902 was to seek funds for the construction of new buildings and the friars' removal from the academy.

Giovanni Ricci's history of the of Taiyuan vicariate noted that after Fiorentini arrived he "immediately ordered the rebuilding of the cathedral and other churches that the Boxers had burned, and within the space of seven years . . . all that had been burned by the Boxers was restored."[48] Fiorentini's attention to the mission's architectural presence, along with his efforts to expand the number of Catholics in central Shanxi, resulted in such an increase that the diocesan register of faithful surpassed that of the pre-Boxer era.[49] A large swath of uncultivated and unoccupied land near Taiyuan's north gate was purchased for the new Franciscan cathedral (fig. 6.3), and construction progressed so quickly that by 1905 the massive church was complete. On 31 December 1905 Bishop Agapito Fiorentini presided over the rite of consecration.[50] The new mother church of Shanxi was named after the Immaculate

FIGURE 6.3. The reconstructed Cathedral of the Immaculate Conception after the original church's destruction by Boxers in 1900. The Franciscan cathedral was completed in 1905 and was built along with a large cluster of Franciscan buildings in the northern part of the city. Source: Archivio Curia Generalizia Ordo Fratrum Minorum, Rome.

Conception of the Blessed Virgin Mary, and an inscription above the main entrance dedicated the cathedral to Saints Joseph and Francis of Assisi.[51] The building was a towering new Catholic edifice in Shanxi's capital, and its completion marked the beginning of an enduring campaign to restore, and magnify, the imposing spiritual presence of the Franciscan mission.

In conjunction with the cathedral's construction, Fiorentini commissioned a new residence for himself and the clergy of the vicariate; after the two-story dormitory was complete, the Lingde Academy was vacated and restored to the local authorities. New orphanages, a hospital and smaller clinic, and sixty-three new churches were all under construction within the first year of Fiorentini's arrival; and after his first retirement in 1910, his successor, Bishop Eugenio Massi, continued the ambitious campaign of reconstruction. Other than establishing a new press for the propagation of the faith in Shanxi, Massi promoted the work of the Franciscan Missionaries of Mary, who had by then returned to Shanxi and were in need of a new convent. In 1905 the sisters had relocated to Taiyuan from their smaller residence at Dongergou in order to manage the newly built Saint Joseph's Hospital, a girl's school, and a swiftly growing orphanage.[52]

The Taiyuan convent included two buildings, one for the Chinese sisters, who wore black habits, and another for the Franciscan Missionaries of Mary, who wore white; an underground tunnel connected the two buildings so they "could avoid the busy streets."[53] The main work of the sisters in Taiyuan was managing the orphanage, and they labored to accommodate the swelling number of orphans brought to its doors. The orphanage was located immediately south of their new convent, and their duties in caring for the children made significant demands on their time. Li Yuzhang and Li Yuming recount that the orphanage not only accepted ill, handicapped, and abandoned young girls, who were commonly left at the many Franciscan churches in Shanxi, but also accepted "old women without means," which heightened numbers considerably.[54] While the influx of orphans was a burden on the mission's resources, it increased the number of Catholics, as each new orphan was baptized and catechized. And once the orphans were of marriageable age, the sisters often served as matchmakers, finding suitable Catholic husbands for the young women.[55]

Massi's efforts to rebuild the mission's churches, support the work of the sisters, and revivify the Catholic culture of Shanxi resulted in unprecedented growth; by the time Massi was transferred to Shaanxi in 1916, 9,572 new names had been added to the vicariate's register. From 1916 until 1940,

Agapito Fiorentini served again as Taiyuan's bishop, and after his retirement he was replaced by Domenico Luca Capozi. By then, concerns about rebuilding the mission's properties and expanding the number of Catholics had largely given way to new political realities as the national conflict between the forces of Mao Zedong (1893–1976) and Chiang Kai-shek (1887–1975) divided the country into three factions: Communists, Nationalists, and a fractured network of warlords. After the protracted disagreements between Capozi and the native Chinese clergy, which had perhaps delayed his return from a trip to Rome, he returned to Taiyuan to urgent deliberations regarding the "Communist question." As China's Communist rule grew more certain, directives from Rome began to reconfigure Shanxi's Catholic operations. Following establishment of the People's Republic of China under the Communists in 1949, Capozi was arrested in September 1951 and the foreign administration of the Franciscan mission in Shanxi was effectively ended. Owing to the Boxer indemnity funds, the careful organization of Taiyuan's post-Boxer bishops, and Shanxi's Catholic physical presence—the rebuilt "fortress of God"—the Franciscan mission had laid a foundation strong enough to prepare the Catholic community for a renewed confrontation. Before his arrest Bishop Capozi entrusted the establishment of the anti-Communist church organization, the Legion of Mary, to Father Hao Nai (1914–1970), who was directed to train Shanxi's young Catholics for resistance against the forces of "atheistic Communism," the church's new spiritual enemy.[56]

REMEMBRANCE AND EXPANSION

In the wake of the Boxer Uprising, the process of rebuilding the Catholic population of Shanxi, or as the missionaries put it, "the army of God," was complicated by the growing company of local bandits and the ongoing clash between Nationalists and Communists. In addition, beginning in 1937 the constant aerial bombing by Japanese planes began to threaten Catholic buildings and lives. The first task of the Franciscans after returning to war-torn Shanxi in 1901 was to commemorate the "soldiers" who had fallen in "spiritual battle," and this task continued apace despite the turbulent internal and external threats to China's stability that changed unpredictably from year to year. After beginning their assigned task to collect information about the martyred Catholics of Shanxi, Fathers Barnabas Nanetti da Cologna and Francesco Saccani discovered that far more people had died than the few foreign and Chinese Christians beheaded in Yuxian's yamen on 9 July 1900. Information about these other, newly recognized martyrs resulted in numerous memorial stelae and published works in both China and the West. Additionally, long and exacting accounts, drafted in formalized ecclesial Latin, were presented to the Vatican's Congregation for the Cause of Saints, then called the Congregation of Rites, to be consulted when considering future canonizations.

Among memorials of the deaths of Chinese Christians were five memorial stelae erected to celebrate the more than one hundred persons who defiantly presented their necks to the executioner in a Taiyuan courtyard after Yuxian's 14 July edict. Nanetti da Cologna and Saccani also collected local Christian songs that remembered Chinese Catholics who had heroically resisted Boxer attacks. One rhyme recounted:

> There was a Catholic woman,
> She was young and lovely.
> After her husband was killed,
> A Boxer seized her and left.
> He wished to take her home,
> And make her his wife.
> Resolute!—she would rather die than follow,
> The Boxer forced her on his back and held her tight.
> With all her strength she bit his arm,
> And blood flowed in large drops.
> The Boxer struggled to no avail,
> And with scornful words he let her go.[57]

The subject of this song was the daughter of a respected local Catholic woman named Lucia Wang, and refrains such as this, even today, add a patina of veneration to older Shanxi Catholic families who continue to preserve the memories of their ancestors who suffered during the Boxer Uprising.

The best-known commemorative monuments in Shanxi were those narrating the deaths of the Christians who died on 9 July, and these were erected at the collective request of the Protestant and Catholic foreign missionaries, though they were paid for by the local Chinese authorities. In many ways the erection of these monuments was an intentional victory over Yuxian, whose popularity among Shanxi's local literati aggravated the returning Catholics. Upon returning, the missionaries could not help but note the large stone monument erected outside Taiyuan's south gate honoring the virtue and actions of the former governor, who had beleaguered foreigners and their "heterodox" religion.[58] Franciscans and Protestants both petitioned to have the stele replaced; and as the court turned against the Boxers, local gentry whose names were inscribed on the tablet's face also grew anxious to remove it from public view. When Yuxian's replacement entered Taiyuan in 1901, the local gentry "made all haste to protect themselves by pulling the erection down and destroying the stone of which it had been built. The site was subsequently used by the foreigner-friendly Qing official, Shên, for a monument in European style, whereupon was written the Decree expressing the Imperial sorrow for the massacres and plundering that had taken place."[59] The replacement monument, which was built in a Chinese rather than a European style, was destroyed in 1966 during the Cultural Revolution, but the Franciscan archive in Rome has preserved the text of the stele, as well as photographs taken by visiting friars.

Another commemorative stele, drafted by Cen Chunxuan, covered by a *ting* pavilion (*tingzi*), was installed at the former railway bureau, or Pig-Head Alley, where the missionaries and Chinese Christians were lodged before their executions at Yuxian's yamen (fig. 6.4). The archive of the Franciscan Missionaries of Mary has preserved a handwritten draft of the monument's narrative inscription:

> The Son of Heaven here commemorates the missionaries of Shanxi who were cruelly slaughtered unexpectedly, and it has been ordered that the official in charge of the area where they were killed record the names of the missionaries for posterity. Now I have been appointed the magistrate of Shanxi and solemnly honor the will of the Court. Thus . . . I decreed that representatives from the Foreign Affairs Bureau assemble craftsmen and set a date to begin construction, which is now complete and officials have been asked to make a record of the affair. Looking into the rebellion of 1900, the Protestant and Roman Catholic missionaries encountered difficulties and were willing to die for their benevolent way, and in all 150 people died. . . . I commend those faithful missionaries who repeatedly encountered difficulties and cruelty.[60]

After this preface, Cen fixed his remarks on the Franciscan missionaries who died on 9 July: "Governor Yuxian treacherously detained them here [at Pig-Head Alley] . . . outrageously seizing them and slaughtering them at the door of the governor's yamen. . . . I, Cen, transmit this in the capital (Taiyuan) to exonerate [the martyrs]."[61] At the demand of foreign authorities,

FIGURE 6.4. The pavilion that enclosed the two commemorative stelae erected in 1901 as a tribute to the Christian martyrs executed at Yuxian's prefectural yamen on 9 July 1900. Source: Archivio Curia Generalizia Ordo Fratrum Minorum, Rome.

the former railway bureau was demolished and transformed into a public garden, in the center of which was featured the large pavilion atop the stone version of Governor Cen's memorial address.[62] It was a sweeping victory for the Franciscan mission; Yuxian had fled and was beheaded by the court's order, the memorial extolling his antiforeignism was replaced with a newly installed pro-Christian monument, and a lofty pavilion was constructed in Pig-Head Alley advertising the court's desire that the virtue and suffering of the Catholics in Taiyuan "be never forgotten."[63]

Remembrance was an important component of strengthening the "army of God," as past Christians who had died from persecution functioned as perennial examples of those who had chosen the "permanence of heaven" over the "transience of the world"; the Franciscan mission applied itself energetically to the task of producing a Chinese analogue to the *Roman Martyrology*. The result was that in addition to public monuments of the spiritual and earthly battles in Shanxi during the Boxer Uprising, a large body of martyrdom narratives began to appear in Shanxi and Europe. One of the more popular accounts retells the killing of Father Peter Zhao Yuqian (1836–1900) (fig. 6.5), who was among the most admired Chinese priests in Shanxi. Having been born in the small village of Heshangzui in 1836 and educated at the Franciscan seminary at Dongergou, Zhao was a favorite of Shanxi's Catholic community for devoting himself to relief efforts during the terrible famine of 1877.[64] Zhao was some one hundred miles away, administering last rites to another Chinese priest, when Yuxian arrested the two bishops and their companions. Having heard of the sudden rise of Boxer activities in the province, Father Zhao shaved his head, dressed like a common laborer, and hurried to Taiyuan, where he discovered an empty mission.

The sixty-five-year-old priest fled Taiyuan along with two other Catholics but was discovered by a local woman who suspected that they were Christians and announced their whereabouts to nearby Boxers; the woman also claimed they intended to poison the village wells at the behest of the European missionaries.[65] Zhao and his companions escaped to another village, Zhoujiagou, but they were discovered by their Boxer pursuers immediately after entering a teahouse: "The chief Boxer, carrying a trident, burst open the door and seized him," and he "then pinned the priest to the wall with his trident and called to the others to come in and bind all three."[66] The men tied Zhao's thumbs tightly to his toes and carried him by a pole to nearby Yangjiabao, where they urged him to apostatize.[67] Refusing, Zhao Yuqian was suspended from a high beam, and "a Boxer raised his spear and thrust it through his abdomen"; he was left hanging there to slowly bleed to death through the evening.[68] The other two were beheaded.

Similar stories were published in Chinese books such as *The Glorious Crown of Shanxi Catholicism* (Shanxi Tianzhujiao zhi rongguan), which were popularized in Shanxi after the Boxer Uprising to memorialize the "army of martyrs" who died in 1900. These accounts often were accompanied by meticulous stories of miracles and a shared cultural interest of the Catholic Church and the native popular culture of Shanxi. A female relative of Father Zhao who had suffered "a growth in the eye for ten years" reportedly prayed to her kinsman, asking him to heal her ailment. "No sooner had she finished her prayer," Giovanni Ricci asserts, "than she was immediately cured."[69] Zhao and his two companions were interred at Yangjiabao, where a monument was later erected to commemorate their deaths. Other native

FIGURE 6.5. Father Peter Zhao Yuqian, OFM, a local Chinese Franciscan who was killed by Boxers in 1900. Zhao was among the many Chinese victims who acquired a large public following in Shanxi after the Boxer Uprising. Source: Archivio Curia Generalizia Ordo Fratrum Minorum, Rome.

Chinese martyrs were said to have appeared to the living in visions and to have rendered countless favors to those who sought intercession by them as members of the Church Triumphant in heaven.

The magical incantations and the particular female magical efficacy of the Red Lanterns, the failed invulnerability of the Boxers, and the court's volte-face turn against these heavenly warriors were swiftly transformed into popular anti-Boxer disdain in Shanxi, as "superstition" (*mixin*) and sentiments of cultural antagonism slowly succumbed to the pressures of Western modernity, Japanese aggression against China, and the advent of China's Communist age. Foreign revenge against court and Boxer atrocities was considered by some to have been nearly as appalling as Boxer outrages. Chinese Christian victims of the Boxer Uprising were quickly forgotten, if thought of much at all, in nonmissionary accounts of 1900, and the task of remembrance and reconstruction continued once the famines were over. But while most of Shanxi's population was turning its gaze toward political questions—Communist versus Nationalist—the post-Boxer-era Shanxi Catholic community did not slacken its imagined, or real, "spiritual battle."

NOTES

PROLOGUE

1   Luo Guanzhong, *Sanguo yanyi* [Romance of the Three Kingdoms] (Yangzhou: Jiangsu guangling guji keyinshe, 1996), 110, recto and verso. All translations into English are my own unless noted otherwise.

2   Zhang Deyi and Jia Lili, *Taiyuan shihua* [Concise history of Taiyuan] (Taiyuan: Shanxi renmin chubanshe, 2000), 161.

3   Ibid.

4   Revelation (Revised Standard Version), 12:7.

5   From the Chaplet of Saint Michael; Ann Ball, *A Litany of Saints* (Huntington, IN: Our Sunday Visitor, 1993), 161. The Chaplet of Saint Michael the Archangel is a chaplet traditionally said to have derived from a private revelation by the Archangel Michael to the Portuguese Carmelite nun Antónia d'Astónaco and was approved by Pope Pius IX in 1851.

6   R. G. Tiedemann, *Reference Guide to Christian Missionary Societies in China: From the Sixteenth Century to the Twentieth Century* (Armonk, NY: M. E. Sharpe, 2009), 27.

7   For studies of women missionaries in China, some of which include accounts of Catholic women, see for example Jane Hunter, *The Gospel of Gentility: American Women Missionaries in Turn-of-the-Century China* (New Haven, CT: Yale University Press, 1984); Dana L. Robert, ed., *Gospel Bearers, Gender Barriers: Missionary Women in the Twentieth Century* (Maryknoll, NY: Orbis Books, 2002); and Mary Taylor Huber and Nancy C. Lutkehaus, eds., *Gendered Missions: Women and Men in Missionary Discourse and Practice* (Ann Arbor: University of Michigan Press, 1999). By and large, standard works on the Jesuit enterprise in China contain only passing mention of women. See for example George H. Dunne, *Generation of Giants: The Story of the Jesuits in China in the Last Decades of the Ming Dynasty* (London: Burns and Oates, 1962); Charles E. Ronan, and Bonnie B. C. Oh, eds., *East Meets West: The Jesuits in China, 1582–1773* (Chicago: Loyola University

Press, 1988); and the more recent Liam Matthew Brockey, *Journey to the East: The Jesuit Mission to China, 1579–1724* (Cambridge, MA: Harvard University Press, 2007).

8   Henrietta Harrison has written a biography of Liu, so I will not repeat her work with a long biography of my own. See *The Man Awakened from Dreams: One Man's Life in a North China Village, 1857–1942* (Stanford, CA: Stanford University Press, 2005).

9   R. G. Tiedemann, "The Church Militant: Armed Conflict between Christians and Boxers in North China," in *The Boxers, China, and the World*, ed. Robert Bickers and R. G. Tiedemann (Lanham: Rowman and Littlefield, 2007), 18.

10   Georg Evers, "My Experiences with Asian Theology," in Leonard Fernando, ed., *Seeking New Horizons, Festschrift in honor of Dr. M. Amaladoss, SJ* (Delhi: Vidya-jyoti, 2002), 121.

11   Xiang Lanxin, *The Origins of the Boxer War: A Multinational Study* (London: Routledge Curzon, 2003), 355.

12   Bob Whyte, *Unfinished Encounter: China and Christianity* (London: Collins, 1988), 138.

1. TAIYUAN, FROM MISSION TO DIOCESE

1   ASV, *Congr. Riti.*, Processus 4623, Article 8, 38.

2   Liu Anrong, *Shanxi Tianzhujiao shi yanjiu (1620–1949)* (Historical research on Roman Catholicism in Shanxi) (Taiyuan: Beiyue wenyi chubanshe, 2011), 34. For a brief discussion of the early Jesuit presence in Shanxi and Shaanxi, see Nicolas Standaert, *Chinese Voices in the Rites Controversy: Travelling Books, Community Networks, Intercultural Arguments* (Rome: Institutum Historicum Societas Iesu, 2012), 150–153.

3   Liam Matthew Brockey, *Journey to the East: The Jesuit Mission to China, 1579–1724* (Cambridge, MA: Harvard University Press, 2007), 328.

4   Qin Geping, *Taiyuan jiaoqu jianshi* (A concise history of the diocese of Taiyuan) (Taiyuan: Catholic Diocese of Taiyuan, 2008), 7. In an exhaustive history of Taiyuan, *Taiyuan shigao* (Draft history of Taiyuan), the first Catholic mission-ary, Michel Trigault, is said to have entered Taiyuan in 1635, rather than 1633. See Huang Zheng, ed., *Taiyuan shigao* (Taiyuan: Shanxi renmin chubanshe, 2003), 416–417.

5   Biblioteca da Ajuda, Jesuítas na Ásia Collection at Biblioteca da Ajuda (Lisbon) (hereafter BAJA), 49-V-14:692r., Manuel Jorge, SJ, Annual Letter, Society of Jesus (hereafter AL) from the Northern Residences, Vice Province 1660. Beijing, 20 July 1662.

6   Ibid.

7   Ibid.

8   Qin Geping, *Taiyuan jiaoqu jianshi*, 8.

9   For this quote about Vagnone, see BAJA, 49-V-8:716v., Lazzaro Cattaneo, SJ, AL Vice Province 1630, Hangzhou, 12 September 1631.

10   Nicolas Standaert, ed., *Handbook of Christianity in China*, vol. 1, *635–1800* (Leiden, Netherlands: Brill, 2001), 534–575.

11   "It was a difficult time for Chinese Catholics: In 1724 the Yongzheng emperor proscribed their religion, European missionaries were expelled from China or forced into hiding, Chinese Catholic communities were driven underground, and the church was weakened by apostasy as well as persecution." Robert E. Entenmann, "Christian Virgins in Eighteenth-Century Sichuan," in *Christianity in China: From the Eighteenth Century to the Present*, ed. Daniel H. Bays (Stanford, CA: Stanford University Press, 1996), 180.

12   Huang Zheng, *Taiyuan shigao*, 417.

13   For a general study of the first Franciscan and Dominican friars to enter China, see Wang Shujie, ed., *Tianzhujiao zaoqi chuanru Zhongguo shihua* (A history of the early entrance of Catholicism into China) (Puqi, China: Neibu duwu, 1993), 172–175.

14   See Li Yuzhang and Li Yuming, *Shanxisheng Taiyuanshi Tianzhujiao baizhounian tekan* (One hundred years of Shanxi Province Taiyuan Catholicism commemorative issue) (Taiyuan: Budefanyin, 2006).

15   Bishop Giovanni's letter is quoted in Arthur Christopher Moule, *Christians in China before the Year 1550* (New York: Society for Promoting Christian Knowledge, 1930), 173.

16   The nomenclature of the distinction "Nestorian" has grown more nuanced in light of recent scholarship, and I acknowledge that *Church of the East* or *East Syrian Church* are perhaps better titles. I have retained *Nestorian* largely for convenience, because that is the name assigned to East Syrian Christians in all Roman Catholic sources to date. I thank Christopher D. Johnson for helping me with this important distinction and refer the reader to the study of Syrian Orthodoxy by Volker L. Menze, *Justinian and the Making of the Syrian Orthodox Church* (Oxford: Oxford University Press, 2008).

17   For a consideration of Montecorvino and the first Roman Catholic appearance in Khanbaliq (Beijing), see Yang Jingjun, *Beijing Tianzhujiao shi* (A history of Catholicism in Beijing) (Beijing: Zongjiao wenhua chubanshe, 2009), 12–21.

18   After 1578, Portuguese friars had a church and friary stationed in Macao and were able to sustain their work in China on a smaller scale. See Arnulf Camps and Pat McCloskey, *The Friars Minor in China (1294–1955), Especially the Years 1925–55, Based on the Research of Friars Bernard Willeke and Domenico Gandolfi, O.F.M.* (Rome: Franciscan Institute, 1995), 14–15. For another discussion of the Franciscan mission in China before 1900, see Marion A. Habig, *In Journeyings Often: Franciscan Pioneers in the Orient* (New York: Franciscan Institute, 1953).

19   Qin Geping, *Taiyuan jiaoqu jianshi*, 8.

20   Ibid.

21   Antonio de Santa Maria Caballero, "Respuesta a un papel que an sacado contra los religiosos de la Orden de Santo Domingo y de S. Francesco de la Mission de China, los Reverendos Padres de la Compañía de aquel Reyno, o el Procurador de dhas. Provincias y Missiones en su nombre, llamado Bartolome Roboredo, que reside en

el Colegio de la Compañía de esta ciudad de Manilla." Ms., Archivo de la Provincia del Santo Rosario [Archives of the Dominican Province of the Holy Rosary], Manila and Avila, *Ritos Chinois*, vol. 70: ff. 507–568; copy vol. 67: ff. 79–138, "Quinta Cosa," f. 116r.

See Eugenio Menegon, *Ancestors, Virgins, and Friars: Christianity as a Local Religion in Late Imperial China* (Cambridge, MA: Harvard University Press, 2009), 83.

22 Anselm M. Romb, OFM, Conv. *Mission to Cathay: The Biography of Blessed Odoric of Pordenone* (Paterson, NJ: Saint Anthony Guild Press, 1956), 136.

23 The jurisdictional history of Shanxi's ecclesial boundaries during the eighteenth and nineteenth centuries is complex, and perhaps the most exhaustive study of the province's Catholic mission is Liu Anrong's *Shanxi Tianzhujiao shi yanjiu*, which exactingly outlines the province's ecclesial precincts and chronologically charts every Jesuit and Franciscan missionary to have served there.

24 For a study of the Franciscan mission in China from 1784 to 1785, see Bernard H. Willeke, *Imperial Government and Catholic Missions in China during the Years 1784–1785* (Saint Bonaventure, NY: Franciscan Institute, 1948). For a discussion of Shanxi during that time see pp. 92–95.

25 Roger R. Thompson, "The Chinese Countryside and the Modernizing State," in Bays, *Christianity in China*, 57.

26 For a more detailed account of the five articles in this letter, see ibid.

27 Zhongyang yanjiuyuan jindaishi yanjiusuo, eds., *Jiaowu jiaoan dang* (Missionary incidents archives) 7 vols. (Taipei: Zhongyang yanjiuyuan jindaishi yanjiusuo, 1974), 4:320.

28 For a brief history of the 1870 Church of the Immaculate Conception in Taiyuan, see Qin Geping, *Taiyuan jiaoqu jianshi*, 97; and Li Yuzhang and Li Yuming, *Shanxisheng Taiyuanshi Tianzhujiao*, 21–36.

29 See Qin Geping, *Taiyuan jiaoqu jianshi*, 119.

30 See ibid. The Geliaogou church is the oldest surviving Catholic church in the Taiyuan Diocese and is still in use by the Christian community there. The towers were destroyed by the Boxers in 1900 but were restored in 1901.

31 Qin Geping, *Taiyuan jiaoqu jianshi*, 129.

32 ACGOFM, *Sinae 1870–1904*, 243.

33 ACGOFM, *Acta Ordinis Fratrum Minorum*, vol. 5, 1886, 129.

34 Zhang Deyi and Jia Lili, *Taiyuan shihua* [Concise history of Taiyuan] (Taiyuan: Shanxi renmin chubanshe, 2000), 159.

35 Georges Hauptmann, "François Joseph Meistermann, 1850–1923: Barnabé d'Alsace, Franciscain O.F.M.—Missionaire apostolique Archéologue— architecte/ bâtisseur—écrivain—Historien de la Terre Sainte" (unpublished manuscript, 2008), 10–14.

36 See Qin Geping, *Taiyuan jiaoqu jianshi*, 12.

37 See Li Yuzhang and Li Yuming, *Shanxisheng Taiyuanshi Tianzhujiao*, 38.

38 See Liu Anrong, *Shanxi Tianzhujiao*, 39.

39 Gabriel Grioglio, OFM, 21 October 1857, Archives de l'Oeuvre de la Propagation

de la Foi, Oeuvres Pontificales Missionaires Centre de Lyon (hereafter AOPF), E101–1 Chansi indivis, 14906.

40 Quoted in Henrietta Harrison, *The Missionary's Curse and Other Tales from a Chinese Catholic Village* (Berkeley: University of California Press, 2013), 74.

41 See Liu Anrong, *Shanxi Tianzhujiao*, 39. This episode demonstrates the sometimes tense relationship between Chinese and European priests in Shanxi. In 1859 Bishop Grioglio and a group of native clergy under his direction had an acidic disagreement, the precise cause of which was apparently unreported. The result was that Grioglio suspended the Chinese priests, the priests complained to the Propaganda Fide in Rome, and Rome responded by suspending Grioglio. Only after extended ecclesial mediation was Grioglio restored to harmony with the Chinese priests in Shanxi. See Camps and McCloskey, *Friars Minor in China (1294–1955)*, 25.

42 Li Yuzhang and Li Yuming, *Shanxisheng Taiyuanshi Tianzhujiao*, 38–39.

43 Liu Anrong, *Shanxi Tianzhujiao*, 40.

44 Li Yuzhang and Li Yuming, *Shanxisheng Taiyuanshi Tianzhujiao*, 38.

45 Giovanni Ricci, *Historia Vicariatus Taiyuanfu: Ab ejus origine usque ad dies nostros (1700–1928)* (Beijing: Congregationis Missionis, 1929), 109.

46 For an account of this famine see Kathryn Edgerton-Tarpley, *Tears from Iron: Cultural Responses to Famine in Nineteenth-Century China* (Berkeley: University of California Press, 2008).

47 Saint Bartholomew-on-the-Tiber is located on a small island on the Tiber in Rome. The basilica church "rises on the ruins of an ancient Roman temple," and in 1694 the Franciscans established a college on the island for the missionary preparation of friars. See Marco Pupillo, *St. Bartholomew's on the Tiber Island: A Thousand Years of History and Art* (Milan: Edizioni Angelo Guerini, 1998), 7.

48 Pacifique-Marie Chardin, *Les missions franciscaines en Chine: Notes géographiques et historiques* (Paris: Auguste Picard, 1915), 85.

49 See Tianzhujiao Taiwan diqu zhujiao xuansheng weiyuanhui zhubian (Taiwan Roman Catholic Bishops Committee), eds., *Zhonghua xundao shengren zhuan* (Biographies of China's martyr saints) (Taipei: Tianzhujiao Taiwan diqu zhujiao xuan wiyuanhui, 2000), 237.

50 Qin Geping, *Taiyuan jiaoqu jianshi*, 26. Also see Luigi Lanzi, *Francesco Fogolla: Apostoli in Cina* (Parma: Convento SS. Annunziata, 1997), 11.

51 Qin Geping, *Taiyuan jiaoqu jianshi*, 26.

52 Chardin, *Les missions franciscaines en Chine*, 87.

53 Qin Geping, *Taiyuan jiaoqu jianshi*, 27. See Francesco Fogolla, OFM, *La Muraglia Cinese Relazione Crito-Scientifics Illustrata* (Turin: Tipografia G. Lerossi, 1898).

54 Chardin, *Les missions franciscaines en Chine*, 87–88.

55 R. J. Forrest, "Report of R. J. Forrest, Esq., H. B. M. Consul at Tien-tsin, and Chairman of the Famine Relief Committee at Tien-tsin." In *China's Millions* (November 1879), 135–136.

56 Chardin, *Les missions franciscaines en Chine*, 88.

57 Li Yuzhang and Li Yuming, *Shanxisheng Taiyuanshi Tianzhujiao*, 41.

58 Ibid. Also see ACGOFM, *Acta Ordinis Fratrum Minorum*, vol. 19, 1900 (Rome), 192.

59 Qin Geping, *Taiyuan jiaoqu jianshi*, 28.

60 Li Yuzhang and Li Yuming, *Shanxisheng Taiyuanshi Tianzhujiao*, 41.

61 Qin Geping, *Taiyuan jiaoqu jianshi*, 28.

62 See ibid; and Taiyuan Diocese Archive (hearafter TDA). At present the Taiyuan Diocese Archive has no systematic organization, and scholarly consultation requires patient sifting through loose materials.

63 See Qin Geping, *Taiyuan jiaoqu jianshi*, 29. Also see Chardin, *Les missions franciscaines en Chine*, 100–101.

64 For a lengthy account of Bishop Eugenio Massi's missionary work at Shaanxi's Tongzhou vicariate, see Pietro Moretti, *Su le Rive del Fiume Giallo: Storia di una Missione Francescana in Cina* (Ancona, Italy: Biblioteca Francescana, 1955).

65 Qin Geping, *Taiyuan jiaoqu jianshi*, 31.

66 Ibid. For another brief account of Massi's work in Shanxi, see Moretti, *Su le Rive del Fiume Giallo*, 67–68.

67 Qin Geping, *Taiyuan jiaoqu jianshi*, 31.

68 *The Canberra Times*, 9 November 1937.

69 These tunnels, now used for storage, are beneath the seminary buildings at Dongergou, buildings that are presently used as a diocesan retreat house. It appears that the principal interest of the Japanese was Shanxi's rich resources, especially the coal around Datong.

70 See the cover photo and text, "La béatification des martyrs de Chine: La parole du souverain pontife," *Annales des Franciscaines Missionaires de Marie* 55 (January 1947): 1–7. The original beatification homily by Pope Pius XII was given on 27 November 1946. Also see Qin Geping, *Taiyuan jiaoqu jianshi*, 33.

71 Qin Geping, *Taiyuan jiaoqu jianshi*, 33.

72 Ibid.

73 See Li Yuzhang and Li Yuming, *Shanxisheng Taiyuanshi Tianzhujiao*, 42, and Qin Geping, *Taiyuan jiaoqu jianshi*, 34.

74 See Harrison, *The Missionary's Curse*, 148.

75 See Liu Anrong, *Shanxi Tianzhujiao*, 44–45.

76 Ibid., 65.

77 Georges Goyau, *Missionaries and Martyrs: Mother Mary of the Passion and the Franciscan Missionaries of Mary*, trans. George Telford (Anand, India: Anand Press, 1944), 16–17.

78 Ibid., ii.

79 *The Franciscan Missionaries of Mary* (London: Burns, Oates and Washbourne, 1926), 4.

80 Ibid., 13.

81 While hagiographers interested in Assunta's life have far outnumbered those who have written about the other Franciscan Missionaries of Mary who served in China, books have been published on the life of Marie-Hermine de Jesus, several of which appear in the notes and bibliography of the present study. The

most exhaustive work on her life is, perhaps, the anonymous book *Vie de la Mere Marie-Hermine de Jésus et de ses Compagnes Massacrées au Chan-si (China), le 9 Juillet 1900* (Rome: L'Institute des Franciscaines Missionaires de Marie, 1902).

82   Louis Nazaire Bégin, *Life of Mother Marie-Hermine of Jesus: Massacred in Shan-si (China) July 9th, 1900* (Quebec: Archeveque de Quebec, 1910), 23.

83   Giovanni Ricci, *Gigli e Rose Ossia le Sette Protomartiri dell'Instituto delle Francescane Missionarie di Maria: Massaccrate in Cina il 9 Luglio 1900* (Levanto, Italy: Tipografia dell'Immaculata, 1919), 11–12.

84   Ibid. 1–8.

85   Goyau, *Missionaries and Martyrs*, 8.

86   Justina Fanego, *In Order to Give Life: A Community That Delivered Itself Up to Death*, trans. Sheila Patenaude (Clamecy, France: Nouvelle Imprimerie Laballery, 2000), especially page 69.

87   Ibid., 67.

88   *The Newly Canonized Martyr-Saints of China* (Taipei: Chinese Regional Bishops Conference, 2000), 88.

89   Fanego, *In Order to Give Life*, 72.

90   Ibid., 73.

91   Tianzhujiao Taiwan diqu zhujiao xuansheng weiyuanhui zhubian, *Zhonghua xundao shengren zhuan*, 272–273.

92   See R. G. Tiedemann, *Reference Guide to Christian Missionary Societies in China: From the Sixteenth Century to the Twentieth Century* (Armonk, NY: M. E. Sharpe, 2009), 56–57 and 70–71.

93   Goyau, *Missionaries and Martyrs*, 21.

94   *Shanxi Tianzhujiao zhi rongguan* (The glorious crown of the Roman Catholic Church in Shanxi (Taiyuan: Shanxi Taiyuan jiaoqu, 1946), 29.

95   Goyau, *Missionaries and Martyrs*, 14. The photograph of the martyred Delbroucq was published in George Monchamp, *A Sketch of the Life of Father Victorin Delbrouck, a Franciscan Martyr of Our Days* (Paterson, NJ: Province of the Most Holy Name, 1910), 76. This idea was not uncommon among Catholic missionary orders in China, even until the twentieth century. When the French Jesuits in Shanghai grew understaffed, they wrote to the American Jesuits for reinforcements. Father Eugene Beauc, SJ, Mission Superior of the French Jesuits, wrote in a letter to Father Joseph Piet, SJ, of the California Province, that those who apply to the China mission should expect "to live, to toil, to sacrifice all, and to die in China— with the hope of martyrdom." Eugene Beauc, SJ, to Joseph Piet, SJ, 20 February 1928. California Province Jesuit Archives, Santa Clara, California.

96   Li Yuzhang and Li Yuming, *Shanxisheng Taiyuanshi Tianzhujiao*, 126.

97   See Pamela Kyle Crossley, *The Manchus* (Cambridge, MA: Blackwell, 1997), 4–6.

98   AFMM, letter from Marie-Hermine de Jesus, FMM, 17 December 1899.

99   Liu Dapeng, *Jinci zhi* [Jinci Temple gazetteer], in *Yihetuan zai Shanxi diqu shiliao* [Historical sources on Boxers in Shanxi], ed. Qiao Zhiqiang (Taiyuan: Shanxi renmin chubanshe, 1980), 7.

2. BOXERS AND LOCAL GODS

1   Liu Dapeng, *Jinci zhi* [Jinci Temple gazetteer], in *Yihetuan zai Shanxi diqu shiliao* [Historical sources on Boxers in Shanxi], ed. Qiao Zhiqiang (Taiyuan: Shanxi renmin chubanshe, 1980), 9.

2   See the *Henan qihuang tieleitu* (Peculiar pictorial depictions of famine in Henan to invoke tears from iron). These woodblock images are preserved in the *Si sheng gao zai tu qi* [Preliminary pictorial report on the famines of the four provinces (Shandong, Henan, Shanxi, and Zhili)], in *Qi yu jin Zhi zhenjuan zhengxin lu* [Commentary on the accounts of relief contributions for Shandong, Henan, Shanxi, and Zhili] (n.p., 1881).

3   *Si sheng gao zai tu qi*, 13 recto.

4   Ibid. Kathryn Edgerton-Tarpley poignantly describes this image in her study of nineteenth-century famine in northern China: "Famished onlookers watch from behind a tree, while others rush to join the feast. The figures are barefoot and ragged, the tree has been stripped of all its bark and leaves by the starving populace, and the corpse, which is little more than skin and bones, lies face down in the dust. There is no sense that even one of the living persons in the print has any intention of preventing the man with the knife from stripping the corpse of its flesh." *Tears from Iron: Cultural Responses to Famine in Nineteenth-Century China* (Berkeley: University of California Press, 2008), 219.

5   For a lengthier discussion of Shanxi's famines from 1875 to 1880, see Alvyn Austin, *China's Millions: The China Inland Mission and Late Qing Society, 1832–1905* (Grand Rapids, MI: William B. Eerdmans, 2007), 139–150.

6   Kathryn Edgerton-Tarpley, interview with Tan Ruhua, age eighty-five, 5 April 2001, Shangzhuang village, Yuanqu county, Shanxi, in *Tears from Iron*, 9.

7   Correspondence from Yizhoufu in *North China Herald*, 17 December 1897.

8   Correspondence from North Jiangsu in *North China Herald*, 30 May 1898.

9   TDA, Shanxi Boxer Announcement, Guangxu 26th Reign Year (1900), Notice 1. Also see Qiao Zhiqiang, ed., *Yihetuan zai Shanxi diqu shiliao*, 1.

10   Archibald E. Glover, who along with his family fled from Shanxi during the height of Boxer violence, recounts an encounter en route in which they were discovered during a rain procession. "They halted opposite us. Then cries and curses were heard, soon there was battering at the gate; stones and brick-bats were flung over the wall and the gate house into the courtyard where our own quarters were. . . . They again withdrew, shouting threats of revenge should the drought continue." Glover, *A Thousand Miles of Miracle: The Tragic True Story of Persecution during the Boxer Rebellion in China* (1904; repr., Station Approach, UK: OMF Publishing, 2000), 20.

11   ACGOFM, Letter from Théodoric Balat, OFM, 5 December 1899. Also in Léon de Kerval, *Deux Martyrs Français de l'Ordre des Frères Mineurs: Le R. P. Théodoric Balat et le Fr. André Bauer, Massacrés en Chine le 9 Juillet 1900*, 2nd ed. (Paris: Prime, 1906), 215.

12   Ebenezer Henry Edwards, *Fire and Sword in Shansi: The Story of the Martyrdom*

of Foreigners and Chinese Christians (London: Oliphant, Anderson and Ferrier, 1903), 54–55.

13   OCA, Jennie Clapp, Pitkin Genealogy, Leith Papers.

14   An example of the Mainland Chinese scholarly view of the Boxer Uprising may be seen in Ren Yanli, ed., *Zhongguo Tianzhujiao: Jichu zhishi* [Chinese Catholicism: A foundational understanding] (Beijing: Zongjiao zongjiao wenhua chubanshe, 2005), 275–284.

15   A more exhaustive account of the rise of the Boxers throughout northern China can be found in Joseph Esherick's *The Origins of the Boxer Uprising*, and I shall only briefly recapitulate those origins in order to contextualize the Boxers of Shanxi. See *The Origins of the Boxer Uprising* (Berkeley: University of California Press, 1987), especially chapters 6 and 7.

16   *Huibao* (Church newspaper), no. 153, 21 February 1900. In Esherick, *Origins of the Boxer Uprising*, 136.

17   Giovanni Ricci, *The Franciscan Martyrs of the Boxer Rising* (Dublin: Franciscan Missionary Union Merchants' Quay, 1932), 7.

18   Ibid., 7.

19   A small number of scholars in recent years have attempted to lighten the violent tenor of this Boxer motto, such as Jane Elliot in her "revised" consideration of the Boxer Uprising. Elliot, who goes to acrobatic lengths to exonerate the Boxers, has creatively rendered *Fu Qing mieyang* as "Uphold the dynasty! Expel the foreigners!" Such a translation not only misrepresents the meaning of the motto but also misrepresents the larger corpus of Boxer placards and, indeed, their behavior. The term *mie*, for example, cannot in any way be taken in this context to mean "expel" but more accurately implies to "wipe out," "exterminate," or even "annihilate." When Boxers attacked foreigners and Christian churches in 1900 they called out *"sha, sha,"* or "kill, kill!" There are no instances of Boxers shouting "Go away!" during their attacks. While several salutary assertions are made in Elliot's revisionist study, it is nonetheless riddled with similar misrepresentations and inaccuracies. See Elliot, *Some Did It for Civilisation, Some Did It for Their Country: A Revised View of the Boxer War* (Hong Kong: Chinese University of Hong Kong Press, 2002), xxvi.

20   *Qingshigao* [Draft history of the Qing] (Beijing: Zhonghuashuju, 1977), juan 455, 12: 633. Translated and quoted in Chiang Ying-ho, "Literary Reactions to the Kengtzu Incident (1900)" (PhD diss., University of California, Berkeley, 1982), 6.

21   See *Gugong bowuyuan Ming Qing danganbu: Yihetuan dang'an shiliao* (Forbidden City Museum Archives: Society of Righteous Harmony Archive Historical Materials) (Beijing: Zhonghuashuju, 1959), 196.

22   *Qingshigao*, juan 465, 12: 633, 6.

23   Qin Geping, *Taiyuan jiaoqu jianshi* [A concise history of the diocese of Taiyuan] (Taiyuan: Catholic Diocese of Taiyuan, 2008), 322. Other scholars have attempted a more nuanced, even somewhat sympathetic, portrayal of Yuxian, most notably Joseph Esherick in his brief biography in *Origins of the Boxer Uprising*, 190–193.

24   Qin Geping, *Taiyuan jiaoqu jianshi*, 322.

25   Ibid. For the date of Yuxian's appointment to Shanxi, see Edwards, *Fire and Sword in Shansi*, 51.

26   Liu Dapeng, *Jinci zhi*, 10.

27   Qin Geping, *Taiyuan jiaoqu jianshi*, 322.

28   ACGOFM, Letter from André Bauer, OFM, 6 May 1900. Quoted in Georges Goyau, *Missionaries and Martyrs: Mother Mary of the Passion and the Franciscan Missionaries of Mary*, trans. George Telford (Anand, India: Anand Press, 1944), 32.

29   Ricci, *Franciscan Martyrs of the Boxer Rising*, 11.

30   Edwards, *Fire and Sword in Shansi*, 56.

31   See Zhang Deyi and Jia Lili, *Taiyuan shihua* [Concise history of Taiyuan] (Taiyuan: Shanxi renmin chubanshe, 2000), 160.

32   Daniel L. Overmyer, *Local Religion in North China in the Twentieth Century: The Structure and Organization of Community Rituals and Beliefs* (Leiden, Netherlands: Brill, 2009), 27.

33   Liu Dapeng, *Jinci zhi*, 7.

34   Ibid., 8–9.

35   Ibid., 9.

36   Ibid.; Zhang Deyi and Jia Lili, *Taiyuan shihua*, 161.

37   Zhang Deyi and Jia Lili, *Taiyuan shihua*, 161.

38   Mark Meulenbeld, "Chinese Religion in the Ming and Qing Dynasties," in *The Wiley-Blackwell Companion to Chinese Religions*, ed. Randall L. Nadeau (Malden, MA: Wiley-Blackwell, 2012), 126.

39   Jean DeBernardi, "Teachings of a Spirit Medium," in *Religions of China in Practice*, ed. Donald S. Lopez Jr. (Princeton, NJ: Princeton University Press, 1996), 230.

40   For a brief description of such ceremonies connected to the veneration of Lord Guan, see Tam Wai Lun, "Religious Festivals in Northern Guandong," in John Lagerwey, ed., *Religion and Chinese Society*, vol. 2, *Taoism and Local Religion in Modern China* (Hong Kong: Chinese University Press, 2004), 824.

41   Qin Geping, *Taiyuan jiaoqu jianshi*, 315.

42   For an account of the collaborative attack by the Boxers and Qing militia against Zhujiahe village, see Anthony E. Clark, *China's Saints: Catholic Martyrdom during the Qing (1644–1911)* (Bethlehem, PA: Lehigh University Press; Lanham. MD: Rowman and Littlefield, 2011), 99–112.

43   For a brief discussion of Shanxi Boxer attacks and Catholic resistance see Henrietta Harrison, "Village Politics and National Politics: The Boxer Movement in Central Shanxi," in *The Boxers, China, and the World*, ed. Robert Bickers and R. G. Tiedemann (Lanham, MD: Rowman and Littlefield, 2007), 1–15.

44   Zhang Deyi and Jia Lili, *Taiyuan shihua*, 161.

45   Qin Geping, *Taiyuan jiaoqu jianshi*, 315.

46   I was informed by the Shanxi scholar Liu Anrong that her research on popular religion and Catholicism around Taiyuan shows that Catholics and popular religionists during the Boxer era and today consider the Lord of Heaven (Catholic)

and Old Man Heaven (popular religion) to be the same God/god, which places an ironic twist on the fact that both groups believed in a spiritual battle between their gods during the Boxer era.

47 See Lu Jingqi and Cheng Xiao, eds., *Yihetuan yuanliu shiliao* [Historical materials related to the Origins of the Society of Righteous Harmony] (Beijing: Renmin Daxue, 1980), 105–106.

48 TDA, Shanxi Boxer Announcement, Guangxu 26th Reign Year (1900), Notice 1. Also see Qiao Zhiqiang, *Yihetuan zai Shanxi diqu shiliao*, 1.

49 TDA, Shanxi Boxer Announcement, Guangxu 26th Reign Year (1900), Notice 5. Also see Qiao Zhiqiang, *Yihetuan zai Shanxi diqu shiliao*, 3.

50 TDA, Shanxi Boxer Announcement, Guangxu 26th Reign Year (1900), Notice 5. Also see Qiao Zhiqiang, *Yihetuan zai Shanxi diqu shiliao*, 3.

51 TDA, Shanxi Boxer Announcement, Guangxu 26th Reign Year (1900), Notice 8. See also Qiao Zhiqiang, *Yihetuan zai Shanxi diqu shiliao*, 3–4. In my translations of the character names from *Xiyouji*—Tangseng, Shaseng, Zhubajie, and Wukong—I have employed the readable English equivalents of Arthur Waley. For a brief discussion of possession rites invoking gods from popular fiction, such as Monkey, see Esherick, *Origins of the Boxer Uprising*, 62.

52 TDA, Shanxi Boxer Announcement, Guangxu 26th Reign Year (1900), Notice 8. See also Qiao Zhiqiang, *Yihetuan zai Shanxi diqu shiliao*, 4.

53 Reprinted in *The Boxer Rising: A History of the Boxer Trouble in China*, 2nd ed. (Shanghai: Shanghai Mercury, 1901), 1.

54 Edwards, *Fire and Sword in Shansi*, 54.

55 Ibid.

56 ASV, *Congr. Riti.*, Processus 4623, p. 256.

57 TDA, Shanxi Boxer Announcement, Guangxu 26th Reign Year (1900), Notice 7. Also see Qiao Zhiqiang, *Yihetuan zai Shanxi diqu shiliao*, 3.

58 TDA, Shanxi Boxer Announcement, Guangxu 26th Reign Year (1900), Notice 7. Also see Qiao Zhiqiang, *Yihetuan zai Shanxi diqu shiliao*, 3.

59 TDA, Shanxi Boxer Announcement, Guangxu 26th Reign Year (1900), Notice 7. Also see Qiao Zhiqiang, *Yihetuan zai Shanxi diqu shiliao*, 4. The phrase *duan chuan yihequan shenhui* is tentatively rendered here; it could also read something like: "transmits down to the Fists of Righteous Harmony Spirit Society."

60 TDA, Shanxi Boxer Announcement, Guangxu 26th Reign Year (1900), Notice 12. Also see Qiao Zhiqiang, *Yihetuan zai Shanxi diqu shiliao*, 5.

61 Paul A. Cohen, *History in Three Keys: The Boxers as Event, Experience, and Myth* (New York: Columbia University Press, 1997), 171.

62 Boxer notices, for example, began to include antidote formulae to save victims from foreign poison. Ibid., 95.

63 TDA, Shanxi Boxer Announcement, Guangxu 26th Reign Year (1900), Notice 11. Also see Qiao Zhiqiang, *Yihetuan zai Shanxi diqu shiliao*, 5. It is tempting here to read significance into the colors employed in Boxer mythologies; red signifies happiness and prosperity (Chinese Red Lantern women), while white is China's funerary color and signifies death and inauspiciousness (foreign white-lantern magic).

64 TDA, Shanxi Boxer Announcement, Guangxu 26th Reign Year (1900), Notice 1. Also see Qiao Zhiqiang, *Yihetuan zai Shanxi diqu shiliao*, 1.

65 TDA, Shanxi Boxer Announcement, Guangxu 26th Reign Year (1900), Notice 13. Also see Qiao Zhiqiang, *Yihetuan zai Shanxi diqu shiliao*, 6.

66 TDA, Shanxi Boxer Announcement, Guangxu 26th Reign Year (1900), Notice 5. Also see Qiao Zhiqiang, *Yihetuan zai Shanxi diqu shiliao*, 3.

67 Liu Dapeng, *Qianyuan suoji* [Casual notes from within the garden], in Qiao Zhiqiang, *Yihetuan zai Shanxi diqu shiliao*, 28.

68 For this information I am indebted to Liu Anrong, who provided me with an unpublished manuscript, in 2011, of her field research on popular religious practices in Shanxi near the area of Taiyuan.

69 For further reading on Shanxi's unique religious admixture, see Liu Anrong, "Catholic and Chinese Folk Religion during the Republican Era in the Region of Taiyuan, Shanxi," in *A Voluntary Exile: Chinese Christianity and Cultural Confluence since 1552*, ed. Anthony E. Clark (Bethlehem, PA: Lehigh University Press; Lanham, MD: Rowman and Littlefield, 2014).

70 Again, I am grateful to Liu Anrong for this information.

71 ACGOFM, letter from Francesco Fogolla, OFM, 1 February 1900. Quoted in Théobald Aumasson, OFM, *La croix sur la pagode: Le B^x Théodoric Balat et ses compagnons martyrs*, 2nd ed. (Brive, France: Editions Echo des Grottes, 1947), 61.

72 Giovanni Ricci, *Gigli e Rose Ossia le Sette Protomartiri dell'Instituto delle Francescane Missionarie di Maria: Massaccrate in Cina il 9 Luglio 1900* (Levanto, Italy: Tipografia dell'Immaculata, 1919), 73.

73 Ephesians 6:12.

3. CATHOLICS AND FOREIGN GODS

1 In Li Renkai, ed., *Zhili yihetuan diaocha ziliao xuanbian* [A material investigation into selected documentary excerpts related to the Zhili Yihetuan] (Shijiazhuang, China: Hebei jiaoyu chubanshe, 2001), 161–162.

2 "Hymn of Departure" intoned to missionaries leaving for the China mission. See George M. Stenz, *Life of Father Richard Henle, S.V.D.: Missionary in China* (Techny, IL: Mission Press, S.V.D., 1921), 45.

3 Correspondence from Father Emeric Langlois de Chavagnac, SJ, Fuzhou, China, 1701, in *Lettres édifiantes et curieuses écrites des missions étrangères par quelques missionaires de la Compagnie de Jésus* (Paris: n.p., 1717–1774), 9: 345–347.

4 Correspondence from Father François Noël, SJ, China, 1703, in ibid., 4: 94–95.

5 Eugenio Menegon, *Ancestors, Virgins, and Friars: Christianity as a Local Religion in Late Imperial China* (Cambridge, MA: Harvard University Press, 2009), 208.

6 Anselm M. Romb, *Mission to Cathay: The Biography of Blessed Odoric of Pordenone* (Paterson, NJ: Saint Anthony Guild Press, 1956), 136.

7 Ibid., 23.

8 Other Protestant missionary accounts represent the view that China suffered from widespread demonic possession. Archibald E. Glover notes encounters with

possessed "witches," and in one passage of his memoirs he recounts an instance of a possessed host: "What was our distress when she suddenly became demon-possessed—a most distressing sight to witness. . . . She simply sat on her doorstep looking straight before her, with dulled eyes, dead to all expression and apparently going off into a swoon. Later she began an incantation, the weird strain of which made one's flesh creep." *A Thousand Miles of Miracle in China: A Personal Record of God's Delivering Power from the Hands of the Imperial Boxers of Shan-si* (London: Pickering and Inglis, 1904), 29.

9   John L. Nevius, *Demon Possession and Its Allied Themes: Being an Inductive Study of Phenomena of Our Times* (London: George Redway, 1897), 17.

10   Ibid., 18.

11   See Peter Fleming, "Chosen for China: The California Province Jesuits in China 1928–1957; A Case Study in Mission and Culture" (PhD diss., Graduate Theological Union, Berkeley, CA, 1987); also see Robert Streit, *Catholic Missions in Figures and Symbols: Based on the Vatican Missionary Exhibition 1926* (Boston: Society for the Propagation of the Faith, 1927), 57.

12   Fleming, "Chosen for China," 4.

13   Cardinal Francis Spellman, "Homily to Catholic Students Mission Crusade," *Jesuit Missions*, no. 19 (January–February 1945), 3. The homily was delivered at Saint Patrick's Cathedral, New York, 1944.

14   Henrietta Harrison notes another popular deity in the Buddhist tradition who may be set against Michael the Archangel as an analogue protector. This deity is the Bodhisattva Weituo, Skanda in Sanskrit, and is commonly known as the protector of the Buddhist teaching and the monasteries that preserve and spread that teaching. See *The Missionary's Curse and Other Tales from a Chinese Catholic Village* (Berkeley: University of California Press, 2013), 34–35.

15   See Alban Butler, *Lives of the Saints* (Norwalk, CT: Easton Press, 1995), 3: 677–680; the four-volume work was originally printed in 1756–1759. Also see *Pictorial Lives of the Saints* (New York: Benziger Brothers, 1922), 473–474. The entries related to Saint Michael the Archangel are in conjunction with the feast of Saint Michael, celebrated on September 29.

16   Revelation 12:7.

17   See Kenneth Scott Latourette, *A History of Christianity*, vol. 2 (New York: Harper-Collins, 1981).

18   Fleming, "Chosen for China," 30.

19   See Pierre-Marie-Alphonse Favier, *Péking, histoire et description* (Lille, France: Desclée de Bouwer, 1900), 269–270. Translated in Arnulf Camps, "The Chinese Martyrs among the 120 Martyrs of China, Canonized on the 1st of October 2000," in *Silent Force: Native Converts in the Catholic China Mission*, ed. Rachel Lu Yan and Philip Vanhaelemeersch (Leuven, Belgium: Ferdinand Verbiest Institute, 2009), 528–529.

20   By 1914 the global number of people living under foreign rule was 700 million, more than one-third of the world's population at that time. Jakob Baumgartner, "The Expansion of Catholic Missions from the Time of Leo XIII until World War

II," in *History of the Church*, ed. Hubert Jedin (New York: Crossroads, 1981), 10: 557.

21   See Gerald A. McCool, *Catholic Theology in the Nineteenth Century* (New York: Seabury Press, 1977), 21–24.

22   This was also an era of ecclesial "tidying" of all aspects of church operations and belief; for example, in 1864 Pope Pius IX anathematized eighty theological and philosophical propositions in his encyclical *Syllabus of Errors*;. And in the First Vatican Council's *Pastor Aeternus*, the pope was declared infallible in matters of faith and morals.

23   José Eugenio Borao, ed., *Spaniards in Taiwan* (Taipei: SMC, 2001), 2: 192.

24   In Louis Nazaire Bégin, *Life of Mother Marie-Hermine of Jesus: Massacred in Shan-si (China) July 9th, 1900* (Quebec: Archeveque de Quebec, 1910), 57.

25   I thank Christopher Johnson for pointing this out to me.

26   Luciano Morra, "I Boxer e la Chiese Cattolica in Cina nei secoli XIX e XX" (PhD diss., Pontificia Universitas Gregoriana, Rome, 1995), 89–90.

27   Benedict Anderson, *Imagined Communities: Reflections on the Origin and Spread of Nationalism* (New York: Verso, 1991).

28   George H. Dunne, *Generation of Giants: The Story of the Jesuits in China in the Last Decades of the Ming Dynasty* (London: Burns and Oates, 1962), 370. While it is tempting to consign pejoratively all nineteenth-century missionary perspectives to pugilistic prose and Sinophobia, such a view would misrepresent the Franciscan mission in Shanxi, which adopted a much more nuanced manner of preaching the Christian message to non-Christian Chinese.

29   Tertullian, *The Apology* (Whitefish, MT: Kessinger Publishing, 2001), 50. Originally published in the 2nd century CE.

30   Ephesians 6:12.

31   Pacifique-Marie Chardin, *Les missions franciscaines en Chine: Notes géographiques et historiques* (Paris: Auguste Picard, 1915), 87.

32   Georges Goyau, *Missionaries and Martyrs: Mother Mary of the Passion and the Franciscan Missionaries of Mary*, trans. George Telford (Anand, India: Anand Press, 1944), 6 and 8.

33   Bégin, *Life of Mother Marie-Hermine*, 11.

34   Cipriano Silvestri, *La Testimonianza del Sangue: Biografie dei Beati Cinesi Uccisi il 4, 7 e 9 Luglio 1900* (Rome: S. Guiseppe al Triomfale, 1943), 64.

35   Romb, *Mission to Cathay*, 25.

36   Silvestri, *La Testimonianza del Sangue*, 64.

37   See Giovanni Ricci, *Historia Vicariatus Taiyuanfu: Ab ejus origine usque ad dies nostros (1700–1928)* (Beijing: Congregationis Missionis, 1929), 127, plate 30.

38   While most Catholic orders did in fact ordain Chinese clergy, the Franciscan order appears to have been more favorable to the indigenization of "native clergy." An even more igneous question among the orders was the consecration of bishops. Until 1926 the only Chinese priest to have been made a bishop was the Dominican Gregory Luo Wenzao, OP (1616–1691).

39   See Arnulf Camps and Pat McCloskey, *The Friars Minor in China (1294–1955), Especially the Years 1925–55, Based on the Research of Friars Bernard Willeke and*

Domenico Gandolfi, O.F.M. (Rome: Franciscan Institute, 1995), 11–12.

40   Also see Qin Geping, *Taiyuan jiaoqu jianshi* [A concise history of the diocese of Taiyuan] (Taiyuan: Catholic Diocese of Taiyuan, 2008), 355. Wang Tingrong is also known as Wang Ruose, or Joseph Wang.

41   Harrison, *The Missionary's Curse*, 66.

42   For a brief discussion of Frédéric-Vincent Lebbe and his legacy, see *Histoires Chinoises du Père Lebbe* (Leuven, Belgium: Secrétariat de la Jeunesse catholique chinoise, 1928).

43   See Paul Goffard and Albert Sohier, eds., *Lettres du Père Lebbe* (Paris: Tournai, 1960), 137–158. Also in Fleming, "Chosen for China," 43.

44   Silvestri, *La Testimonianza del Sangue*, 51.

45   Ibid., 51–52.

46   Ibid., 52.

47   For records, historical photographs, and transcriptions of these commemorative structures and stelae, see the collections related to the Catholic Diocese of Taiyuan at ACGOFM and TDA.

48   "Les Martyrs de Chine fêtés à Paris," *Annales des Franciscaines Missionaires de Marie* 55 (February 1947): 22.

49   Ibid.

50   Ibid., 23.

51   AFMM. Letter from Marie-Hermine de Jesus, FMM, 6 May 1900. Quoted in Georges Goyau, *Missionaries and Martyrs: Mother Mary of the Passion and the Franciscan Missionaries of Mary*, trans. George Telford (Anand, India: Anand Press, 1944), 25–26.

52   ACGOFM, letter from Théodoric Balat, OFM, 5 December 1899.

53   ACGOFM, report from Bishop Gregorio Grassi, OFM, 30 April 1897.

54   Camps and McCloskey, *The Friars Minor in China*, 27.

55   Ibid.

56   ACGOFM, letter from André Bauer, OFM, 30 May 1899.

57   Chardin, *Les missions franciscaines en Chine*, 85.

58   Camps and McCloskey, *The Friars Minor in China*, 25.

59   Today, even though this region is no longer directly affiliated with the Franciscan order, most Shanxi churches still feature statues or large paintings of Saint Francis or Saint Anthony. While, as I have already suggested, the Franciscan view of the Church Militant did not assume or promote physical conflict with the native Chinese, whom they hoped to convert to Christianity, the Ecclesia Militans view did assume an inevitable spiritual, if not cultural, antagonism with China. And, this expectation was accompanied by the anticipation of martyrdom, which could not occur without violent conflict.

60   See Ricci, *The Franciscan Martyrs of the Boxer Rising*, 13.

61   Quoted in Ricci, *The Franciscan Martyrs of the Boxer Rising* (Dublin: Franciscan Missionary Union Merchants' Quay, 1932), 10–11.

62   See *Zhongguo Tianzhujiao shouce* [Directory of the Roman Catholic Church in China] (Hebei Province: Hebei xindeshe chubanshe, 2010), 94. This handbook was

published in 2010; unofficial reports have estimated as many as ninety thousand Catholics in the Taiyuan Diocese today. For some the question remains whether this growth represents the victory of spiritual warfare, or it is facilitated by the absence of such militant rhetoric.

63   Paul Richard Bohr, *Famine in China and the Missionary: Timothy Richard as Relief Administrator and Advocate of National Reform, 1876–1884* (Cambridge, MA: East Asian Research Center, Harvard University Press, 1972), xv.

64   *North China Herald*, 24 June 1879, 619.

65   *Wanguo gongbao* [The globe magazine] (Shanghai), 28 September 1877, 94–95; modified from the translation in *Report of the Committee of the China Famine Relief Fund* (Shanghai: American Presbyterian Mission Press, 1879), 19.

66   Tianzhujiao Taiwan diqu zhujiao xuansheng weiyuanhui zhubian, eds., *Zhonghua xundao shengren zhuan* [Biographies of China's martyr saints] (Taipei: Tianzhujiao Taiwan diqu zhujiao xuan wiyuanhui, 2000), 240.

67   Ibid., 240. While not stated explicitly in current sources, Fogolla's commission to build this church may have been a gesture of thanksgiving for the end of the drought.

68   Barnabas Nanetti da Cologna, OFM, *Nel Settentrionale San-si: Diario* (Florence: Ufficio della "Rassegna Nazionale," 1903), 2. The only complete copy of this invaluable source I could find was located in the stacks of the former Jesuit library at Zikawei (Xujiahui), Shanghai. While there I was able to photograph the entire journal, which has helped to fill in the large gaps of historical narrative missing in Chinese sources. An abridgement can be found in Barnabas Nanetti da Cologna, "Nel Settentrionale San-si," in *La Rassegna Nazionale*, vol. 133, anno 25 (Florence: Presso L'Ufficio del Periodico, 1908), 86–118.

69   Nanetti da Cologna, *Nel Settentrionale San-si*, 3.

4. RED LANTERN WOMEN AND FRANCISCAN SISTERS

1   Barnabas Nanetti da Cologna, *Nel Settentrionale San-si: Diario* (Florence: Ufficio della "Rassegna Nazionale," 1903), 11.

2   For the emergence of the Red Lanterns in these areas see *Shandong yihetuan diaocha ziliao jiaoyanshi* [Research department investigative documents on the Shandong Boxers] (Jinan: Zhongguo shehui kexueyuan jindaishi yanjiusuo jindaishi ziliao bianjishi, 1980), 131–135.

3   Joseph W. Esherick, *Origins of the Boxer Uprising* (Berkeley: University of California Press, 1987), 235.

4   For an exhaustive account of Boxer violence against North Church and all of Beijing, see J. M. Planchet, *Documents sur les martyrs de Pékin pendant la persecution des Boxeurs* (Beijing: Imprimerie des Lazaristes, 1922).

5   Pierre-Marie-Alphonse Favier, *The Heart of Pekin: Bishop A. Favier's Diary of the Siege, May-August, 1900*, ed. J. Freri (Boston: Marlier, 1901), 24.

6   Arthur Judson Brown, *New Forces in Old China: An Inevitable Awakening*, 2nd ed. (New York: F. H. Fleming, 1904), 199.

7   A brief analysis of Favier's connection to the French protectorate and the siege against his cathedral in 1900 can be found in Ernest P. Young, *Ecclesiastical Colony: China's Catholic Church and the French Religious Protectorate* (Oxford: Oxford University Press, 2013), 73–77.

8   Chiang Ying-ho, "Literary Reactions to the Keng-tzu Incident (1900)" (PhD diss, University of California, Berkeley, 1982), 100.

9   Esherick, *Origins of the Boxer Uprising*, 297. See also Zhongfang, "Gengzi jishi" (Records of the Events of 1900), in *Zhongguo shehui kexueyuan jindaishi yanjiusuo jindaishi ziliao bianjishi* [Chinese Contemporary Social Science Research Institute, compiled documentary materials] (Beijing: Zhonghuashuju, 1978), 9–78.

10   Quoted in Esherick, *Origins of the Boxer Uprising*, 297.

11   For Red Lantern organizational structure see Nankai daxue lishixi, eds., "Tianjin diqu Yihetuanyundong diaocha baogao" [Investigative report on the Boxer Movement in the area of Tianjin] (Tianjin: Nankai daxue lishixi, 1956), 40–42.

12   Quoted in Paul H. Cohen, *History in Three Keys: The Boxers as Event, Experience, and Myth* (New York: Columbia University Press, 1997), 139. See Liu Mengyang, *Tianjin quanfei* [The Boxer bandits of Tianjin] (Beijing: Beijing chubanshe, 1997).

13   For a reprint of this image, see V. M. Alekseev, *Kitayskaya narodnaya kartina: Dukhovnaya zhizn' starogoKitaia v narodnykh izobrazheniyakh* [The Chinese folk picture: The spiritual life of old China in folk graphic art] (Moscow: Izdatelstvo Nauka, 1966). Another interesting early representation of a Red Lantern woman can be found in *Jing-Jin quanfei jilüe* [A concise account of the Boxer bandits of Beijing and Tianjin] (Hong Kong: Xiangang shuju, 1901). In this image the woman is similarly depicted carrying a red lantern, though she also is featured as a very frail young woman with impossibly small bound feet.

14   Zhang Deyi and Jia Lili, *Taiyuan shihua* [Concise history of Taiyuan] (Taiyuan: Shanxi renmin chubanshe, 2000), 162.

15   Liu Dapeng, *Qianyuan suoji*, in Zhang Deyi and Jia Lili, *Taiyuan shihua*, 162.

16   Liu Dapeng, *Qianyuan suoji*, in Qiao Zhiqiang, ed., *Yihetuan zai Shanxi diqu shiliao* [Historical sources on Boxers in Shanxi] (Taiyuan: Shanxi renmin chubanshe, 1980), 29–30.

17   Ibid.

18   Ibid.

19   Ibid., 29.

20   For a brief description of Guanyin, see Kevin Trainor, ed., *Buddhism* (Oxford: Oxford University Press, 2001), 136–139; and for Nüwa, see Yuan Ke, ed. *Zhongguo shenhua chuanshu cidian* [Dictionary of terms related to Chinese mythology] (Taipei: Huashi chubanshe, 1987), 26–27.

21   Liu Dapeng, *Qianyuan suoji*, in Qiao Zhiqiang, ed., *Yihetuan zai Shanxi diqu shiliao*, 29.

22   See Diana Preston, *The Boxer Rebellion: The Dramatic Story of China's War on Foreigners That Shook the World in the Summer of 1900* (New York: Walker, 2000), 107.

23   Liu Dapeng, *Qianyuan suoji*, in Qiao Zhiqiang, ed., *Yihetuan zai Shanxi diqu shiliao*, 29.

24   Ibid., 30.

25   George Lynch, *Impressions of a War Correspondent* (London: Georges Newnes, 1901), 196.

26   Liu Dapeng, *Qianyuan suoji*, in Qiao Zhiqiang, ed., *Yihetuan zai Shanxi diqu shiliao*, 29.

27   Ibid.

28   Liu Mengyang, *Tianjin quanfei*, 19–20.

29   Liu Dapeng, *Qianyuan suoji*, in Qiao Zhiqiang, ed., *Yihetuan zai Shanxi diqu shiliao*, 30.

30   Ibid.

31   John Paul II, "Mary's Enmity toward Satan Was Absolute," *L'Osservatore Romano*, 5 June 1996, 11.

32   *The Franciscan Missionaries of Mary* (London: Burns, Oates and Washbourne, 1926), 23.

33   AFMM, letter from Marie-Hermine de Jesus, FMM, 9 February 1899.

34   Ibid., 26 February 1899.

35   Ibid., 9 February 1899.

36   Quoted in *Vie de la mere Marie-Hermine de Jesus et de ses compagnes massacrees au Chan-si (Chine), le juillet 1900*, 173.

37   Departure Ceremony Sermon, quoted in ibid., 178.

38   Justina Fanego, *In Order to Give Life: A Community That Delivered Itself Up to Death*, trans. Sheila Patenaude (Clamecy, France: Nouvelle Imprimerie Laballery, 2000), 74.

39   AFMM. Letter from Maria Amandina, FMM, March 1899.

40   Ibid., 16 May 1899.

41   In *Vie de la mere Marie-Hermine de Jesus et de ses compagnes massacrees au Chan-Si (Chine), le juillet 1900*, 204.

42   Quoted in ibid., 217.

43   Giovanni Ricci, *Gigli e Rose Ossia le Sette Protomartiri dell'Instituto delle Francescane Missionarie di Maria: Massaccrate in Cina il 9 Luglio 1900* (Levanto, Italy: Tipografia dell'Immaculata, 1919), 5.

44   Robert E. Entenmann, "Christian Virgins in Eighteenth-Century Sichuan," in *Christianity in China: From the Eighteenth Century to the Present*, ed. Daniel H. Bays (Stanford, CA: Stanford University Press, 1996), 180.

45   Ricci, *Gigli e Rose*, 6.

46   Quoted in *Vie de la mere Marie-Hermine de Jesus et de ses compagnes massacrees au Chan-Si (Chine), le juillet 1900*, 246–247.

47   Ibid., 255.

48   AFMM. Letter from Marie-Hermine de Jesus, FMM, 6 September 1899.

49   AFMM. Letter from Maria Amandina, FMM, 16 May 1899.

50   Ibid.

51 Leo XIII, *Mirae Caritatis* (1902), 9.

52 Ricci, *Gigli e Rose*, 8.

53 See, for example, letter from Marie-Hermine de Jesus, FMM, in *Vie de la mere Marie-Hermine de Jesus et de ses compagnes massacrees au Chan-Si (Chine), le juillet 1900 1900*, 168.

54 AFMM. Letter from Marie-Hermine de Jesus, FMM, 9 February 1899.

55 Ibid., 1 September 1899.

56 Ibid., 24 January 1900.

57 Ibid., 10 September 1899.

58 Ibid., 6 May 1900.

59 Ibid., 25 June 1900.

60 Ibid., 25 June 1900.

61 Ibid., 24 January 1900.

62 In Ebenezer Henry Edwards, *Fire and Sword in Shansi: The Story of the Martyrdom of Foreigners and Chinese Christians* (London: Oliphant, Anderson and Ferrier, 1903), 278.

63 Ibid., 279.

64 For Giovanni Ricci's Latin translations of Governor Yuxian's edicts issued in Shanxi during the summer of 1900, see relevant passages in ASV, *Congr. Riti.*, Processus 4629. Translations of official rescripts such as these, included in the Vatican's collected materials consulted for the causes for beatification and canonization, also can be found scattered throughout the Vatican's other materials. See, for example, ASV, *Congr. Riti.*, Processus 4623 and 4628. The ASV documents are voluminous—several thousands of pages in handwritten ecclesial Latin—and present a daunting task to any scholar attempting to make use of these important narratives, interrogations, and notices.

65 The implication of this line is vague but may suggest the avoidance of conversion to Christianity.

66 ACGOFM, Yuxian Decree, 5 July 1900. Archibald Glover's memoirs include an edict, which he dates to 25 June 1900, also written by Governor Yuxian: "Foreign religions are reckless and oppressive, disrespectful to the gods and oppressive to the people. The 'Righteous People' [viz., the Boxers] will burn and kill. Your judgments from Heaven are about to come. Turn from the false and revert to the true. Is it not benevolence to exhort you people of the Christian religion? Therefore be quick and reform. If you do your duty, you are good people. If you do not repent, there will be no opportunity for second thoughts. For this purpose is this proclamation put forth. Let all comply with it." *A Thousand Miles of Miracle in China: A Personal Record of God's Delivering Power from the Hands of the Imperial Boxers of Shan-si* (London: Pickering and Inglis, 1904), 21.

67 Mother Marie-Hermine, writing in May, appeared suspicious about the veracity of the rumors circulating about the destruction of railways and churches, and the potential of violence against the Franciscan mission in Shanxi: "We do not know what is truth in all these stories, however, we are worried about nothing." There was no way of predicting in advance how quickly things would change for the

seven sisters, both in the weather and in the severity of social unrest that spread through northern China as quickly as the rains fell to earth. AFMM. Letter from Marie-Hermine de Jesus, FMM, 20 May 1900.

5. FRIARS, MAGISTRATES, AND THE FISTS OF RIGHTEOUS HARMONY

1   In *Vie de la mere Marie-Hermine de Jesus et de ses compagnes massacrees au Chan-Si (Chine), le juillet 1900*, 306.

2   In Fortunato Margiotti, *Il Cattolicismo nello Shansi dalle Origini al 1738* (Rome: Edizioni "Sinica Franciscana," 1958), 594–596.

3   Ibid., 594. I have modified Margiotti's Italian translation of this edict based on the original Chinese version.

4   In Zhang Deyi and Jia Lili, *Taiyuan shihua* [Concise history of Taiyuan] (Taiyuan: Shanxi renmin chubanshe, 2000), 162.

5   Li Di [Li Wenyu], *Quanhuoji* [Record of Boxer calamities] (Shanghai: Shanghai tushanwan yinshuguan, 1909), 332.

6   Ibid., 333.

7   Ibid.

8   Qin Geping, *Taiyuan jiaoqu jianshi* [A concise history of the diocese of Taiyuan] (Taiyuan: Catholic Diocese of Taiyuan, 2008), 322.

9   See Li Di, *Quanhuoji*, 333.

10   See ibid., 334; and Zhang Deyi and Jia Lili, *Taiyuan shihua*, 162.

11   ACGOFM, Yuxian Decree, 12 July 1900.

12   Liu Dapeng, *Qianyuan suoji*, in Qiao Zhiqiang, ed., *Yihetuan zai Shanxi diqu shiliao* [Historical sources on Boxers in Shanxi] (Taiyuan: Shanxi renmin chubanshe, 1980), 31. While there were examples of Western political and economic designs on China, it appears that these rumors of a collaborative missionary-native Christian insurgence in Shanxi were contrived to support Yuxian's aspiration to eradicate foreigners and Christianity in his jurisdiction.

13   In Ebenezer Henry Edwards, *Fire and Sword in Shansi: The Story of the Martyrdom of Foreigners and Chinese Christians* (London: Oliphant, Anderson and Ferrier, 1903), 50.

14   In ibid., 51.

15   Paul A. Cohen, "Christian Missions and Their Impact to 1900," in *The Cambridge History of China*, ed. John King Fairbank (London: Cambridge University Press, 1978), vol. 10, pt. 1, p. 543.

16   *The Roman Martyrology*, trans. Raphael Collins (Fitzwilliam, NH: Loreto, 2000), 272–273. Originally published in 1749.

17   Li Di, *Quanhuoji*, 333.

18   Pierre-Marie-Alphonse Favier, *The Heart of Pekin: Bishop A. Favier's Diary of the Siege, May-August, 1900*, ed. J. Freri (Boston: Marlier, 1901), 52.

19   In Henry Mazeau, *The Heroine of Pe-Tang: Hélène de Jaurias, Sister of Charity (1824–1900)*, trans. by an Ursuline, Grandniece of Hélène de Jaurias (New York: Benziger Brothers, 1928), 221.

20   In ibid., 51.

21   Pierre-Xavier Mertens, *The Yellow River Runs Red: A Story of Modern Chinese Martyrs*, trans. C. C. Martindale from the French, *Du sang chrétien sur le fleuve juane* (Saint Louis, MO: B. Herder, 1936; repr., trans. Beryl Pearson, Saint Louis, MO: B. Herder, 1939), 32.

22   Ibid., 31. Also see Anthony E. Clark, *China's Saints: Catholic Martyrdom during the Qing (1644–1911)* (Bethlehem, PA: Lehigh University Press; Lanham. MD: Rowman and Littlefield, 2011), 102–110.

23   See R. G. Tiedemann, "The Church Militant: Armed Conflicts between Christians and Boxers in North China," in *The Boxers, China, and the World*, ed. Robert Bickers and R. G. Tiedemann (Lanham, MD: Rowman and Littlefield, 2007), 28–29.

24   Li Di, *Quanhuoji*, 333.

25   For transcriptions of the commemorative stelae produced and preserved at Guchengying, on which the Boxer attacks on the village are narrated, see TDA, Guchengying Stelae Transcriptions, Guangxu 34th Reign Year (1908); also see Qin Geping, *Taiyuan jiaoqu jianshi*, 341–345. For the Vatican's record of the Guchengying incident see ASV, *Congr. Riti.*, Processus 4623, vol. 5, which contains 321 pages of detailed information. Guchengying is transliterated in the Processus as "Ku-tcen-in," and the document outlines the circumstances of the martyrdoms of 129 Christians. These materials were compiled and recorded by Barnabas Nanetti da Cologna, Francesco Saccani, and Giovanni Ricci at Dongergou village.

26   During the exhaustive process of gathering testimonies regarding the lives and deaths of candidates for beatification or canonization, Ricci and his confreres conducting the interviews required each witness to sign a sworn deposition attesting to the veracity of their claims. These sworn depositions were imposed upon both Christians and non-Christians and were checked against each other to corroborate the accounts of Catholic witnesses against those of nonbelievers. The depositions were signed by the witness and included in both Chinese and Latin a cautionary phrase saying that those who perjure will suffer "automatic excommunication by the Supreme Pontiff" (*excommunicationis latae sentae a qua nonnisi a Summo Pontifice),* which can be absolved by sacramental confession "only at the moment of death" (*praeterquam in mortis articulo absolve possim*). For the original deposition see ASV, *Congr. Riti.*, Processus 4629, 17–30, "Formula juramenti testis." These depositions include the original names of the Chinese witnesses providing testimonies, though the handwritten text of these transcriptions is in some areas unclear. For other examples of depositions that are typeset, and thus easier to decipher, see ASV, *Congr. Riti.*, Processus 4629, 44–46.

27   ACGOFM, letter from Father Antonio, OFM, to Giovanni Ricci, OFM, 3 January 1907. In Giovanni Ricci, *Barbarie e trionfi ossia le vittime illustri del San-Si in Cina nella persecuzione del 1900*, 2nd ed. (Florence: Tipografia Barbera, 1909), 613.

28   Ma Jianzhong, *Strengthen the Country and Enrich the People: The Reform Writings of Ma Jianzhong, 1845–1900*, trans. Paul John Bailey (Richmond, Surrey, U.K.: Curzon, 1998), 58. Ma Jianzhong was the younger brother of the famous former-Jesuit

and founder of Fudan University, Ma Xiangbo (1840–1939), who was a popular activist and supporter of China's national identity and self-strengthening movements.

29   Ibid., 58.

30   Wilbur J. Chamberlain and Georgia Louise Chamberlain, *Ordered to China: Letters of Wilbur J. Chamberlain, Written from China While under Commission from the New York "Sun" during the Boxer Uprising of 1900 and the International Complications Which Followed* (New York: Frederick A. Stokes, 1903), 43. David Silbey describes this scenario well: "The railway, modern and efficient, was reshaping the Chinese economy and violently displacing thousands, if not millions, from their livelihoods." *The Boxer Rebellion and the Great Game in China* (New York: Hill and Wang, 2012), 39.

31   AFMM. Letters from Marie-Hermine de Jesus, FMM, 20 May and 6 June 1900, respectively.

32   Ibid., 6 June 1900. Without knowing why, she had correctly combined these two Chinese perceptions: the railroad lines, which had disrupted the flow of qi and had angered China's gods, were cut to restore qi, mollify the gods, and relieve the drought.

33   AFMM. Letter from Marie-Hermine de Jesus, FMM, 25 June 1900.

34   Ibid., 6 June 1900.

35   Ricci, *Barbarie e trionfi*, 600. Details regarding the precise date and time of the Franciscans' arrest vary. July 2 is sometimes mentioned as the date of arrest, and 4 o'clock in the afternoon has been noted as the time they were escorted to "Pig-Head Alley." See for example, Georges Goyau, *Missionaries and Martyrs: Mother Mary of the Passion and the Franciscan Missionaries of Mary*, trans. George Telford (Anand, India: Anand Press, 1944), 35; and Tianzhujiao Taiwan diqu zhujiao xuansheng weiyuanhui zhubian, eds., *Zhonghua xundao shengren zhuan* [Biographies of China's martyr saints] (Taipei: Tianzhujiao Taiwan diqu zhujiao xuan wiyuanhui, 2000), 230. Giovanni Ricci's account, which is set on 5 July 1900, is the most likely, especially as the commemorative inscription installed at Pig-Head Alley in 1901 read: "Qui omnes die 5 Iulii anni 1900—Huc insidiose traducli—Per quatuordies ibidem—Detenli sunt." Unfortunately this inscription, as well as nearly all of the commemorative stelae related to the Boxer Uprising in Shanxi, was destroyed during the Cultural Revolution between 1966 and 1967. See *Barbarie e trionfi*, 601.

36   Ricci, *Barbarie e trionfi*, 600.

37   Tianzhujiao Taiwan diqu zhujiao xuansheng weiyuanhui zhubian, eds., *Zhonghua xundao shengren zhuan*, 230. Also see Ricci, *Barbarie e trionfi*, 599.

38   Li Di, *Quanhuoji*, 334.

39   Ricci, *Barbarie e trionfi*, 602.

40   Ibid. Also see Nat Brandt, *Massacre in Shansi* (Syracuse, NY: Syracuse University Press, 1994), 228. Near the end of Archibald Glover's account of his family's escape from Shanxi, he also notes the renewed showers. "Never have I seen such rain. All

day and far into the night it poured and poured." *A Thousand Miles of Miracle in China: A Personal Record of God's Delivering Power from the Hands of the Imperial Boxers of Shan-si* (London: Pickering and Inglis, 1904), 146.

41   In Ricci, *Barbarie e trionfi*, 604.

42   Giovanni Ricci, *Gigli e Rose Ossia le Sette Protomartiri dell'Instituto delle Francescane Missionarie di Maria: Massaccrate in Cina il 9 Luglio 1900* (Levanto, Italy: Tipografia dell'Immaculata, 1919), 87–88.

43   ASV, *Congr. Riti.*, Processus 4623, p. 258.

44   The most extensive collection of materials on the Sino-Missionary conflicts in Shanxi during the Boxer Uprising is held in the Vatican's Secret Archives (ASV); one of the more exhaustive sources in this repository is ASV, *Congr. Riti.*, Processus 4623, consisting of six volumes (six handwritten codices in one folio). The first volume, titled "Transumptum Processus Apostolici Servorum Dei Episcopi Gregorii Grassi et loc.," contains introductory materials pertaining to the European and native Chinese martyrs attached to the Franciscan mission in Shanxi. For accounts of predominantly Chinese martyrs of Shanxi in 1900, see ASV, *Congr. Riti.*, Processus 4624, which consists of a single codex.

45   See Ricci, *Barbarie e trionfi*, 610.

46   See ibid., 611.

47   Ricci, *Gigli e Rose*, 88.

48   For narrative descriptions and witness testimonies see ASV, *Congr. Riti.*, Processus 4623–4624, 4627–4629, and 4434–4435, passim.

49   Brandt, *Massacre in Shansi*, 229.

50   Ricci, *Barbarie e trionfi*, 618.

51   Edwards notes that the Protestants "appear to have made no resistance—as indeed it would have been useless." *Fire and Sword in Shansi*, 72.

52   Tianzhujiao Taiwan diqu zhujiao xuansheng weiyuanhui zhubian, eds., *Zhonghua xundao shengren zhuan*, 230.

53   Liu Dapeng, *Qianyuan suoji*, in Qiao Zhiqiang, ed., *Yihetuan zai Shanxi diqu shiliao*, 31–32.

54   Ibid., 32.

55   UOSC, Dr. Charles F. Johnson Papers (Ax 268). Box I, Folio p. 66. Another contemporary Protestant account of the Taiyuan incident is the journal of the Shanxi missionary Eva Jane Price, which is held at the Houghton Library, Harvard University. The most relevant entry is 1 August 1900. For a published version of the journal with related photographs of the Protestant mission in Shanxi around 1900, see Eva Jane Price, *China Journal, 1889–1900: An American Missionary Family during the Boxer Rebellion* (New York: Charles Scribner's Sons, 1989).

56   UOSC, Dr. Charles F. Johnson Papers (Ax 268). Box I, Folio pp. 68–69.

57   Ricci, *Barbarie e trionfi*, 618.

58   Li Di, *Quanhuoji*, 339.

59   Barnabas Nanetti da Cologna, *Nel Settentrionale San-si: Diario* (Florence: Ufficio della "Rassegna Nazionale," 1903), 18.

60   Ibid., 20.

61   Ricci, *Gigli e Rose*, 88.

62   Li Di, *Quanhuoji*, 339.

63   Ricci, *Gigli e Rose*, 92.

64   Li Di, *Quanhuoji*, 340. The extreme violence of the Taiyuan incident described by the witnesses is unlikely to have been exaggerated. Even more frightful examples of late-Qing execution, including public slicing and the piling of dismembered bodies on streets, are discussed, accompanied by photographic images, in Timothy Brook, Jérôme Bourgon, and Gregory Blue's study of public torture and execution in China, *Death by a Thousand Cuts* (Cambridge, MA: Harvard University Press, 2008).

65   Goyau, *Missionaries and Martyrs*, 37.

66   One helpful source to compare against more hagiographical narratives of the 9 July 1900 incident is the 263-page annotated booklet of testimonies contained in the Vatican archives. See ASV, *Congr. Riti.*, Processus 4628. This source contains less-embellished narratives of the events.

67   Louis Nazaire Bégin, *Life of Mother Marie-Hermine of Jesus: Massacred in Shan-si (China) July 9th, 1900* (Quebec: Archeveque de Quebec, 1910), 62–63.

68   Jonathan Goforth, *By My Spirit* (Minneapolis: Bethany Publishing, 1964), 63.

69   Nanetti da Cologna, *Nel Settentrionale San-si*, 21.

70   See Liu Dapeng, *Qianyuan suoji*, in Qiao Zhiqiang, ed., *Yihetuan zai Shanxi diqu shiliao*, 30–33.

71   Qin Geping, *Taiyuan jiaoqu jianshi*, 320.

72   Ibid., 318.

73   Giovanni Ricci, *The Franciscan Martyrs of the Boxer Rising* (Dublin: Franciscan Missionary Union Merchants' Quay, 1932), 77.

74   Ibid.

75   Ibid.

76   Nearly all the commemorative monuments in Shanxi were destroyed during the Cultural Revolution, though some Catholic villagers were able to bury monuments before the arrival of Red Guards. Three of the four stelae at Guchengying, for example, were hidden and have been recovered in recent years, and I was able to photograph each one and transcribe its inscription. The monument at Yangjiabao was unfortunately destroyed, though photographs and detailed transcriptions of the monument are held at the Taiyuan Diocesan Archive, which is presently overseen by a priest who resides outside of China. Several of the stelae inscriptions have been published in Qin Geping's *Taiyuan jiaoqu jianshi*. The monuments at Guchengying, as of my last visit there in 2010, were being installed in a memorial pavilion next to the Catholic church.

77   TDA, Guchengying stelae inscriptions, Guangxu *Gengnian*, 1900.

78   TDA, Yangjiabao stele inscription, Guangxu *Gengnian*, 1900. Also see Qin Geping, *Taiyuan jiaoqu jianshi*, 345–348.

79   Ricci, *Franciscan Martyrs of the Boxer Rising*, 78.

80   Ibid.

81   Ibid., 79.

82   Giovanni Ricci, *Avec les Boxeurs Chinois* (Brive, France: "Échos des Grottes," 1949), 13.

83   Ban Gu, *The History of the Former Han Dynasty*, vol. 1, trans. Homer H. Dubs (Baltimore: Waverly Press, 1938), 30.

84   Ibid.

85   Sima Qian, *Shiji* (Records of the grand historian) (Beijing: Zhonghuashuju, 1982), 348. The two-millennia-old trope of paranormal emanations that denote heaven's endorsement, and similar miracles ascribed to Catholic martyrs in 1900, are too analogous to disregard.

86   Tianzhujiao Taiwan diqu zhujiao xuansheng weiyuanhui zhubian, eds., *Zhonghua xundao shengren zhuan*, 63. Also see Clark, *China's Saints*, 79.

87   G. de Montgesty [Gabriel Larigaldie], *Two Vincentian Martyrs: Blessed Francis Regis Clet, C.M., Blessed John Gabriel Perboyre, C. M.*, trans. Florence Gilmore (Maryknoll, NY: Catholic Foreign Mission Society of America, 1925), 176.

88   In Qin Geping, *Taiyuan jiaoqu jianshi*, 321.

89   Ricci, *Gigli e Rose*, 92.

90   Ibid., 94.

91   Ricci, *Avec les Boxeurs Chinois*, 20.

92   Ibid., 21.

93   The Eight Allied Armies, or "Eight-Nation Alliance," included Japan, Germany, Russia, France, the United Kingdom, the United States, Austria-Hungary, and Italy.

94   Qin Geping, *Taiyuan jiaoqu jianshi*, 312.

6. REVENGE AND RECONSTRUCTION

1   J. O. P. Bland and E. Backhouse, *China under the Empress Dowager: Being the History of the Life and Times of Tzu Hsi* (Philadelphia: J. B. Lippincott, 1910), 349.

2   Huang Zheng, ed., *Taiyuan shigao* [Draft history of Taiyuan] (Taiyuan: Shanxi renmin chubanshe, 2003), 423.

3   Ibid., 424.

4   Ibid.

5   Shen Tun-ho [Shen Dunhe], *Recollections of a Chinese Official: With Some Sidelights on Recent History* (Shanghai: North-China Herald, 1903), 26.

6   Huang Zheng, *Taiyuan shigao*, 424.

7   Qin Geping, *Taiyuan jiaoqu jianshi* [A concise history of the diocese of Taiyuan] (Taiyuan: Catholic Diocese of Taiyuan, 2008), 323.

8   Ibid.

9   Huang Zheng, *Taiyuan shigao*, 424.

10   Manfred Görtemaker, *Deutschland im 19. Jahrhundert: Entwicklungslinien* (Opladen, Germany: Leske and Budrich, 1996), 367. The last line of this speech is now infamous, but Kaiser Wilhelm II was already known for his anti-Asianism years before he uttered these words. During the first half-century following the Boxer Uprising, Western views of China were decidedly pejorative. Western representations of China before the Boxer era, however, vacillated between naive

adulation, such as the idyllic depictions of the Chinese "philosopher king" and the caricatured Chinese beauties in European chinoiserie popularized in mid-to-late-seventeenth-century Europe, and the occasional imaginings of the "Yellow Peril," a phrase coined, regrettably, by Kaiser Wilhelm in 1895. For an example of late-nine-teenth-century uses of that term, see G. G. Rupert, *The Yellow Peril* (Britton, UK: Union Publishing, 1911); Kaiser Wilhelm's use of this term is mentioned on p. 9.

11   In Roger Thomson, "Military Dimensions of the 'Boxer Uprising' in Shanxi Prov-
     ince," in *Warfare in Chinese History*, ed. Hans J. Van de Ven (Leiden, Netherlands:
     Brill, 2000), 313.

12   Ibid., 131.

13   Amar Singh et al., *Reversing the Gaze: Amar Singh's Diary, a Colonial Subject's
     Narrative of Imperial India* (Boulder, CO: Westview Press, 2002), 130.

14   Ibid.

15   See Hans J. Van de Ven, "Robert Hart and Gustav Detring during the Boxer Rebel-
     lion," *Modern Asian Studies* 40, no. 3 (2006): 631–662.

16   David Silbey, *The Boxer Rebellion and the Great Game in China* (New York: Hill
     and Wang, 2012), 231.

17   Zhang Deyi and Jia Lili, *Taiyuan shihua* [Concise history of Taiyuan] (Taiyuan:
     Shanxi renmin chubanshe, 2000), 165.

18   Ibid. For another account of the coal disputes in Shanxi during the late Qing see
     Huang Zheng, *Taiyuan shigao*, 425–427.

19   Zhang Deyi and Jia Lili, *Taiyuan shihua*, 165.

20   Ibid., 166.

21   Ibid.

22   Ibid., 165.

23   Peter Fleming, "Chosen for China: The California Province Jesuits in China
     1928–1957; A Case Study in Mission and Culture" (PhD diss., Graduate Theological
     Union, Berkeley, CA, 1987), 206.

24   Donald L. Horowitz describes this well: "The fundamental premise of colonial
     rule was the felt unfitness of the ruled to manage their own affairs. In the colonial
     situation, no group, whatever its imputed characteristics or its manifest behavior,
     was permitted to approach the European balance of virtues, lest it imperil the
     European right to rule. Even the more advanced ethnic groups among the colo-
     nized peoples were denigrated. Their perceived industriousness and adaptability
     met with colonial approval at one level, since they served colonial purposes. But
     on another it was simultaneously thought that such groups were too aggressive
     or acquisitive." *Ethnic Groups in Conflict* (Berkeley: University of California Press,
     1985), 160.

25   Fleming, "Chosen for China," 207.

26   In ibid.

27   W. R. Jones, "The Image of the Barbarian in Medieval Europe," *Comparative Stud-
     ies in Society and History* 13 (1971): 377–407.

28   R. G. Tiedemann, "Christianity in a Violent Environment: The North China
     Plain on the Eve of the Boxer Uprising," in *Historiography of the Chinese Catholic*

Church: Nineteenth and Twentieth Centuries, ed. Jérôme Heyndrickx (Leuven, Belgium: Ferdinand Verbiest Foundation, 1994), 140.

29   Pascal M. D'Elia, *Catholic Native Episcopacy in China: Being an Outline of the Formation and Growth of the Chinese Catholic Clergy 1300–1926* (Shanghai: T'usewei Printing Press, 1927), 82.

30   Ibid., 83.

31   The seminarian's name was Zhang Yao. See Liu Anrong, *Shanxi Tianzhujiao shi yanjiu (1620–1949)* [Historical research on Roman Catholicism in Shanxi] (Taiyuan: Beiyue wenyi chubanshe, 2011), 65–66.

32   Qin Geping, *Taiyuan jiaoqu jianshi*, 33.

33   D'Elia, *Catholic Native Episcopacy in China*, 87.

34   *L'Osservatore Romano*, 22 September 1926.

35   D'Elia, *Catholic Native Episcopacy in China*, 91.

36   Fleming, "Chosen for China," 214.

37   Ricci, *The Franciscan Martyrs of the Boxer Rising* (Dublin: Franciscan Missionary Union Merchants' Quay, 1932), 118.

38   Giovanni Ricci, *Vicariatus Taiyuanfu seu Brevis Historia Antiquae Franciscanae Missionis Shansi et Shensi a sua Origine ad Dies Nostros (1700–1928)* (Beijing: Congregationis Missionis, 1929), 120. Ricci notes that Yuxian had given or sold orphan girls to some twenty Qing officials, from whom the Franciscans were unable to retrieve the orphans (120).

39   Shen Tun-ho, *Recollections of a Chinese Official*, 20.

40   Ibid., 20–21.

41   Ebenezer Henry Edwards, *Fire and Sword in Shansi: The Story of the Martyrdom of Foreigners and Chinese Christians* (London: Oliphant, Anderson and Ferrier, 1903), 175.

42   Shen Tun-ho, *Recollections of a Chinese Official*, 20.

43   Ibid.

44   Ricci, *Vicariatus Taiyuanfu*, 120.

45   When Fiorentini first arrived at Taiyuan, there remained only seven European and fourteen native Chinese priests to serve the entire vicariate. The interim administrator of the mission's affairs was Barnabas Nanetti da Cologna, who had written an anxious letter to von Waldersee the previous year requesting a "strong army" to come to Taiyuan to protect the Catholics from ongoing dangers in Shanxi. Fiorentini was confronted with tremendous uncertainty when he began his episcopal duties in Taiyuan. For da Cologna's letter to von Waldersee, see Edwards, *Fire and Sword in Shansi*, 167–168.

46   Arthur Sowerby, *North China Herald* (February), quoted in Edwards, *Fire and Sword in Shansi*, 170–171.

47   Edwards, *Fire and Sword in Shansi*, 169.

48   Ricci, *Vicariatus Taiyuanfu*, 122.

49   Ibid.

50   Ibid. Also see Qin Geping, *Taiyuan jiaoqu jianshi*, 29.

51   Qin Geping, *Taiyuan jiaoqu jianshi*, 98.

52 Li Yuzhang and Li Yuming, *Shanxisheng Taiyuanshi Tianzhujiao baizhounian tekan* [One hundred years of Shanxi Province Taiyuan Catholicism commemorative issue] (Taiyuan: Budefanyin, 2006), 126. The first group of Franciscan Missionaries of Mary sisters to serve in Taiyuan were the seven who were executed in 1900; the second group arrived in Taiyuan in 1902.

53 Ibid. This underground tunnel is still extant in Taiyuan; the property is presently used by a state-owned medical facility.

54 Ibid., 131.

55 Ibid.

56 For materials related to Hao Nai, see TDA and Qin Geping, *Taiyuan jiaoqu jianshi*, 34–35.

57 TDA, "Shanxi Boxer Era Rhyme." Also see Qin Geping, *Taiyuan jiaoqu jianshi*, 322.

58 Although this stele is mentioned in several sources, including Edwards, *Fire and Sword in Shanxi*, 117, and Shen Tun-ho, *Recollections of a Chinese Official*, 26, the complete narrative of the monument is no longer known.

59 Shen Tun-ho, *Recollections of a Chinese Official*, 26.

60 AFMM, "Proclamation by Cen Chunxuan at Taiyuan, Shanxi," 1901.

61 Ibid.

62 See Edwards, *Fire and Sword in Shanxi*, 132, and Shen Tun-ho, *Recollections of a Chinese Official*. 26.

63 AFMM, "Proclamation by Cen Chunxuan at Taiyuan, Shanxi," 1901.

64 Qin Geping, *Taiyuan jiaoqu jianshi*, 325. Also see Ricci, *Franciscan Martyrs of the Boxer Rising*, 28–31.

65 Ricci, *Franciscan Martyrs of the Boxer Rising*, 30; and Qin Geping, *Taiyuan jiaoqu jianshi*, 326.

66 Qin Geping, *Taiyuan jiaoqu jianshi*, 326. Also see Ricci, *Franciscan Martyrs of the Boxer Rising*, 30.

67 Qin Geping, *Taiyuan jiaoqu jianshi*, 326.

68 Ibid.

69 Ricci, *Franciscan Martyrs of the Boxer Rising*, 31.

GLOSSARY OF CHINESE CHARACTERS

Baiyi　白衣

Ban Gu　班固

Baolian　寶蓮

Beige　北格

Beijing　北京

Beijing Tianzhujiao shi 北京天主教史

Beimen Dongtoudao　北門東頭道

Beitang　北堂

Budeyi　不得已

Caozhou　曹洲

Cen Chunxuan　岑春煊

Cheng Hede　成和德

Chen Guodi　陳國砥

Cheng Xiao　程嘯

Chiang Kai-shek　(Jiang Jieshi) 蔣介石

Chong Qi　崇綺

Chuanjiaoshi yu jindai Zhongguo　傳教
　士與近代中國

Cixi　慈禧

Dabeimen　大北門

Damo (Bodhidharma)　達摩

dao qiang bu ru　刀槍不入

Da Qing lichao shilu　大清歷朝實錄

Datong　大同

Da Yingguo　大英國

dingwu qihuang　丁戊奇荒

Dongergou　洞兒溝

Dong Fuxiang　董福祥

Dongtang　東堂

Duan　端

duan chuan yihequan shenhui　端傳義
　和拳神會

En Hai　恩海

ermaozi　二毛子

Fengshenghe　風聲河

Fengtai　豐台

Fujian　福建

Fu Qing mieyang　扶清滅洋

Fuxi　伏羲

Fuzhou　福州

gege　哥哥

Geliaogou　圪瞭溝

Gengzi　庚子

"Gengzi jishi"　庚子記

Guan　關

Guandong　廣東

Guangxu　光緒

[177]

Guangxu sannian 光緒三年

Guanyin 觀音

Gu Changsheng 顧長聲

Guchengying 古城營

Gugong bowuyuan Ming Qing danganbu 故宮博物院檔案部：義和團檔案史料

Gugong bowuyuan Ming Qing danganbu: Yihetuan dang'an shiliao 故宮博物院檔案部：義和團檔案史料

Guo Qizi 郭七子

Guozijian 國子監

Han 漢

Han Feizi 韓非子

Hanhua 漢化

Hankou 漢口

Hanlin 翰林

Hao Nai 郝鼐

Haotian 昊天

Hebei 河北

Heiyi 黑衣

Henan qihuang tieleitu 河南奇荒鐵淚圖

He Zongxun 何宗遜

hongdengzhao 紅燈照

hongdou 紅豆

Huangyecun 黃冶村

Huang Zheng 黃征

Hu Handu 許涵度

Huibao 會報

huizhang 會長

Hu Xingyuan 胡興元

Jia Lili 賈莉莉

Jia Luosa 賈羅撒

Jiangzhou 絳州

jiaoren 教人

Jiaowu jiaoan dang 教務教案檔

jiatangye 家堂爺

Jinci 晉祠

Jinci zhi 晉祠誌

Jing-Jin quanfei jilüe 京津拳匪紀略

Jingxian 涇縣

"Jinshi chuqi Zhongguo minju dui xifang xuanjiao shengxianghua de fanying" 僅是初期中國民聚對西方宣教聖像畫的反應

Jinzhong 金鐘

jizhe 笄者

Kangxi 康熙

Ke Xuebin 柯學斌

Kong Xiangxi 孔祥熙

Lanzhou 蘭州

li 里

Liangquandao 梁泉道

libai 禮拜

Li Bingheng 李秉衡

Li Di 李杕 (Li Wenyu 李問漁)

Li Hongzhang 李鴻章

Lingde 令德

Li Renkai 黎仁凱

Li Shiheng 李士恒

Liu Anrong 劉安榮

Liu Bang 劉邦

Liu Dapeng 劉大鵬

Liu E 劉鶚

Liuhe 六合

Liu Mengyang 劉孟揚

Liyuantun 梨園屯

Li Yuming 李毓明

Li Yuzhang 李毓章

Luanfu 潞安府

Lu Jingqi 陸景琪

Luo Guanzhong 羅貫中

Lü Shiqiang   呂實強

Ma Jianzhong   馬建忠
"Maliya fangji chuanjiao xiuhui zai Hua
    zhi chuanjiao shiye"   瑪利亞方濟會
    在華之傳教事業
maodun   矛盾
Mao Zedong   毛澤東
maozi   毛子
Ma Xiangbo   馬相伯
Menggaoweinuo zongxiuyuan   孟高維
    諾總修院
mixin   迷信

Nanchengjiao   南城角
Nanjing   南京
Nankai daxue lishixi   南開大學歷史系
Nantang   南堂
Nüwa   女媧

Pingding   平定
Pingyang   平陽

qi   氣
Qianyuan suoji   潛園瑣記
Qiao Zhiqiang   喬志強
Qin   秦
Qing   清
Qin Geping   秦格平
Qingshigao   清史稿
*Qing zhongqianqi Xiyang Tianzhujiao zai
    Hua huodong dang'an shiliao*   清中
    前期西洋天主教在華活動檔案史料
Qin Shihuangdi   秦始皇帝
Qi yu jin Zhi zhenjuan zhengxin lu   齊豫
    晉直賑捐微信錄
Quanhuoji   拳禍記

Ren Yanli   任延黎
Ruan Xiumei   阮羞美

Sanguo yanyi   三國演義
Sanxian   三賢
Shaanxi   陝西
Shandong   山東
*Shandong yihetuan diaocha ziliao jiao-
    yanshi*   山東義和團調查資料教研室
Shanghai   上海
Shangyingcun   上營村
Shanxi   山西
*Shanxisheng Taiyuanshi Tianzhujiao
    baizhounian tekan*   山西省太原市天
    主教百週年特刊
Shanxisheng yanjiuzhongxin   山西省研
    究中心
Shanxi Tianzhujiao shi yanjiu   山西天主
    教史研究
Shanxi Tianzhujiao zhi rongguan   山西
    天主教之榮冠
Shanxi tongzhi   山西通志
Shaseng   沙僧
sha sha shao shao   殺殺燒燒
Shengmu   聖母
Shengmuhui   聖母會
Shiji   史記
Shuiliaotai   水鐐臺
Sima Qian   司馬遷
Si sheng gao zai tu qi   四省告災圖啟
Sunzi   孫子

Taibei (Taipei)   台北
Taiyuan   太原
Taiyuanfu   太原府
Taiyuan jiaoqu jianshi   太原教區簡史
Taiyuan shigao   太原史稿
Taiyuan shihua   太原史話

Tangseng　唐僧

Taohuawu　桃花塢

Tiancun　田村

Tianjin　天津

"Tianjin diqu Yihetuanyundong diaocha baogao"　天津地區義和團運動調查報告

Tianjin quanfei　天津拳匪

Tianzhujiao　天主教

Tianzhujiao Taiwan diqu zhujiao xuansheng weiyuanhui zhubian　天主教台灣地區主教宣聖委員會主編

Tianzhujiao zaoqi chuanru Zhongguo shihua　天主教早期傳入中國史話

Tianzhutang　天主堂

tingzi　亭子

Tongzhou　同洲

Tuixiangzhai riji　退想齋日記

Wang Jingshan　王靜山

Wang Shujie　王書偕

Wang Tingrong　王挺榮

Wanguo gongbao　萬國公報

Wangxia　望廈

Wenshui　文水

Wuchang　武昌

Wukong　悟空

Xi'an　西安

Xiaodian　小店

xiaoshennü　小神女

xiaoshun　孝順

xiaoshuo　小說

Xiaozhan　小站

Xie Jiafu　謝家福

Xijiacun　西家村

Xin Bozhi　辛伯植

Xiru ermu zi　西儒耳目子

Xishiku　西什庫

Xiyouji　西遊記

Xu Guangqi　徐光啓

Xu Tong　徐桐

Yang Guangxian　楊光先

Yangjiabao　楊家堡

Yang Jingjun　楊靖筠

Yan Liang　顏良

Yasongda zouguo de lu qianbei fuwu　雅松達走過的路謙卑服務

Ye Chuandao　葉傳導

Ye Mingchen　葉名琛

Yihequan　義和拳

Yihetuan　義和團

Yihetuan yuanliu shiliao　義和團源流史料

Yihetuan yundong　義和團運動

Yihetuan zai Shanxi diqu shiliao　義和團在山西地區史料

yin　隱

yingshen saihui　迎神賽會

Yonghegong　雍和宮

Yongzheng　雍正

Yu　孟

Yuan　元

Yuan Ke　袁珂

Yuci　榆次

Yu gaoge zhu : Wang (Leisi) Shiwei shengping xiaoji　獄高歌主：王（類思）世偉生平小記

Yu Liang　瑜亮

Yuxian　毓賢

Ze　澤

Zhang Deyi　張德一

Zhang Xin　張信

Zhao Yuqian　趙毓謙

Zhili　直隸

Zhili yihetuan diaocha ziliao xuan-
　　bian　直隸義和團調查資料選編

Zhongfang　仲芳

Zhongguo diyi lishi danganguan　中國第
　　一歷史檔案館

Zhongguo fengsuhua　中國風俗化

Zhongguo guanshen fanjiao de yuanyin
　　(1860–1874)　中國官紳反教的原因
　　(一八六令至一八七四)

Zhongguo shehui kexueyuan jindaishi
　　yanjiusuo jindaishi ziliao bianjishi
　　中國社會科學院近代史研究所近代史
　　資料編輯室

Zhongguo shenhua chuanshuo cidian
　　中國神話傳說辭典

Zhongguo Tianzhujiao: Jichu zhishi　中國
　　天主教：基礎知識

Zhongguo Tianzhujiao qiji xin jia-
　　onan　中國天主教及其新教難

Zhongguo Tianzhujiao shouce　中國天
　　主教手冊

Zhonghua xundao shengren zhuan　中華
　　殉道聖人傳

zhongjun　中軍

zhonglou　鐘樓

Zhongyang yanjiuyuan jindaishi yanjiu-
　　suo　中央研究院近代史研究所

Zhou Cang　周倉

Zhubajie　豬八戒

Zhujiahe　朱家河

Zhutouxiang　豬頭巷

zixin　自新

Zongli Yamen　總理衙門

BIBLIOGRAPHY

ACGOFM (Archivio Curia Generalizia Ordo Fratrum Minorum), *Sinae 1870–1904; Sinae 1897–99*, vol. 11, SK551; *Sinae 1900–03*, vol. 12, SK552; SM/219, 64; SM/219, 75.

Alekseev, V. M. *Kitayskaya narodnaya kartina: Dukhovnaya zhizn' starogoKitaia v narodnykh izobrazheniyakh* [The Chinese folk picture: The spiritual life of old China in folk graphic art]. Moscow: Izdatelstvo Nauka, 1966.

Anderson, Benedict. *Imagined Communities: Reflections on the Origin and Spread of Nationalism.* New York: Verso, 1991.

Armstrong, Regis J., J. A. Wayne Hellmann, and William J. Short. *Francis of Assisi: Early Documents.* Vol. 1. New York: New City Press, 1999.

ASV (Archivio Segreto Vaticano), *Congr. Riti.*, Processus 4623–4624; *Congr. Riti.*, Processus 4627–4629; *Congr. Riti.*, Processus 4434–4435.

Atlas hierarchicus: Descriptio geographica et statistica Sanctae Romanae Ecclesiae. Paderborn, Germany: Saint Boniface Press, 1929.

Aumasson, Théobald. *La croix sur la pagode: Le B* Théodoric Balat et ses compagnons martyrs.* 2nd ed. Brive, France: Editions Echo des Grottes, 1947.

Austin, Alvyn. *China's Millions: The China Inland Mission and Late Qing Society, 1832–1905.* Grand Rapids, MI: William B. Eerdmans, 2007.

Ball, Ann. *A Litany of Saints.* Huntington, IN: Our Sunday Visitor, 1993.

Ballaster, Ros. *Fabulous Orients: Fictions of the East in England, 1662–1785.* Oxford: Oxford University Press, 2005.

Ban Gu. *The History of the Former Han Dynasty.* Vol. 1. Translated by Homer H. Dubs. Baltimore: Waverly Press, 1938.

Barnes, A. A. S. *On Active Service with the Chinese Regiment: A Record of Operations of the First Chinese Regiment in North China from March to October 1900.* London: Grant Richards, 1902.

Bays, Daniel H., ed. *Christianity in China: From the Eighteenth Century to the Present.* Stanford, CA: Stanford University Press, 1996.

———. *A New History of Christianity in China.* Malden, MA: Wiley-Blackwell, 2012.

Beals, Z. Chas. *China and the Boxers: A Short History on the Boxer Outbreak, with Two Chapters on the Sufferings of Missionaries and a Closing One on the Outlook.* New York: M. E. Munson, 1901.

Bégin, Louis Nazaire. *Life of Mother Marie-Hermine of Jesus: Massacred in Shan-si (China) July 9th, 1900.* Quebec: Archeveque de Quebec, 1910.

Benedict XIV. "De servorum Dei beatificatione et Beatorum canonizatione." *Prato* 1839–1841, Lib. III.

———. "Letter to Bishops, Priests, Consecrated Persons and Lay Faithful of the Catholic Church in the People's Republic of China." *Homily on the Mount of the Beatitudes* (Israel, 24 March 2000), 5. Published in *L'Osservatore Romano,* English edition, 29 March 2000.

Bernard, Henri. *La découverte de nestoriens mongols aux ordos et l'histoire ancienne du christianisme en extreme-orient.* Tientsin, China: Hautes etudes, 1935.

Bickers, Robert, and R. G. Tiedemann, eds. *The Boxers, China, and the World.* Lanham, MD: Rowman and Littlefield, 2007.

Biografia del P. Guiseppe Maria Gambaro di Galliate (Novara): Morto per la fede in Cina nella persecuzione del 1900 assieme a un numero raccolte dal P. Giovanni Ricci. Rome: Collegio S. Antonio, 1912.

Bland, J. O. P., and E. Backhouse. *China under the Empress Dowager: Being the History of the Life and Times of Tzu Hsi.* Philadelphia: J. B. Lippincott, 1910.

Blarer, M. T. de. *La bienheureuse Marie Hermine de Jésus et ses compagnes, franciscaines missionnaires de marie, massacres le 9 juillet 1900 a Tai-yuan-fou (Chine).* Vanves, France: n.p., 1947.

Bohr, Paul Richard. *Famine in China and the Missionary: Timothy Richard as Relief Administrator and Advocate of National Reform, 1876–1884.* Cambridge, MA: East Asian Research Center, Harvard University Press, 1972.

Borao, José Eugenio, ed. *Spaniards in Taiwan.* Vol. 2. Taipei: SMC, 2001.

Bornemann, Fritz. *As Wine Poured Out: Blessed Joseph Freinademetz, SVD: Missionary in China, 1879–1908.* Rome: Divine Word Missionaries, 1984.

Borst-Smith, Ernest F. *Caught in the Chinese Revolution: A Record of Risks and Rescue.* London: T. Fisher Unwin, 1912.

Bosshardt, R. A. *The Restraining Hand: Captivity for Christ in China.* London: Hodder and Stoughton, 1936.

The Boxer Rising: A History of the Boxer Trouble in China. 2nd ed. Shanghai: Shanghai Mercury, 1901.

Brandt, Joseph van den. *Les Lazaristes en Chine, 1697–1935*. Beijing: Notices Bibliographiques, 1936.

Brandt, Nat. *Massacre in Shansi*. Syracuse, NY: Syracuse University Press, 1994.

Brockey, Liam Matthew. *Journey to the East: The Jesuit Mission to China, 1579–1724*. Cambridge, MA: Harvard University Press, 2007.

Brook, Timothy, Jérôme Bourgon, and Gregory Blue. *Death by a Thousand Cuts*. Cambridge, MA: Harvard University Press, 2008.

Broomhall, Marshall, ed. *Martyred Missionaries of the China Inland Mission*. London: Morgan and Scott, 1901.

Brown, Arthur Judson. *New Forces in Old China: An Inevitable Awakening*. 2nd ed. New York: F. H. Fleming, 1904.

Budge, S. E. Wallis. *The Monks of Kublai Khan, Emperor of China*. London: Religious Tract Society, 1928.

Bulfoni, Clara, and Anna Pozzi. *Lost China: The Photographs of Leone Nani*. Milan: Skira, 2003.

Bulletin of the Catholic University of Peking (Archabbey Press, Beatty, PA), no. 1 (September 1926).

Bulletin of the Catholic University of Peking (Archabbey Press, Latrobe, PA), no. 6 (July 1920).

Bureaux de l'oeuvre de al sainte-enfance. *Le bienheureux Paul Tchen, premier martyr de la Ste-enfance*. Paris: Bureaux de L'œvre de la Sainte-Enfance, 1927.

Butler, Alban. *Lives of the Saints*. 4 vols. Norwalk, CT: Easton Press, 1995. Original edition printed in 1756–1759.

Caballero, Antonio de Santa Maria. "Respuesta a un papel que an sacado contra los religiosos de la Orden de Santo Domingo y de S. Francesco de la Mission de China, los Reverendos Padres de la Compañía de aquel Reyno, o el Procurador de dhas. Provincias y Missiones en su nombre, llamado Bartolome Roboredo, que reside en el Colegio de la Compañía de esta ciudad de Manilla." Ms., Archivio de la Provincia del Santo Rosario [Archives of the Dominican Province of the Holy Rosary], Manila and Avila. *Ritos Chinois*, vol. 70: ff. 507–568; copy vol. 67: ff. 79–138.

Cameron, Nigel. *Barbarians and Mandarins: Thirteen Centuries of Western Travelers in China*. New York: John Weatherhill, 1970.

Camps, Arnulf, and Pat McCloskey. *The Friars Minor in China (1294–1955), Especially the Years 1925–55, Based on the Research of Friars Bernard Willeke and Domenico Gandolfi, O.F.M.* Rome: Franciscan Institute, 1995.

Cary-Elwes, Columba. *China and the Cross: Studies in Missionary History*. London: Longmans, Green, 1957.

Casserly, Gordon. *The Land of the Boxers, or China under the Allies*. New York: Longmans, Green, 1903.

Castel, E. *Rose of China (Marie-Therese Wang), 1917–1932*. Translated by Basil Stegmann. New York: Benziger Brothers, 1934.

Cavalli, Teofilo. *I Figli della Lotta: B. Gregorio Grasso, B. Francesco Fogolla, B. Elia Facchina, Francescani*. Milan: Instituto di Propaganda Libraria, 1946.

Cerasa, Nicola. *Breve storia della missione di Taiyuan Shansi Cina*. Rome: Provincia Romana dei Frati Minori, 1988.

Chaigneau, Placide. *Aller simple pour la Chine: Lettres de Placide Chaigneau, missionaire vendéen (1865–1897)*. La Roche-sur-Yon, France: Centre Vendéen de Recherches Historiques, 2001.

Chamberlain, Wilber J., and Georgia Louise Chamberlain. *Ordered to China: Letters of Wilber J. Chamberlain, Written from China While under Commission from the New York "Sun" during the Boxer Uprising of 1900 and the International Complications Which Followed*. New York: Frederick A. Stokes, 1903.

Chang Hsin-pao. *Commissioner Lin and the Opium War*. Cambridge, MA: Harvard University Press, 1964.

Chang, Mark K. *A Historical Sketch of the Catholic Church in China*. Tainan, Taiwan: Window Press, 1986.

Charbonnier, Jean-Pierre. *Christians in China, A.D. 600–2000*. Translated by M. N. L. Couve de Murville. San Francisco: Ignatius Press, 2007. Originally published as *Histoire des Chrétiens de Chine*. Paris: Les Indes Savantes, 2002.

———. *Les 120 Martyrs de Chine: Canonisés le 1er Octobre 2000*. Paris: Églises D'Asie, 2000.

Chardin, Pacifique-Marie. *Les missions franciscaines en Chine: Notes géographiques et historiques*. Paris: Auguste Picard, 1915.

Chesneaux, Jean, ed. *Popular Movements and Secret Societies in China, 1840–1950*. Stanford, CA: Stanford University Press, 1972.

Chiang Ying-ho. "Literary Reactions to the Keng-tzu Incident (1900)." PhD diss., University of California, Berkeley, 1982.

Chine et Ceylan. Abbeville, France: Imprimerie C. Paillart, 1898–1902.

Chine et Ceylan: Lettres des Missionaires de la Compagnie de Jésus: Notices sur les Martyrs du Tche-li Sud-Est. Abbeville, France: Imprimerie C. Paillart, 1901.

Chine, Ceylan, Madagascar: Lettres des Missionnaires Francais de la Compagnie de Jesus, Province de Champagne. 12 (March–June 1903).

The Chinese Church as Revealed in the National Christian Conference Held in Shanghai, Tuesday, May 2, to Thursday, May 11, 1922. Shanghai: Oriental Press, 1922.

Christian, George G. *SS. Augustine Zhao Rong and Companions: Martyrs of China.* New York: Dominican Friars, Province of Saint Joseph, 2005.

Chung, Mary Keng Mun, ed. *Beating Devils and Burning Their Books: Views of China, Japan, and the West.* Ann Arbor, MI: Association for Asian Studies, 2010.

Chung, Mary Keng Mun. *Chinese Women in Christian Ministry: An Intercultural Study.* New York: Peter Lang, 2005.

Clark, Anthony E. *China's Saints: Catholic Martyrdom during the Qing (1644–1911).* Bethlehem, PA: Lehigh University Press; Lanham, MD: Rowman and Littlefield, 2011.

———. "Early Modern Chinese Reactions to Western Missionary Iconography." *Southeast Review of Asian Studies* 30 (2008): 5–22.

———. *A Voluntary Exile: Chinese Christianity and Cultural Confluence since 1552.* Bethlehem, PA: Lehigh University Press; Lanham, MD: Rowman and Littlefield, 2014.

Clark, Francis X. *Asian Saints: The 486 Catholic Canonized Saints and Blesseds of Asia.* 2nd ed. Quezon City, Philippines: Claretian Communications, 2000.

Clements, Paul H. *The Boxer Rebellion: A Political and Diplomatic Review.* New York: Columbia University, 1915.

Cohen, Paul H. *China and Christianity: The Missionary Movement and the Growth of Chinese Antiforeignism, 1860–1870.* Cambridge, MA: Harvard University Press, 1963.

———. *History in Three Keys: The Boxers as Event, Experience, and Myth.* New York: Columbia University Press, 1997.

Coltman, Robert, Jr. *Beleaguered in Beijing: The Boxer's War against the Foreigner.* Philadelphia: F. A. Davis, 1901.

Compte, Louis le. *Un Jésuit à Pékin: Nouveaux mémoires sur l'état présent de la Chine 1687–1692.* Paris: Phébus, 1990.

Conger, Sarah Pike. *Letters from China: With Particular Reference to the Empress Dowager and the Women of China.* Chicago: A. C. McClurge, 1909.

Cordara, Giulio Cesare. *On the Suppression of the Society of Jesus: A Contemporary Account.* Translated by John P. Murphey. Chicago: Loyola Press, 1999.

Cracco, Amedeo. *La prefettura apostolica di Sanyuan, Cina-Shensi.* Sanyuan, China: Tung-yuan-fang, 1933.

Criveller, Gianni. *The Martyrdom of Alberico Crescitelli: Its Context and Controversy.* Hong Kong: Holy Spirit Study Centre, 2004.

———. *Preaching Christ in Late Ming China: The Jesuits' Presentation of Christ from Matteo Ricci to Giulio Aleni.* Taipei: Ricci Institute, 1997.

Cronin, Vincent. *The Wise Man from the West*. London: Harvill Press, 1999.

Crossley, Pamela Kyle. *The Manchus*. Cambridge, MA: Blackwell, 1997.

Crouch, Archie R. *Rising through the Dust: The Story of the Christian Church in China*. New York: Friendship Press, 1948.

Cuenot, Joseph. *Kwangsi: Land of the Black Banners*. London: B. Herder, 1942.

Da Qing lichao shilu (Veritable records of successive reigns of the Great Qing). Xinjing: Da Manzhou Diguo Guowuyuan, 1937. Reprint, Beijing: Zhonghuashuju, 1986–1987.

Dawson, Christopher. *Mission to Asia*. Toronto: University of Toronto Press, 1998.

———. *The Mongol Mission: Narratives of the Franciscan Missionaries in Mongolia and China in the Thirteenth and Fourteenth Centuries*. London: Sheed and Ward, 1955.

Dean, William. *The China Mission: Embracing a History of the Various Missions of All Denominations among the Chinese*. New York: Sheldon, 1859.

Dease, Alice. *Bluegowns: A Golden Treasury of Tales of the China Missions*. Maryknoll, NY: Catholic Foreign Missions Society, 1927.

Dehergne, Joseph. *Répertoire des Jésuites de Chine de 1552 à 1800*. Rome: Institutum Historicum Societas Iesu, 1973.

D'Elia, Pascal M. *The Catholic Missions in China: A Short Sketch of the History of the Catholic Church in China from the Earliest Records to Our Own Days*. Shanghai: Commercial Press, 1934.

———. *Catholic Native Episcopacy in China: Being an Outline of the Formation and Growth of the Chinese Catholic Clergy 1300–1926*. Shanghai: T'usewei Printing Press, 1927.

Devine, W. *The Four Churches of Peking*. London: Burns, Oates and Washbourne, 1930.

Donovan, John F. *The Pagoda and the Cross: The Life of Bishop Ford of Maryknoll*. New York: Charles Scribner's Sons, 1967.

Ducourneau, Jean-Yves. "'To the Extremes of Love': Francis Regis Clet (1748–1820), Priest of the Congregation of the Mission, Martyr in China." Translated by John Rybolt. *Vincentiana*, www.vincentiana.famvin.org.

Dufresse, Gabriel-Taurin. Letter. October 26, 1800. In *Nouvelles lettres édifiantes*. Vol. 3. Paris: Société des Missions Étrangères de Paris.

Duiker, William J. *Cultures in Collision: The Boxer Rebellion*. San Rafael, CA: Presidio Press, 1978.

Dujardin, Carine. *Missionering en Moderniteit: De Belgische Mindbroeders in China, 1872–1940*. Leuven, Belgium: Leuven University Press, 1996.

Dunch, Ryan. *Fuzhou Protestants and the Making of a Modern China, 1857–1927*. New Haven, CT: Yale University Press, 2002.

Dunne, George H. *Generation of Giants: The Story of the Jesuits in China in the Last Decades of the Ming Dynasty*. London: Burns and Oates, 1962.

Edgerton-Tarpley, Kathryn. *Tears from Iron: Cultural Responses to Famine in Nineteenth-Century China*. Berkeley: University of California Press, 2008.

Edwards, Ebenezer Henry. *Fire and Sword in Shansi: The Story of the Martyrdom of Foreigners and Chinese Christians*. London: Oliphant, Anderson and Ferrier, 1903.

Elliot, Jane E. *Some Did It for Civilisation, Some Did It for Their Country: A Revised View of the Boxer War*. Hong Kong: Chinese University of Hong Kong, 2002.

Elman, Benjamin A. *On Their Own Terms: Science in China, 1550–1900*. New Haven, CT: Yale University Press, 2001.

Esherick, Joseph W. *The Origins of the Boxer Uprising*. Berkeley: University of California Press, 1987.

Fairbank, John King, ed. *The Cambridge History of China*. Vol. 10, part 1. London: Cambridge University Press, 1978.

Fanego, Justina. *In Order to Give Life: A Community That Delivered Itself Up to Death*. Translated by Sheila Patenaude. Clamecy, France: Nouvelle Imprimerie Laballery, 2000.

Favier, Pierre-Marie-Alphonse. *The Heart of Pekin: Bishop A. Favier's Diary of the Siege, May-August, 1900*. Edited by J. Freri. Boston: Marlier, 1901.

———. *Péking, histoire et description*. Lille, France: Desclée de Brouwer, 1900.

Fazzini, Gerolamo. *The Red Book of Chinese Martyrs*. San Francisco: Ignatius Press, 2009.

Federici, Emidio. *Beata Maria Assunta (Pallotta): Francescana Missionaria di Maria (1875–1905)*. Rome: Francescane Missionarie di Maria, 1954.

Fernandez, Pablo. *One Hundred Years of Dominican Apostolate in Formosa (1859–1958)*. 1959. Reprint, Taipei: SMC, 1994.

Fernando, Leonardo, ed. *Seeking New Horizons: Festschrift in Honor of Dr. M. Amaladoss, SJ*. Delhi: Vidyajyoti, 2002.

Fleming, Peter. "Chosen for China: The California Province Jesuits in China 1928–1957; A Case Study in Mission and Culture." PhD diss., Graduate Theological Union, Berkeley, CA, 1987.

Fleming, Peter S. *The Siege at Peking*. Hong Kong: Oxford University Press, 1983.

Foccroulle, Luc, et al. *Tonnerre en Chine: Vincent Lebbe*. Taipei: Kuangchi Press, 1997.

Fogolla, Francesco. *La Muraglia Cinese Relazione Crito-Scientifics Illustrata*. Turin: Tipografia G. Lerossi, 1898.

Forrest, R. J. "Report of R. J. Forrest, Esq., H. B. M. Consul at Tien-tsin, and Chairman of the Famine Relief Committee at Tien-tsin." *China's Millions* (November 1879): 134–139.

Forsyth, Robert Coventry. *The China Martyrs of 1900: A Complete Roll of the Christian Heroes Martyred in China in 1900, with Narratives of Survivors*. London: Religious Tract Society, 1904.

Foster, L. S. *Fifty Years in China: An Eventful Memoir of Tarleton Perry Crawford, D.D.* Nashville: Bayless-Pullen, 1909.

Four Jesuits Martyred in China in the 20th Century. Taipei: Taiwan Roman Catholic Bishops Committee, 2000.

The Franciscan Missionaries of Mary. London: Burns, Oates and Washbourne, 1926.

Francis of Assisi and Clare of Assisi. *Francis and Clare: The Complete Works*. Translated by Regis J. Armstrong, OFM Cap., and Ignatius C. Brady. New York: Paulist Press 1982.

Fülöp-Miller, René. *Macht und Geheimnis der Jesuiten*. 1891. Reprint, Leipzig: Grethlein, 1929.

Gabet, Le R. P. *Les missions catholiques en chine en 1846: Coup d'œil sur l'état des missions de chine présenté au saint-père le pape pie IX*. 1848. Reprint, Paris: Valmonde Édition, 2006.

Gandolfi, Domenico. "Cenni di Storia del vicariato apostolico di Taiyuanfu Shansi, Cina 1930–1952." *Studi Francescani* 84 (1987): 299–360.

Gascoyne-Cecil, William. *Changing China*. London: James Nisbet, 1910.

Gasperetti, Elio. *In God's Hands: The Life of Blessed Alberic Crescitelli of the Missionaries of Saints Peter and Paul, P.I.M.E.* Detroit: Missionaries of Saints Peter and Paul, 1955.

Gernet, Jacques. *China and the Christian Impact*. Translated by Janet Lloyd. Cambridge: Cambridge University Press, 1985. Originally published in French as *Chine et christianisme*. Paris: Editions Gallimard, 1982.

Ghellinck, Joseph de. *Les Franciscains en Chine Aux XIIIe–XIVe Siècles (Ambassadeurs et Missionaires)*. 2 vols. Leuven, Belgium: Xaveriana, 1927.

Ghéon, Henri. *Les Trois Sagesses du Vieux Wang: Drame chinois en quatre tableaux*. Paris: André Blot, 1927.

Giles, Brother. *Yentou New Year: A Life of Brother Benedict Jensen, Franciscan Missionary in China*. Oakland, CA: Franciscan Fathers, 1959.

Giles, Lancelot. *The Siege of the Peking Legations: A Diary*. Nedlands: University of Western Australia Press, 1970.

Gillman, Ian, and Hans-Joachim Klimkeit. *Christians in Asia before 1500*. Ann Arbor: University of Michigan Press, 1999.

Gilson, Charles. *The Lost Column: A Story of the Boxer Rebellion in China*. 1910. Reprint, London: Oxford University Press, 1924.

Girardot, Norman J. *The Victorian Translation of China: James Legge's Oriental Pilgrimage*. Berkeley: University of California Press, 2002.

Glorie Serafiche: Cenni Biografici Dei Ven. Servi di Dio, Mons. Gregorio Grassi, Mons. Francesco Fogolla, Padre Elia Facchini. Parma: Premiate Tipografie Riunite Donati, 1927.

Glover, Archibald E. *A Thousand Miles of Miracle: The Tragic True Story of Persecution during the Boxer Rebellion in China*. 1904. Reprint, Station Approach, UK: OMF Publishing, 2000.

Gobien, Charles le. *Histoire de l'édit de l'empereur de la Chine en faveur de la religion chrétienne: Avec un éclaircissement sur les honneurs que les chinois rendent à Confucius et aux morts*. Paris: Anisson, 1698.

Goffard, Paul, and Albert Sohier, eds. *Lettres du Père Lebbe*. Paris: Tournai, 1960.

Goforth, Jonathan. *By My Spirit*. Minneapolis: Bethany Publishing, 1964.

Golvers, Noël, ed. *The Christian Mission in China in the Verbiest Era: Some Aspects of the Missionary Approach*. Leuven, Belgium: Ferdinand Verbiest Foundation, 1999.

Görtemaker, Manfred. *Deutschland im 19. Jahrhundert: Entwicklungslinien*. Opladen, Germany: Leske and Budrich, 1996.

Goyau, Georges. *Missionaries and Martyrs: Mother Mary of the Passion and the Franciscan Missionaries of Mary*. Translated by George Telford. Anand, India: Anand Press, 1944.

Gray, Jack. *Rebellions and Revolutions: China from the 1800s to 2000*. 2nd ed. Oxford: Oxford University Press, 2002.

Gray, John Henry. *China: A History of the Laws, Manners and Customs of the People*. Mineola, NY: Dover, 2002.

Greenberg, Michael. *British Trade and the Opening of China, 1800–1842*. Cambridge: Cambridge University Press, 1951.

Guadalupi, Gianni. *China through the Eyes of the West: From Marco Polo to the Last Emperor*. Vercelli, Italy: White Star, 2004.

Gu Changsheng. *Chuanjiaoshi yu jindai zhongguo* [Missionaries and modern China]. Shanghai: Shanghai renmin chubanshe, 2004.

Gugong bowuyuan Ming Qing danganbu: Yihetuan dang'an shiliao [Forbidden City Museum Archives: Society of Righteous Harmony Archive Historical Materials]. Beijing: Zhonghuashuju, 1959.

Guiness [Taylor], Geraldine. *One of China's Scholars: The Culture and Conversion of a Confucianist.* London: Morgan and Scott, 1900.

Gunn, Geoffrey C. *First Globalization: The Eurasian Exchange, 1500–1800.* Lanham, MD: Rowman and Littlefield, 2003.

Habig, Marion A. *In Journeyings Often: Franciscan Pioneers in the Orient.* New York: Franciscan Institute, 1953.

———. *Pioneering in China: The Story of the Rev. Francis Xavier Engbring, O.F.M.: First Native American Priest in China, 1857–1895.* Chicago: Franciscan Herald Press, 1930.

Hacker, Arthur. *China Illustrated: Western Views of the Middle Kingdom.* Hong Kong: Tuttle, 2004.

Hagspiel, Bruno. *Along the Mission Trail.* Vol. 4, *In China.* Techny, Illinois: Mission Press, S.V.D., 1927.

Hanson, Eric O. *Catholic Politics in China and Korea.* Maryknoll, NY: Orbis Books, 1980.

Harrison, Henrietta. *The Man Awakened from Dreams: One Man's Life in a North China Village, 1857–1942.* Stanford, CA: Stanford University Press, 2005.

———. *The Missionary's Curse and Other Tales from a Chinese Catholic Village.* Berkeley: University of California Press, 2013.

———. "Rethinking Missionaries and Medicine in China: The Miracles of Assunta Pallotta, 1905–2005." *Journal of Asian Studies* 71, no. 1 (February 2012): 127–148.

Hartwich, Richard. *Steyler Missionare in China II. Bichof A. Henninghaus ruft Steyler Missionsschwestern, 1904–1910.* Rome: Apud Collegium Verbi Divini, 1985.

Hattaway, Paul. *China's Book of Martyrs (AD 814–Present).* Carlisle, U.K.: Piquant Editions, 2007.

———. *China's Christian Martyrs.* Grand Rapids, MI: Monarch Books, 2007.

Hauptmann, Georges. "François Joseph Meistermann, 1850–1923: Barnabé d'Alsace, Franciscain O.F.M.—Missionaire apostolique Archéologue— architecte/ bâtisseur—écrivain—Historien de la Terre Sainte" (unpublished manuscript, 2008.

Hay, Malcolm. *Failure in the Far East: Why and How the Breach between the Western World and China First Began.* London: Neville Spearman, 1956.

Headland, Isaac Taylor. *Chinese Heroes: Being a Record of Persecutions Endured by Native Christians in the Boxer Uprising.* New York: Eaton and Mains, 1902.

Hefley, James C., and Marti Hefley. *China: Christian Martyrs of the 20th Century.* Milford, MI: Mott Media, 1978.

Hefner, Robert, ed. *Conversion to Christianity: Historical and Anthropological Perspectives on a Great Transformation.* Berkeley: University of California Press, 1993.

Henry, B. C. *The Cross and the Dragon; or, Light in the Broad East.* New York: Anson D. F. Randolph, 1885.

Henry, Léone. *Le Siège du Pé-t'ang dans Pékin en 1900: Le Commandant Paul Henry et ses trente Marins.* Beijing: Des Lazaristes du Pé-t'ang, 1910.

Henty, G. A. *With the Allies to Pekin: A Tale of the Relief of the Legations.* New York: Charles Scribner's Sons, 1903.

Hewlett, W. Meyrick. *The Siege of the Legations: June to August, 1900.* London: Pewtress, 1900.

Heyndrickx, Jérôme. *Historiography of the Chinese Catholic Church: Nineteenth and Twentieth Centuries.* Leuven, Belgium: Ferdinand Verbiest Foundation, 1994.

———. *Philippe Couplet, S.J. (1623–1693): The Man Who Brought China to Europe.* Nettetal, Germany: Steyler Verlag, 1990.

Hibbert, Christopher. *The Dragon Wakes: China and the West, 1793–1911.* Newton Abbot, U.K.: Readers Union, 1971.

Hillgarth, J. N., ed. *Christianity and Paganism, 350–750.* Philadelphia: University of Pennsylvania Press, 1986.

Histoires Chinoises du Père Lebbe. Leuven, Belgium: Secrétariat de la Jeunesse catholique chinoise, 1928.

Hollweck, P. Joseph. *Joseph Freinademetz: Ein Leben im Dienst der Menschen Chinas.* Nettetal, Germany: Steyler Verlag, 2003.

Hooker, Mary. *Behind the Scenes in Peking: Being Experiences during the Siege of the Legations.* London: John Murray, 1910.

Horowitz, Donald L. *Ethnic Groups in Conflict.* Berkeley: University of California Press, 1985.

Hsiang, Paul Stanislaus. *The Catholic Missions in China during the Middle Ages (1294–1368).* Cleveland: John T. Zubal, 1984. First produced as a dissertation at Catholic University of America, 1949.

Huang Zheng, ed. *Taiyuan shigao* (Draft history of Taiyuan). Taiyuan: Shanxi renmin chubanshe, 2003.

Huber, Mary Taylor, and Nancy C. Lutkehaus, eds. *Gendered Missions: Women and Men in Missionary Discourse and Practice.* Ann Arbor: University of Michigan Press, 1999.

Huber, Raphael M. *A Documented History of the Franciscan Order: From the Birth of Saint Francis to the Division of the Order under Leo X, 1182–1517.* Milwaukee, WI: Nowiny Publishing, 1944.

Hubrecht, Alph. *Les martyrs des Tientsin (21 Juin 1870).* Beijing: Imprimeries des Lazaristes, 1928.

Hummel, Arthur W., ed. *Eminent Chinese of the Ch'ing Period.* Vol. 1. 1943. Reprint, Taipei: SMC, 1991.

Hunter, Alan, and Kim-Kwong Chan. *Protestantism in Contemporary China.* Cambridge: Cambridge University Press, 1993.

Hunter, Jane. *The Gospel of Gentility: American Women Missionaries in Turn-of-the-Century China.* New Haven, CT: Yale University Press, 1984.

Iriarte, Lazaro. *Franciscan History: The Three Orders of Saint Francis of Assisi.* Chicago: Franciscan Herald Press, 1982.

Isoré, Remi. "La chrétienté de Tchao-kia-tchoang sur le pied de guerre (Journal du P. Isoré)." *Chine et Ceylon* 1, no. 2 (April 1899).

Jami, Catherine, and Hubert Delahaye, eds. *L'Europe en Chine: Interactions scientifiques, religieuses et culturelles aux XVIIe et XVIIIe siècles.* Paris: Collège de France, Institut des Hautes Etudes Chinoises, 1993.

Jedin, Hubert, ed. *History of the Church.* Vol. 10. New York: Crossroads, 1981.

Jenkins, Robert C. *The Jesuits in China and the Legation of Cardinal de Tournon.* London: David Nutt, 1894.

Jensen, Lionel M. *Manufacturing Confucianism: Chinese Traditions and Universal Civilization.* Durham, NC: Duke University Press, 1997.

Jing-Jin quanfei jilüe [A concise account of the Boxer bandits of Beijing and Tianjin]. Hong Kong: Xiangang shuju, 1901.

Jing Shan. *The Diary of His Excellency Ching-Shan: Being a Chinese Account of the Boxer Troubles.* Translated by J. J. L. Duyvendak. Leiden, Netherlands: Brill, 1924.

John Paul II. "Cappella Papale for the Canonization of 123 New Saints." Homily of John Paul II (Sunday, 1 October 2000).

———. "Homily for the Canonization of Saint John Gabriel Perboyre. " Translated by Stanislaus Brindley. *Vincentiana,* www.vincentiana.famvin.org.

———. "Mary's Enmity toward Satan Was Absolute." *L'Osservatore Romano,* 5 June 1996.

———. "Pope's Homily at the Mass of Beatification of Salesian Martyrs on Sunday, 15 May." *L'Osservatore Romano,* 23 May 1983.

———. *Tertio Millennio Adveniente.* 10 November 1994.

Jones, W. R. "The Image of the Barbarian in Medieval Europe." *Comparative Studies in Society and History* 13 (1971): 377–407.

Journal de la Mission du Koúy-tchou (Chine). Paris: n.p., 1861–1862.

Kearney, James F. *The Four Horsemen Ride Again*. Shanghai: T'ou-sè-wè, 1940.

Kelly, John S. *A Forgotten Conference: The Negotiations at Peking, 1900–1901*. Paris: Librarie Minard, 1963.

Kemp, E. G. *Reminiscences of a Sister: S. Florence Edwards of Taiyuanfu*. London: Carey Press, 1919.

Keown-Boyd, Henry. *The Boxer Rebellion*. New York: Dorset, 1991.

———. *The Fists of Righteous Harmony: A History of the Boxer Uprising in China in the Year 1900*. London: Leo Cooper, 1991.

Kerval, Léon de. *Deux Martyrs Français de l'Ordre des Frères Mineurs: Le R. P. Théodoric Balat et le Fr. André Bauer, Massacrés en Chine le 9 Juillet 1900*. 2nd ed. Paris: Prime, 1906.

———. *Le R. P. Hugolin de Doullens ou le vie d'un Frère Mineur Missionnaire en Chine aux XIXe siècle*. Vanves, France: Imprimerie Franciscaine Missionaire, 1902.

———. *Le R. P. Théodoric Balat et le Fr. Andre Bauer, massacres en Chine le 9 Juillet 1900: Apercus biographiques*. Paris: Vic et Amat, 1903.

Ketler, Isaac C. *The Tragedy of Paotingfu: An Authentic Story of the Lives, Services and Sacrifices of the Presbyterian, Congregational and China Inland Missionaries Who Suffered Martyrdom at Paotingfu, China, June 30th and July 1, 1900*. New York: Fleming H. Revell, 1902.

Ke Xuebin (Anthony E. Clark). "Jinshi chuqi Zhongguo minju dui xifang xuanjiao shengxianghua de fanying" [Initial Chinese reactions to missionary propaganda in images]. *Guoji Hanxue* 30 (2011).

Kindopp, Jason, and Carol Lee Hamrin, eds. *God and Caesar in China: Policy Implications of Church-State Tensions*. Washington, DC: Brookings Institution Press, 2004.

Kohr, H. O. *The Escort of an Emperor: A Story of China during the Great Boxer Movement*. N.p.: H. O. Kohr, 1910.

Kuhn, Philip A. *Rebellion and Its Enemies in Late Imperial China: Militarization and Social Structure, 1796–1864*. Cambridge, MA: Harvard University Press, 1970.

Ku Wei-ying and Koen De Ridder. *Authentic Chinese Christianity: Preludes to its Development (Nineteenth and Twentieth Centuries)*. Leuven Chinese Studies IX. Leuven, Belgium: Leuven University Press, 2001.

Ladany, Laszlo. *The Catholic Church in China*. New York: Freedom House, 1987.

Lagerwey, John, ed. *Religion and Chinese Society*. Vol. 2, *Taoism and Local Religion in Modern China*. Hong Kong: Chinese University Press, 2004.

Laitinen, Kauko. *Chinese Nationalism in the Late Qing Dynasty: Zhang Binglin as an Anti-Manchu Propagandist.* London: Curzon Press, 1990.

Lander, Arnold Henry Savage. *China and the Allies.* 2 vols. New York: Charles Scribner's Sons, 1901.

Lang, Vitalis. *Das Apostolische Vikariat Tsinanfu: Franziskanische Missionsarbeit in China.* Werl, Germany: Provinzial-Missionsverwaltung, 1929.

Lanzi, Luigi. *Francesco Fogolla: Apostoli in Cina.* Parma: Convento SS. Annunziata, 1997.

———. *Francesco Fogolla: Missionario e Martire.* Parma: Edito dai Frati Minori, 1996.

Latourette, Kenneth Scott. *A History of Christianity.* Vol. 2. New York: HarperCollins, 1981.

———. *A History of Christian Missions in China.* 1929. Reprint, New York: Russell and Russell, 1967.

Launay, Adrien. *Histoire des Missions de Chine: Mission du Kouy-Tcheou.* 3 vols. Paris: Societe des Missions-Etrangeres, 1907, 1908.

———. *Les Cinquante-Deux Serviteurs de Dieu Français, Annamites, Chinois, Mis à Mort pour la Foi en Extrême Orient de 1815–1856.* Paris: Societe des Missions-Etrangeres, 1893.

Launay, Marcel. *Hélène de Chappotin et les Franciscaines de Marie.* Paris: Les Éditions du Cerf, 2001.

Lavin, Paul, and Robert Lavin. *The Iron Man of China: An American Missionary's Story.* Fitzwilliam, NH: Loreto, 2005.

Lazich, Michael C. *E. C. Bridgman (1801–1861), America's First Missionary to China.* Lewiston, NY: Edwin Mellon Press, 2000.

Le avventure di un missionarie in Cina: Memorie di Mons. Luigi Moccogatta, O.F.M.; raccolte per cura del P. Giovanni Ricci, O.F.M. Modena, Italy: Arcivescovile, 1909.

Leclercq, Jaques. *"Église Vivant" Vie du Père Lebbe: Le Tonnerre qui chante au loin.* Paris: Casterman, 1955.

———. *Thunder in the Distance: The Life of Père Lebbe.* Translated by George Lamb. New York: Sheed and Ward, 1958.

Legge, James. *Christianity in China: Nestorianism, Roman Catholicism, Protestantism.* London: Trübner, 1888.

———. *The Nestorian Monument of Hsi-an Fu.* London: Trübner, 1888.

Leo XIII. *Mirae Caritatis* (1902).

Lernoux, Penny, Arthur Jones, and Robert Ellsberg. *Hearts on Fire: The Story of the Maryknoll Sisters.* Maryknoll, NY: Orbis Books, 1993.

Leroy, Henri-Joseph. *En Chine au Tché-Ly S. E.* Paris: Desclée de Brouwer, 1900.

"Les Martyrs de Chine fêtés à Paris." *Annales des Franciscaines Missionaires de Marie* 55 (February 1947): 22.

Lettres édifiantes et curieuses écrites des missions étrangères par quelques missionaires de la Compagnie de Jésus. 32 vols. Paris: n.p., 1717–1774.

Leung, Beatrice. *Sino-Vatican Relations: Problems in Conflicting Authority, 1976–1986.* Cambridge: Cambridge University Press, 1992.

Leung, Beatrice, and Shun-hing Chan. *Changing Church and State Relations in Hong Kong, 1950–2000.* Hong Kong: Hong Kong University Press, 2003.

Leung, Beatrice, and William T. Liu. *The Chinese Catholic Church in Conflict: 1949–2001.* Boca Raton, FL: Universal, 2004.

Leung, Beatrice, and John D. Young. *Christianity in China: Foundations for Dialogue.* Hong Kong: Centre of Asian Studies, University of Hong Kong, 1993.

Levaux, Léopold. *Le Père Lebbe: Apôtre de la Chine modern (1877–1940).* Brussels: Éditions Universitaires, 1948.

Li Di [Li Wenyu]. *Quanhuoji* [Record of Boxer calamities]. Shanghai: Shanghai tushanwan yinshuguan, 1909.

Life of Blessed John Gabriel Perboyre, Priest of the Congregation of the Mission, Martyred in China, September 11th, 1840. Baltimore: John Murphy, 1894.

Li Renkai, ed. *Zhili yihetuan diaocha ziliao xuanbian* [A material investigation into selected documentary excerpts related to the Zhili Yihetuan]. Shijiazhuang, China: Hebei jiaoyu chubanshe, 2001.

Liu Anrong. *Shanxi Tianzhujiao shi yanjiu (1620–1949)* [Historical research on Roman Catholicism in Shanxi]. Taiyuan: Beiyue wenyi chubanshe, 2011.

Liu Dapeng. *Jinci zhi* [Jinci Temple gazetteer]. In *Yihetuan zai Shanxi diqu shiliao* [Historical sources on Boxers in Shanxi], ed. Qiao Zhiqiang. Taiyuan: Shanxi renmin chubanshe, 1980.

———. *Tuixiangzhai riji* [Diary of ponderings from a retirement chamber]. Edited by Qiao Zhiqiang. Taiyuan: Shanxi renmin chubanshe, 1990.

Liu Kwang-Ching, ed. *Orthodoxy in Late Imperial China.* Berkeley: University of California Press, 1990.

Liu Mengyang. *Tianjin quanfei* [The Boxer bandits of Tianjin]. Beijing: Beijing chubanshe, 1997.

Li Yuzhang and Li Yuming. *Shanxisheng Taiyuanshi Tianzhujiao baizhounian tekan* [One hundred years of Shanxi Province Taiyuan Catholicism commemorative issue]. Taiyuan: Budefanyin, 2006.

Lombardi, Teodosio. *Une Grande Ideale: Monsignor Ermengildo Focaccia, O.F.M. Vescovo di Yütze in China.* Bologna: Edizioni Antoniano, 1968.

Lopez, Donald S., Jr., ed. *Religions of China in Practice*. Princeton, NJ: Princeton University Press, 1996.

Loppinot, Comtesse de. *Soeur Marie-Assunta Franciscaine Missionaire de Marie*. Vanves, France: Imprimerie Franciscaine Missionaire, 1924.

L'Osservatore Romano (22 September 1926), no. 21 (23 May 1983), no. 27 (8 July 1991), no. 40 (4 October 2000).

Loti, Pierre. *Les Derniers Jours de Pékin*. Paris: Calmann Lévy, 1900.

Loup, Robert. *Martyr in Tibet: The Heroic Life and Death of Father Maurice Torney, Saint Bernard Missionary to Tibet*. Translated by Charles Davenport. New York: David McKay, 1956.

Loureiro, Rui Manuel. *Na companhia dos livros: Manuscritos e impressos nas missões jesuítas da Ásia Oriental 1540–1620*. Macau, China: Universidade de Macau, 2007.

Lou Tseng-Tsiang [Dom Pierre-Célestin]. *Ways of Confucius and Christ*. Translated by Michael Derrick. London: Garden City Press, 1948.

Lozada, Eriberto P., Jr. *God Aboveground: Catholic Church, Postsocialist State, and Transnational Process in a Chinese Village*. Stanford, CA: Stanford University Press, 2001.

Lu Jingqi and Cheng Xiao, eds. *Yihetuan yuanliu shiliao* [Historical materials related to the origins of the Society of Righteous Harmony]. Beijing: Renmin Daxue, 1980.

Luo Guanzhong. *Sanguoyanyi* [Romance of the Three Kingdoms]. Yangzhou: Jiangsu guangling guji keyinshe, 1996.

Luo Weihong. *Christianity in China*. Translated by Zhu Chenming. Beijing: China Intercontinental Press, 2004.

Lü Shiqiang. *Zhongguo guanshen fanjiao de yuanyin (1860–1874)* [The causes of anti-Christianity among Chinese officials (1860–1874)]. Hong Kong: Xianggang longmen shudian, 1966.

Lutz, Jessie Gregory. *Chinese Politics and Christian Missions: The Anti-Christian Movements of 1920–28*. Notre Dame, IN: Cross Cultural Publications, 1988.

———. *Christian Missions in China: Evangelists of What?* Boston: D. C. Heath, 1965.

Ly, André. *Journal d'André Ly, prêtre chinoise, missionaire et notaire apostolique, 1747–1763*. Edited by Adrien Launey. Paris: Alphonse Picard et fils, 1906.

Lynch, George. *Impressions of a War Correspondent*. London: Georges Newnes, 1901.

———. *The War of Civilizations: Being a Record of a "Foreign Devil's" Experience with the Allies in China*. New York: Longmans, Green, 1901.

Maas, Otto. *Die Wiedereröffnung der Franziskanermission in China in der Neuzeit*. Münster, Germany: Verlag der Aschendorffschen, 1926.

Madsen, Richard. *China's Catholics: Tragedy and Hope in an Emerging Civil Society*. Berkeley: University of California Press, 1998.

Ma Jianzhong. *Strengthen the Country and Enrich the People: The Reform Writings of Ma Jianzhong, 1845–1900*. Translated by Paul John Bailey. Richmond, Surrey, U.K.: Curzon, 1998.

Margiotti, Fortunato. *Il Cattolicismo nello Shansi dalle Origini al 1738*. Rome: Edizioni "Sinica Franciscana," 1958.

Marin, Rosanna. *That They May Have Life!: The Martyrs of Taiyuan-fu and the FMM*. Rome: Franciscan Missionaries of Mary—Generalate, 2000.

Mariotti, Candido. *Un cenno dell'antica missione Francescana in Cina e di quattro Missionari Marchigiani dei tempi recenti*. Quaracchi, Italy: Collegio di S. Bonaventura, 1911.

Martin, Christopher. *The Boxer Rebellion*. London: Abelard-Schuman, 1968.

Martin, W. A. P. *The Siege in Peking: China against the World*. New York: Fleming H. Revell, 1900.

Martyrologium Romanum: Ex Decreto Sacrosancti Oecumenici Concilii Vaticani II Instauratum Auctoritate Ioannis Pauli PP II Promulgatum, Editio Typica. Vatican City: Typis Vaticanis, 2001.

Maryknoll Mission Letters: China. Vol. 1, *Extracts from the Letters and Diaries of the Pioneer Missioners of the Catholic Foreign Mission Society of America*. New York: Macmillan, 1923.

Mateer, A. H. *Siege Days: Personal Experiences of American Women and Children during the Peking Siege*. New York: Fleming H. Revell, 1903.

Mazeau, Henry. *The Heroine of Pe-Tang: Hélène de Jaurias, Sister of Charity (1824–1900)*. Translated by an Ursuline, Grandniece of Hélène de Jaurias. New York: Benziger Brothers, 1928.

Mazzetti, Adriano. *Una santa tutta missionaria Maria Chiara Nanetti*. Rome: Centro Documentazione Santa Francesca Romana, 2009.

McCool, Gerald A. *Catholic Theology in the Nineteenth Century*. New York: Seabury Press, 1977.

McKnight, Brian E. *The Quality of Mercy: Amnesties and Traditional Chinese Justice*. Honolulu: University of Hawai'i Press, 1981.

Medhurst, Walter. *A Dissertation on the Theology of the Chinese with a View to the Elucidation of the Most Appropriate Term for Expressing the Deity, in the Chinese Language*. Shanghai: Mission Press, 1847.

———. *An Inquiry into the Proper Mode of Rendering the Word God in Translating the Sacred Scriptures into the Chinese Language*. Shanghai: Mission Press, 1848.

———. *Of the Word Shin, as Exhibited in the Quotations Adduced under That Word, in the Chinese Imperial Thesaurus, Called the Pei-Wan-Yun-Foo*. Shanghai: Mission Press, 1849.

Menegon, Eugenio. *Ancestors, Virgins, and Friars: Christianity as a Local Religion in Late Imperial China*. Cambridge, MA: Harvard University Press, 2009.

———. "A Different Country, the Same Heaven: A Preliminary Biography of Giulio Aleni, S.J. (1582–1649)." *Sino-Western Cultural Relations Journal* 15 (1993): 27–51.

Meng Hua and Sukehiro Hirakawa, eds. *Images of Westerners in Chinese and Japanese Literature*. Amsterdam: Editiona Rodopi B.V., 2000.

Menz, Kilian. "Relatio Persecutionis Excitatae in Sinis Anno 1784 et Continuatae Anno 1785." In *Apostolicum*. Vol. 5 (Tsinanfu, China: n.p., 1934).

Menze, Volker L. *Justinian and the Making of the Syrian Orthodox Church*. Oxford: Oxford University Press, 2008.

Mertens, Pierre-Xavier. *Collection des missions la légende dorée en chine: Scenes de la vie de mission au tchely sud-est (vicariat apostolique de sienhsien), deuxième série*. Paris: Vicariat apostolique de Sienhsien, 1926.

———. *The Yellow River Runs Red: A Story of Modern Chinese Martyrs*. Translated by C. C. Martindale from the French, *Du sang chrétien sur le fleuve juane*. Saint Louis, MO: B. Herder, 1936. Reprint, translated by Beryl Pearson, Saint Louis, MO: B. Herder, 1939.

Milani, Luciano. *Per Tre Missionari Francescani: Martirizzati nella Cina*. Bologna: Regia Tipografia, 1900.

Minamiki, George. *The Chinese Rites Controversy from Its Beginning to Modern Times*. Chicago: Loyola University Press, 1985.

Miner, Luella, ed. *Two Heroes of Cathay: An Autobiography and Sketch*. London: Fleming H. Revel, 1903.

Moffett, Samuel Hugh. *A History of Christianity in Asia*. Vol. 1, *Beginnings to 1500*. Maryknoll, NY: Orbis Books, 1998.

———. *A History of Christianity in Asia*. Vol. 2, *1500–1900*. Maryknoll, NY: Orbis Books, 2005.

Monchamp, George. *A Sketch of the Life of Father Victorin Delbrouck, a Franciscan Martyr of Our Days* (Paterson, NJ: Province of the Most Holy Name, 1910).

Monsterleet, Jean. *Martyrs in China*. Translated by Antonia Pakenham. Chicago: Henry Regnery, 1956.

Montgesty, G. de [Gabriel Larigaldie]. *Two Vincentian Martyrs: Blessed Francis Regis Clet, C.M., Blessed John Gabriel Perboyre, C.M.* Translated by Florence Gilmore. Maryknoll, NY: Catholic Foreign Mission Society of America, 1925.

Moorman, John. *A History of the Franciscan Order: From Its Origins to the Year 1517*. Oxford: Oxford University Press, 1968.

Moretti, Pietro. *Su le Rive del Fiume Giallo: Storia di una Missione Francescana in Cina*. Ancona, Italy: Biblioteca Francescana, 1955.

Morra, Luciano. "I Boxer e la Chiese Cattolica in Cina nei secoli XIX e XX." PhD diss., Pontificia Universitas Gregoriana, Rome, 1995.

Moule, Arthur Christopher. *Christians in China before the Year 1550*. New York: Society for Promoting Christian Knowledge, 1930.

Mueller, J. Theodore. *Great Missionaries to China*. Grand Rapids, MI: Zondervan, 1947.

Mungello, David E., ed. *The Chinese Rites Controversy: Its History and Meaning*. Nettetal, Germany: Steyler Verlag, 1994.

———. *Curious Land: Jesuit Accommodation and the Origins of Sinology*. Honolulu: University of Hawai'i Press, 1985.

———. *The Great Encounter of China and the West, 1500–1800*. Lanham, MD: Rowman and Littlefield, 1999.

———. *The Spirit and the Flesh in Shandong, 1650–1785*. Lanham, MD: Rowman and Littlefield, 2001.

Nadeau, Randall L., ed. *The Wiley-Blackwell Companion to Chinese Religions*. Malden, MA: Wiley-Blackwell, 2012.

Nanetti da Cologna, Barnabas. "Nel Settentrionale San-si." In *La Rassegna Nazionale*, vol. 133, anno 25, pp. 86–118. Florence: Presso L'Ufficio del Periodico, 1908.

———. *Nel Settentrionale San-si: Diario*. Florence: Ufficio della "Rassegna Nazionale," 1903.

Nankai daxue lishixi, eds. "Tianjin diqu Yihetuanyundong diaocha baogao" [Investigative report on the Boxer Movement in the area of Tianjin]. Tianjin: Nankai daxue lishixi, 1956.

Naquin, Susan. *Millenarian Rebellion in China: The Eight Trigrams Uprising of 1813*. New Haven, CT: Yale University Press, 1977.

Naquin, Susan, and Evelyn S. Rawski. *Chinese Society in the Eighteenth Century*. New Haven, CT: Yale University Press, 1987.

Neill, Stephen. *The Cross over Asia*. London: Canterbury Press, 1948.

Nevius, John L. *Demon Possession and Its Allied Themes: Being an Inductive Study of Phenomena of Our Times*. London: George Redway, 1897.

New Catholic Encyclopedia. 2nd ed. Detroit: Thomson Gale, 2002.

New Catholic Encyclopedia: Jubilee Volume; The Wojtyla Years. Washington, DC: Catholic University of America, 2001.

The Newly Canonized Martyr-Saints of China. Taipei: Chinese Regional Bishops Conference, 2000.

Nicholls, Bob. *Bluejackets and Boxers: Australia's Naval Expedition to the Boxer Uprising.* Sydney, Australia: Allen and Unwin, 1986.

Nichols, Francis H. *Through Hidden Shensi.* New York: Charles Scribner's Sons, 1902.

Nirenberg, David. *Communities of Violence: Persecution of Minorities in the Middle Ages.* Princeton, NJ: Princeton University Press, 1996.

O'Connor, Richard. *The Spirit Soldiers: A Historical Narrative of the Boxer Rebellion.* New York: G. P. Putnam's Sons, 1973.

Oliphant, Nigel. *A Diary of the Siege of the Legations in Peking during the Summer of 1900.* New York: Longmans, Green, 1901.

O'Malley, Vincent J. *Saints of Asia: 1500 to the Present.* Huntington, IN: Our Sunday Visitor Publishing Division, 2007.

Overmyer, Daniel L. *Local Religion in North China in the Twentieth Century: The Structure and Organization of Community Rituals and Beliefs.* Leiden, Netherlands: Brill, 2009.

Owen, David Edward. *British Opium Policy in China and India.* New Haven, CT: Yale University Press, 1934.

Pedrosa, Ceferino Puebla. *Witnesses of the Faith in the Orient: Dominican Martyrs of Japan, China, and Vietnam.* Translated by Sister Maria Maez. Hong Kong: Provincial Secretariat of Missions Dominican Province of Our Lady of the Rosary, 1989.

Pennington, M. Basil. *Twentieth Century Martyrs of the Cistercian Order of the Strict Observance.* Spencer, MA: Saint Joseph's Abbey, 1997.

Peyrefitte, Alain. *The Immobile Empire.* Translated by Jon Rothschild. New York: Alfred A. Knopf, 1992.

Piazzesi, Victorii. *Acta Sanctae Sedis: In Compendium Opportune Redacta et Illustrata.* Vols. 22, 26. Rome: Sacra Congregatio de Propaganda Fide, 1889–1890, 1893–1894.

Pictorial Lives of the Saints. New York: Benziger Brothers, 1922.

Pius XII. "Letter Apostolic by Which the Venerable Servant of God Maria Assunta Pallotta, Virgin of the Institute of the Franciscan Missionaries of Mary, Is Proclaimed Blessed." Given at Castelgondolfo, 7 November 1954.

Planchet, J. M. *Documents sur les martyrs de Pékin pendant la persecution des Boxeurs.* Beijing: Imprimerie des Lazaristes, 1922.

Porter, Henry D. *William Scott Ament: Missionary of the American Board to China.* New York: Fleming H. Revell, 1911.

Pott, F. L. Hawks. *The Outbreak in China: Its Causes.* New York: Lames Pott, 1900.

Prazniak, Roxann. *Dialogues across Civilizations: Sketches in World History from the Chinese and European Experiences.* Boulder, CO: Westview Press, 1996.

Preston, Diana. *The Boxer Rebellion: The Dramatic Story of China's War on Foreigners That Shook the World in the Summer of 1900.* New York: Walker, 2000.

Price, Eva Jane. *China Journal, 1889–1900: An American Missionary Family during the Boxer Rebellion.* New York: Charles Scribner's Sons, 1989.

Prosperi, Enrico. *La Persecuzione in Cina ed i Missionari Francescani.* Assisi: Tipografia della Porziuncola, 1901.

Pupillo, Marco. *St. Bartholomew's on the Tiber Island: A Thousand Years of History and Art.* Milan: Edizioni Angelo Guerini, 1998.

Purcell, Victor. *The Boxer Uprising: A Background Study.* Cambridge: Cambridge University Press, 1963.

Qiao Zhiqiang, ed. *Yihetuan zai Shanxi diqu shiliao* [Historical sources on Boxers in Shanxi]. Taiyuan: Shanxi renmin chubanshe, 1980.

Qin Geping. *Taiyuan jiaoqu jianshi* [A concise history of the diocese of Taiyuan]. Taiyuan: Catholic Diocese of Taiyuan, 2008.

Qingshigao [Draft history of the Qing]. Beijing: Zhonghuashuju, 1977.

Qi yu jin Zhi zhenjuan zhengxin lu [Commentary on the accounts of relief contributions for Shandong, Henan, Shanxi, and Zhili]. N.p., 1881.

Reilly, Thomas H. *The Taiping Heavenly Kingdom: Rebellion and the Blasphemy of Empire.* Seattle: University of Washington Press, 2004.

Reinders, Eric. *Borrowed Gods: Christian Missionaries Imagine Chinese Religion.* Berkeley: University of California Press, 2004.

Renditions: Chinese Impressions of the West (Chinese University of Hong Kong), nos. 53 and 54 (Spring–Autumn 2000).

Ren Yanli, ed. *Zhongguo Tianzhujiao: Jichu zhishi* [Chinese Catholicism: A foundational understanding]. Beijing: Zhongguo zongjiao wenhua chubanshe, 2005.

Report of the Committee of the China Famine Relief Fund. Shanghai: American Presbyterian Mission Press, 1879.

Ricci, Giovanni. "Acta Martyrum Sinensium Anno 1900 in Provincia San-si Occisorum." *Acta Ordinis Fratrum Minorum 1911–13* (30–32).

———. *Avec les Boxeurs Chinois.* Brive, France: Édition "Écho des Grottes," 1949.

———. *Barbarie e trionfi ossia le vittime illustri del San-Si in Cina nella persecuzione del 1900.* 2nd ed. Florence: Tipografia Barbera, 1909.

———. *Chinese Martyrs of 1900: Tertiaries of Saint Francis.* Melbourne: Australian Catholic Truth Society, 1955.

———. *The Franciscan Martyrs of the Boxer Rising*. Dublin: Franciscan Missionary Union Merchants' Quay, 1932.

———. *Gigli e Rose Ossia le Sette Protomartiri dell'Instituto delle Francescane Missionarie di Maria: Massaccrate in Cina il 9 Luglio 1900*. Levanto, Italy: Tipografia dell'Immaculata, 1919.

———. *Hierarchia Francisciana in Sinis*. Wuchang, China: Ex Typographia Franciscana, 1929.

———. *Historia Vicariatus Taiyuanfu: Ab ejus origine usque ad dies nostros (1700–1928)*. Beijing: Congregationis Missionis, 1929.

———. *Il Fratello di una martire: Memorie del P. Barnabas da Cologna*. Turin: P. Celanza, 1912.

———. *Pagina di Eroismo Cristiano. I Terzari Cinesi Martiri nello Shan-si Settentrionale*. Lonigo, Italy: Tipografia Moderna, 1925.

———. *Vicariatus Taiyuanfu seu Brevis Historia Antiquae Franciscanae Missionis Shansi et Shensi a sua Origine ad Dies Nostros (1700–1928)*. Beijing: Congregationis Missionis, 1929.

Ricci, Matteo. *China in the Sixteenth Century: The Journals of Matthew Ricci: 1583–1610*. Translated by Louis J. Gallagher. New York: Random House, 1953.

———. *Della entrata della Compagnia di Giesù e Christianità nella Cina*. Macerata, Italy: Quodlibet, 2000.

———. *On Friendship: One Hundred Maxims for a Chinese Prince*. Translated by Timothy Billings. New York: Columbia University Press, 2009.

———. *The True Meaning of the Lord of Heaven*. Translated by Douglas Lancashire and Peter Hu Kuo-chen. Taipei: Ricci Institute, 1985.

Rienstra, M. Howard, ed. and trans. *Jesuit Letters from China, 1583–84*. Minneapolis: University of Minnesota Press, 1986.

Ripa, Matteo. *Memoirs of Father Ripa: During Thirteen Years' Residence at the Court of Peking in the Service of the Emperor of China*. London: John Murray, 1844. Reprint, Elibron Classics, 2005, www.elibron.com/english/.

The Rise and Progress of the Boxer Movement in China. Yokohama: FuKuin Printing, 1900.

Robert, Dana L., ed. *Gospel Bearers, Gender Barriers: Missionary Women in the Twentieth Century*. Maryknoll, NY: Orbis Books, 2002.

Robinson, Jack Clark. "Franciscan Spirituality Is Franciscan Missiology." Paper presented at the American Historical Association Annual Meeting, Chicago, 7 January 2012.

The Roman Martyrology. Translated by Raphael Collins. Fitzwilliam, NH: Loreto, 2000. Originally published in 1749.

Romb, Anselm M. *Mission to Cathay: The Biography of Blessed Odoric of Pordenone*. Paterson, NJ: Saint Anthony Guild Press, 1956.

Ronan, Charles E., and Bonnie B. C. Oh. *East Meets West: The Jesuits in China, 1582–1773*. Chicago: Loyola University Press, 1988.

Rossato, P. G. *Ricordo di un martire: P. Angelico Melotto, OFM, 1864–1923*. Hankou, China: Missione Cattolica, 1926.

Rosso, Antonio Sisto. *Apostolic Legations to China of the Eighteenth Century*. South Pasadena, CA: Perkins, 1948.

Rouleau, Francis A. "The Yangchow Latin Tombstone as a Landmark of Medieval Christianity in China." *Harvard Journal of Asiatic Studies* 17, nos. 3–4 (December 1954).

Rousseau, Jean. *Aller simple pour la Chine: Lettres de Placide Chaigneau, missionnaire vendéen (1865–1897)*. La Roche-sur-Yon, France: Centre vendéen de recherches historiques, 2001.

Rowbotham, Arnold H. *Missionary and Mandarin: The Jesuits at the Court of China*. Berkeley: University of California Press, 1942.

Roy, Andrew T. *On Asia's Rim*. New York: Friendship Press, 1962.

Royal, Robert. *Catholic Martyrs of the Twentieth Century: A Comprehensive World History*. New York: Crossroad, 2000.

Ruan Xiumei. "Maliya fangji chuanjiao xiuhui zai Hua zhi chuanjiao shiye" [Events related to the Franciscan missionaries of Mary in China]. Master of philosophy thesis, Department of Chinese, University of Hong Kong, 1994.

Rule, Paul. "From Missionary Hagiography to the History of Chinese Christianity." *Monumenta Serica* 53 (2005): 461–475.

The Rule and the General Constitutions of the Order of Friars Minor. Pulaski, WI: Franciscan Publishers, 1988.

Rupert, G. G. *The Yellow Peril*. Britton, U.K.: Union Publishing, 1911.

Ryan, Thomas F. *China through Catholic Eyes*. Boston: Society for the Propagation of the Faith, 1942.

Salotti, Charles. *Sister Mary Assunta: The Seraphic Flower of the Franciscan Missionaries of Mary*. Translated by Thomas F. Cullen. North Providence, RI: Franciscan Missionaries of Mary, 1931.

Savage-Landor, A. Henry. *China and the Allies*. London: William Heinemann, 1901.

Sellew, Walter A. *Clara Leffingwell: A Missionary*. Chicago: Free Methodist Publishing House, 1907.

Shandong yihetuan diaocha ziliao jiaoyanshi [Research department investigative documents on the Shandong Boxers]. Jinan: Zhongguo shehui kexueyuan jindaishi yanjiusuo jindaishi ziliao bianjishi, 1980.

Shanxisheng yanjiuzhongxin, eds. *Shanxi tongzhi* [Gazetteers of Shanxi]. Beijing: Zhonghuashuju, 1997.

Shanxi Tianzhujiao zhi rongguan [The glorious crown of the Roman Catholic Church in Shanxi]. Taiyuan: Shanxi Taiyuan jiaoqu, 1946.

Shapiro, Sidney. *The Law and Lore of Chinese Criminal Justice.* Beijing: New World Press, 1990.

Sharf, Frederic A., and Peter Harrington. *China, 1900: The Eyewitnesses Speak; The Experience of Westerners in China during the Boxer Rebellion.* London: Greenhill Books, 2000.

Shen Tun-ho [Shen Dunhe]. *Recollections of a Chinese Official: With Some Sidelights on Recent History.* Shanghai: North-China Herald, 1903.

Shih, Joseph. Introduction to *Histoire de l'expédition chrétienne au royaume de la Chine, 1582–1610.* Paris: Desclée de Brouwer, 1978.

Shih, Vincent Y. C. *The Taiping Ideology: Its Sources, Interpretations, and Influences.* Seattle: University of Washington Press, 1967.

Siegmund, George. *Buddhism and Christianity: A Preface to Dialogue.* Tuscaloosa: University of Alabama Press, 1968.

Silbey, David J. *The Boxer Rebellion and the Great Game in China.* New York: Hill and Wang, 2012.

Silvestri, Cipriano. *La Testimonianza del Sangue: Biografie dei Beati Cinesi Uccisi il 4, 7 e 9 Luglio 1900.* Rome: S. Guiseppe al Triomfale, 1943.

Sima Qian. *Shiji* [Records of the grand historian]. Beijing: Zhonghuashuju, 1982.

Simon, R., ed. *Correspondance de Pékin, 1722–1759.* Geneva: Droz, 1970.

Simpson, Bertram Lenox [B. L. Putnam Weale]. *Indiscreet Letters from Peking.* New York: Dodd, Mead, 1919.

Sinarum seu Tuscolana Beatificationis et Canonizationis Servae Dei Mariae Assumptae Pallotta Sororis Professae Instituti Sororum Franciscalium Missionarium Mariae. Rome: Guerra et Mirri, 1923.

Sinarum seu Vicariatus Apostolici Sien-Hsien: Beatificationis seu Declarationis Martyrii Servorum Dei Leonis Ignatii Mangin et Pauli Denn, Sacerdotum Societas Jesu. Rome: Typis Pontificiae Universitas Gregorianae, 1939.

Singh, Amar, et al. *Reversing the Gaze: Amar Singh's Diary, a Colonial Subject's Narrative of Imperial India.* Boulder, CO: Westview Press, 2002.

Smith, Arthur H. *China in Convulsion.* Vols. 1 and 2. New York: Fleming H. Revell, 1901.

———. *The Uplift of China.* New York: Board of Foreign Missions of the Presbyterian Church of the U.S.A., 1907.

Smith, Carl T. *Chinese Christians: Élites, Middlemen, and the Church in Hong Kong.* Hong Kong: Oxford University Press, 1985.

Smith, Stanley P. *China from Within: Or the Story of the Chinese Crisis*. London: Marshall Brothers, 1901.

Soothill, William E. *Timothy Richard of China: Seer, Statesman, Missionary and the Most Disinterested Advisor the Chinese Ever Had*. London: Seeley, Service, 1924.

Spellman, Francis. "Homily to Catholic Students Mission Crusade." *Jesuit Missions*, no. 19 (January–February 1945).

Spence, Jonathan. *The Chan's Great Continent: China in Western Minds*. New York: W. W. Norton, 1998.

———. *God's Chinese Son: The Taiping Heavenly Kingdom of Hong Xiuquan*. New York: W. W. Norton, 1996.

———. *The Memory Palace of Matteo Ricci*. New York: Penguin, 1985.

———. *The Search for Modern China*. 2nd ed. New York: W. W. Norton, 1999.

Standaert, Nicolas, ed. *Chinese Voices in the Rites Controversy: Travelling Books, Community Networks, Intercultural Arguments*. Rome: Institutum Historicum Societas Iesu, 2012.

———. *Handbook of Christianity in China*. Vol. 1, *635–1800*. Leiden, Netherlands: Brill, 2001.

———. *The Interweaving of Rituals: Funerals in the Cultural Exchange between China and Europe*. Seattle: University of Washington Press, 2008.

———. *Yang Tingyun, Confucian and Christian in Late Ming China: His Life and Thought*. Leiden, Netherlands: Brill, 1988.

Steiger, George Nye. *China and the Occident: The Origin and Development of the Boxer Movement*. New Haven, CT: Yale University Press, 1927.

Stenz, George M. *Life of Father Richard Henle, S.V.D.: Missionary in China*. Techny, IL: Mission Press, S.V.D., 1921.

Sticca, Sandro. *Saints: Studies in Hagiography*. Birmingham, NY: Medieval and Renaissance Texts and Studies, SUNY, 1996.

Stratemeyer, Edward. *On to Pekin, or Old Glory in China*. Boston: Lee and Shepard, 1900.

Streit, F. C. *Catholic World Atlas*. Paderborn, Germany: Saint Boniface Press, 1929.

Streit, Robert. *Catholic Missions in Figures and Symbols: Based on the Vatican Missionary Exhibition 1926*. Boston: Society for the Propagation of the Faith, 1927.

Sun, E-tu Zen. *Ch'ing Administrative Terms: A Translation of the Terminology of the Six Boards with Explanatory Notes*. Cambridge, MA: Harvard University Press, 1961.

Sweeten, Alan Richard. *Christianity in Rural China: Conflict and Accommodation in Jiangxi Province, 1860–1900*. Ann Arbor: Center for Chinese Studies, University of Michigan, 1968.

Sylvestre, André. *François-Régis Clet: Prêtre de la Mission, Martyr en Chine, 1748–1820*. Moissac, France, 1998.

——. *Jean-Gabriel Perboyre: Prêtre de la Mission, Martyr en Chine*. Moissac, France: n.p., 1994.

——. *John Gabriel Perboyre, C.M.: China's First Saint*. Translated by John E. Rybolt. Strasbourg, France: Éditions du Signe, 1996.

——. *Vie de Jean-Gabriel Perboyre*. Moissac, France: n.p., 1994.

Tan, Chester C. *The Boxer Catastrophe*. New York: W. W. Norton and Company, 1967.

Tang, Dominique. *Comme ses voies sont insondables! Mémoires 1951–1981*. Hong Kong: Caritas, 1987.

Tang, Edmond, and Jean-Paul Wiest, eds. *The Catholic Church in Modern China, Perspectives*. Maryknoll, NY: Orbis Books, 1993.

Teng, Ssu-yü. *The Taiping Rebellion and the Western Powers: A Comprehensive Survey*. Taipei: Yee Wen, 1977.

Teng, Ssu-yü, and John K. Fairbank. *China's Response to the West: A Documentary Survey, 1839–1923*. Cambridge, MA: Harvard University Press, 1954.

Tennien, Mark. *Chungking Listening Post*. New York: Creative Age Press, 1945.

Tertullian. *The Apology*. Whitefish, MT: Kessinger, 2001. Originally published in the second century CE.

The Theme Song of Assunta. Patterson, NJ: Saint Anthony Guild Press, 1956.

Thiry-Mariste, Ignace. *La Passion des frères Marístes en Chine: 1891–1956*. Paris: Editions Saint Paul, 1956.

Thomas, A. *Histoire de la Mission de Pékin: Depuis les Origines Jusqu'a L'Arrivée des Lazaristes*. Paris: Louis-Michaud, 1923.

Thomson, H. C. *The Case for China*. New York: Charles Scribner's Sons, 1933.

Tianzhujiao Taiwan diqu zhujiao xuansheng weiyuanhui zhubian (Taiwan Roman Catholic Bishops Committee), eds. *Zhonghua xundao shengren zhuan* [Biographies of China's martyr saints]. Taipei: Tianzhujiao Taiwan diqu zhujiao xuan wiyuanhui, 2000.

Tiedemann, R. G. "Controlling the Virgins: Female Propagators of the Faith and the Catholic Hierarchy in China." *Women's History Review* 17, no. 4 (2008): 501–520.

——. *Reference Guide to Christian Missionary Societies in China: From the Sixteenth Century to the Twentieth Century*. Armonk, NY: M. E. Sharpe, 2009.

Timmer, Odorico Timmer. *Acta Martyrum Sinensium Vicariatus Apostolici Shanxi Meridiolanis Anno 1900, Pro Fide Interfectorum Juridice Collecta*. Florence: Ad Claras Aquas, 1919.

——. *Het Apostolisch Vicariaat van Zuid-Shansi in de Eerst Vijf-en-Twintig Jaren van Zijn Bestaan (1890–1915)*. Leiden, Netherlands: Théonville, 1915.

Ting, K. H. *No Longer Strangers*. Edited by Raymond L. Whitehead. Maryknoll, NY: Orbis Books, 1989.

Trainor, Kevin, ed. *Buddhism*. Oxford: Oxford University Press, 2001.

Trigault, Nicolas. *Histoire de l'expedition Chretienne au royaume de la Chine: 1582–1610*. Rome: n.p., 1615.

Tuttle, A. H. *Mary Potter Gamewell and Her Story of the Siege in Peking*. New York: Eaton and Mains, 1907.

Uhalley, Stephen, Jr., and Xiaoxin Wu, eds. *China and Christianity: Burdened Past, Hopeful Future*. Armonk, NY: M. E. Sharpe, 2001.

Valeri, Antonius. *Compendio della vita del B. Giovanni da Triora, Frate Minore: Martirizzato in Cina nel 1816*. Rome: Lucci, 1924.

Van der Sprenkel, Sybille. *Legal Institutions in Manchu China: A Sociological Analysis*. New York: Athlone Press, 1962.

Van de Ven, Hans J. "Robert Hart and Gustav Detring during the Boxer Rebellion." *Modern Asian Studies* 40, no. 3 (2006): 631–662.

——. ed. *Warfare in Chinese History*. Leiden, Netherlands: Brill, 2000.

Venturi, Pietro Tacchi, ed. *Opere Storiche del P. Matteo Ricci, S.I.* Macerata, Italy: n.p., 1913.

Verhaeren, Hubert. *Catalogue de la Bibliothèque du Pé-T'ang*. Beijing: Imprimerie des Lazaristes, 1949.

Vermander, B., ed. *Le Christ Chinois, Héritages et Espérance*. Paris: Desclée de Brouwer, 1998.

Vie de la mere Marie-Hermine de Jesus et de ses compagnes massacrees au Chan-si (Chine), le juillet 1900. Rome: L'Institute des Franciscaines Missionaires de Marie, 1902.

Waite, Carleton Frederick. *Some Elements of International Military Co-operation in the Suppression of the 1900 Antiforeign Rising in China: With Special Reference to Forces of the United States*. Los Angeles: University of Southern California Press, 1935.

Wakeman, Frederic, Jr. and Carolyn Grant, eds. *Conflict and Control in Late Imperial China*. Berkeley: University of California Press, 1975.

Waley-Cohen, Joanna. *The Sextants of Beijing: Global Currents in Chinese History*. New York: W. W. Norton, 1999.

Walsh, James Anthony. *A Modern Martyr: Theophane Vénard*. Maryknoll, NY: Catholic Foreign Mission Society, 1913.

——. *Observations in the Orient: The Account of a Journey to Catholic Mission*

Fields in Japan, Korea, Manchuria, China, Indo-china, and the Philippines. New York: Catholic Foreign Mission Society of America, 1919.

Walton, Joseph. *China and the Present Crisis.* London: Sampson Low, Marston, 1900.

Wang, Dong. *China's Unequal Treaties: Narrating National History.* Lanham, MD: Lexington Books, 2005.

Wang Jingshan. "Yu gaoge zhu: Wang (Leisi) Shiwei shengping xiaoji" [High praise to God in prison: A small record of the whole life of Wang (Leisi) Shiwei]. Unpublished manuscript, Liuhecun, Shanxi, 2000.

Wang Shujie, ed. *Tianzhujiao zaoqi chuanru Zhongguo shihua* [A history of the early entrance of Roman Catholicism into China]. Puqi, China: Neibu duwu, 1993.

Wanguo gongbao [The globe magazine] (Shanghai), 28 September 1877.

Weale, B. L. Putnam. *Indiscreet Letters from Peking: Being the Notes of an Eye-Witness, Which Set Forth in Some Detail, from Day to Day, the Real Story of the Siege and Sack of a Distressed Capital in 1900—the Year of Great Tribulation.* New York: Mead, 1909.

Wedge, Florence. *Franciscan Bishop in China: Most Rev. Rembert C. Kowalski, O.F.M. (1884–), Exiled Bishop of Wuchang, China.* Pulaski, WI: Franciscan Publishers, 1968.

Wei, Louis Tsing-sing. *La Politique Missionaire de la France en Chine, 1842–1856.* Paris: Nouvelles Éditions Latines, 1960.

Wei Yuan. "Examination of the Catholic Religion." In *Haiguo tuzhi* [Illustrated treatise on oceans and countries], translated by Tam Pak Shan. Reprinted in *Renditions,* nos. 53 and 54 (Spring–Autumn 2000).

Wetterwald, Albert. "Une armée chrétienne improvisée: Défence de Wei-tsuen. (Extraits du journal du P. A. Wetterwald)." In *Études* 38e année, vol. 86 (5 March 1901): 660–693.

White, Trumbull, and James P. Boyd. *The Story of China and Her Neighbors: Their Manners, Customs, Life and History, from the Earliest Times to the Present, Including the Boxer Uprising.* N.p.: James P. Boyd, 1900.

Whitehead, James D., et al., eds. *China and Christianity: Historical and Future Encounters.* Notre Dame, IN: Center for Pastoral and Social Ministry, University of Notre Dame Press, 1979.

Whyte, Bob. *Unfinished Encounter: China and Christianity.* London: Collins, 1988.

Wiest, Jean-Paul. "Catholic Images of the Boxers." *American Asian Review* 9, no. 3 (Fall 1991).

———. *Maryknoll in China: A History, 1918–1955.* Maryknoll, NY: Orbis Books, 1988.

Willeke, Bernard H. *Imperial Government and Catholic Missions in China during the Years 1784–1785*. Saint Bonaventure, NY: Franciscan Institute, 1948.

———. "The Report of the Apostolic Visitation of D. Emmanuele Conforti on the Franciscan Missions on Shansi, Shensi and Kansu (1798)." *Archivium Franciscanum Historicum* 84, nos. 1–2 (January–June 1991).

Witek, John W. *Controversial Ideas in China and in Europe: A Biography of Jean-François Foucquet, S.J. (1665–1741)*. Rome: Institutum Historicum Societas Iesu, 1982.

Wolferstan, Bertram. *The Catholic Church in China from 1860 to 1907*. London: Sands and Company, 1909.

Wurth, Elmer, ed. *Papal Documents Related to the New China: 1937–1984*. Maryknoll, NY: Orbis Books, 1985.

Xiang Lanxin. *The Origins of the Boxer War: A Multinational Study*. London: Routledge Curzon, 2003.

Xin Bozhi, ed. *Zhongguo Tianzhujiao qiji xin jiaonan* [Chinese Roman Catholics and their plights]. Hong Kong: Ziyou chubanshe, 1924.

Yamamoto, Sumiko. *History of Protestantism in China: The Indigenization of Christianity*. Tokyo: Institute of Eastern Culture, 2000.

Yan, Rachel Lu, and Philip Vanhaelemeersch, eds. *Silent Force: Native Converts in the Catholic China Mission*. Leuven, Belgium: Ferdinand Verbiest Institute, 2009.

Yang Guangxian. *Budeyi* [I cannot do otherwise]. Shanghai: Shanghai guji chubanshe, 1995. Originally published in 1664.

Yang Jingjun, *Beijing Tianzhujiao shi* [A history of Catholicism in Beijing]. Beijing: Zongjiao wenhua chubanshe, 2009.

Yasongda zouguo de lu qianbei fuwu [Assunta's path of humble service]. Taiyuan: Taiyuan jiaoqu, 2005.

The Yi Ho Tuan Movement of 1900. Beijing: Foreign Languages Press, 1976.

Yip, Ke-che. *Religion, Nationalism and Chinese Students: The Anti-Christian Movement of 1922–1927*. Bellingham: Center for East Asian Studies, Western Washington University, 1980.

Yong Zheng. "The Martyrdom at T'aiyuanfu on the 9th of July, 1900. By an Eyewitness." *North China Herald*, 3 April 1901, 637.

Young, Ernest P. *Ecclesiastical Colony: China's Catholic Church and the French Religious Protectorate*. Oxford: Oxford University Press, 2013.

Yuan Ke, ed. *Zhongguo shenhua chuanshu cidian* [Dictionary of terms related to Chinese mythology]. Taipei: Huashi chubanshe, 1987.

Yu Liang. *Kong Xiangxi* [Biography of Kong Xiangxi]. Hong Kong: Kaiyuan shudian, 1955.

Yu-pin, Paul. *Eyes East*. Paterson, NJ: Saint Anthony Guild Press, 1945.

Zambon, Mariagrazia. *Crimson Seeds: Eighteen PIME Martyrs*. Translated by Steve Baumbusch. Detroit: PIME World Press, 1997.

Zanin, Marius, Auguste Haouisée, and Paul Yu-Pin. *The Voice of the Church in China, 1931–2, 1937–8*. London: Longmans, Green, 1938.

Zavalloni, Roberto. *Martiri della Cina nel 50° della Beatificazione*. Assisi: Edizione Porziuncola, 1996.

Zhang Deyi and Jia Lili. *Taiyuan shihua* [Concise history of Taiyuan]. Taiyuan: Shanxi renmin chubanshe, 2000.

Zhang Longxi. *Mighty Opposites: From Dichotomies to Differences in the Comparative Study of China*. Stanford, CA: Stanford University Press, 1998.

Zheng Yangwen, *The Social Life of Opium in China*. Cambridge: Cambridge University Press, 2005.

Zhongguo diyi lishi danganguan. *Qing zhongqianqi Xiyang Tianzhujiao zai Hua huodong dang'an shiliao* [Archival materials related to Western Catholic activities in China]. 4 Vols. Beijing: Zhonghuashuju, 2003.

Zhongguo shehui kexueyuan jindaishi yanjiusuo jindaishi ziliao bianjishi [Chinese Contemporary Social Science Research Institute, compiled documentary materials]. Beijing: Zhonghuashuju, 1978.

Zhongguo Tianzhujiao shouce [Directory of the Catholic Church in China]. Hebei Province: Hebei xindeshe chubanshe, 2010.

Zhongyang yanjiuyuan jindaishi yanjiusuo, eds. *Jiaowu jiaoan dang* [Missionary incidents archives]. 7 vols. Taipei: Zhongyang yanjiuyuan jindaishi yanjiusuo, 1974.

Zhou, Pierre Bangjiu. *L'aube se lève à l'Est*. Paris: Pierre Téqui, 2000. Published in English as: *Dawn Breaks in the East: A Benedictine Monk's Thirty-Three Year Ordeal in the Prison of Communist China, in Defense of His Faith*. Upland, CA: Serenity, 1992.

INDEX